USA IMMIGRATION GUIDE

USA
IMMIGRATION
GUIDE

with forms

Ramon Carrion

Attorney at Law

Sphinx Publishing
A Division of Sourcebooks, Inc.
Naperville, IL • Clearwater, FL

Third edition, 1998

Published by: **Sphinx® Publishing, A Division of Sourcebooks, Inc.®**

Naperville Office
P.O. Box 372
Naperville, Illinois 60566
(630) 961-3900
Fax: 630-961-2168

Clearwater Office
P.O. Box 25
Clearwater, Florida 33757
(813) 587-0999
Fax: 813-586-5088

Interior Design and Production: Shannon E. Harrington, Sourcebooks, Inc.

This publication is designed to provide accurate and authoritative information in regard to the subject matter covered. It is sold with the understanding that the publisher is not engaged in rendering legal, accounting, or other professional service. If legal advice or other expert assistance is required, the services of a competent professional person should be sought.
From a Declaration of Principles Jointly Adopted by a Committee of the
American Bar Association and a Committee of Publishers and Associations

Library of Congress Cataloging-in-Publication Data
Carrion, Ramon.
    USA immigration guide : with forms / Ramon Carrion.—3rd ed.
        p.   cm.
Includes index.
    ISBN 1-57071-354-5 (pbk.)
    1. Emigration and immigration law—United States—Popular works.
2. Visas—United States—Popular works.   I. Title.
KF4819.6.C37   1998
342.73'082—dc21
                                                                                98-16376
                                                                                CIP

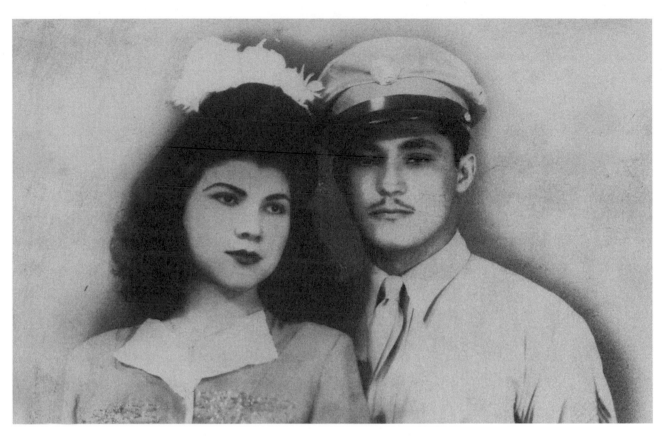

DEDICATION

To the memory of my beloved father, Ramon, and to my mother, Leonor, who were the first and most important "immigrants" in my life. They not only had the vision of a new life in the United States but also the courage to implement that vision. In the spirit of my parents' dreams and motivations, this book is also dedicated to all of you who aspire to participate in the American dream.

CONTENTS

PREFACE

I am sure the reader has heard the expression, "The gift of youth is wasted on the young." The premise of this book is that knowledge of the law is often wasted on the lawyers. We lawyers frequently complain that if our clients had done (or not done) this, that or the other, we could have done a better job resolving their legal problems. Of course, the reason our clients did not do what they should have done was because they did not know what the law required in the first place. The knowledge that our clients needed was not available to them at the time they were making their decisions. Typically, clients take what they believe is reasonably responsible action and then seek out the lawyer for advice or reinforcement after the fact. Since the client has already pursued a given course of action, the legal consultant frequently can only comment on the appropriateness of the client's action. Of course, this is an unfortunate legal irony because lay people, even knowledgeable business people, are not always familiar with technical legal requirements applicable to a specific situation.

In the complex field of immigration and visa law (we'll call it "visa law" in this book) an early mistake can frustrate or, at the least, complicate plans to move individuals and/or their businesses to the United States. We will try to address this situation by explaining in practical terms the philosophy and logic of the United States immigration regimen. In short, this book attempts to be a practical handbook which explains to the foreign person how the U.S. immigration functions.

This book was originally a collection of useful information that I have over the years customarily conveyed to foreign persons during my initial office interviews with them. It was apparent to me that most foreign persons (*aliens*), regardless of their country of origin, were asking the same types of questions. The client wanted to understand the system in order to understand the need to reveal and submit certain types of information. In order to provide a thoroughly useful service to the client, I had to explain much of the background of the law, as well as the philosophy and "mind set" of the U.S. immigration and consular authorities. By thoroughly informing the client, I was able to obtain the proper information which enabled me to provide useful advice in the planning of the client's entry into the United States. This educational process also assisted clients in learning very quickly some of the most important and immediate business and legal norms and customs that they would encounter in the United States. As I began to write this compendium, it grew into this book which I hope will provide readers with some of the insights that I feel are essential in successfully fulfilling their immigration motivations, both long and short term.

Shortly before the writing of this latest edition of this book, the United States enacted the Illegal Immigration Reform and Immigrant Responsibility Act (IIRAIRA). While the title of this law suggests that it was exclusively aimed at controlling illegal immigration to the United States, in fact, it did much more than that. The law created a series of penalties and prohibitions which apply indiscriminately to persons who harbor fraudulent or improper motivations as well as to those whose newly created transgressions are the result of ignorance of the law. Indeed, the current state of the law has likened U.S. immigration policy and practice to the equivalent of a dangerous bureaucratic game of chess in which the stakes are very high indeed. This is because seemingly simple and harmless actions or omissions can, as a result of the interaction of these regulations, have serious complications—very much like a game of chess.

Further complicating the situation for foreign persons is the political climate in which these laws and regulations are enforced. The U.S. Congress has in many instances removed the discretion which the U. S. Immigration and Naturalization Service judges and officials previously exercised and has encouraged these officials to take a "hard line" toward enforcement of the letter of the law. This has resulted in an incongruous situation in which otherwise innocent dependents of a lawfully admitted foreign person can be adjudged as "illegally present" and then barred from the United States for long periods of time.

There is no better antidote to the poison of excessive and arbitrary governmental authority than knowledge and that is the purpose of this book. This book will cover the major provisions of the U.S. visa law as it would apply to a foreign person who is contemplating a move to the United States, whether that move be permanent or temporary. The book will not cover many technical provisions of the law which apply to a person already within the United States. That would be a fitting subject for a much more complete and detailed presentation.

As further described in this preface, the purpose of the book is to educate the foreign person with respect to the policy and philosophy of the United States Immigration regimen as concerns obtaining an appropriate visa for entry into the U.S.A. I do not encourage a lay person to attempt to obtain a visa, other than the visitor's visa (B-1/B-2), to the United States without professional assistance. Consultation with a trained professional legal consultant is greatly encouraged.

There are certain countries in the world where there are especially heavy demands for immigrant visas to the United States or from which there are instances of fraud and abuse with respect to visa application to the United States. The United States consular authorities in those countries are very scrupulous in examining an individual's credentials and intentions when the individual applies for any kind of visa to the

United States. This book should be especially helpful to persons from those countries; however, it will also be helpful to any alien seeking to enter the United States, since it is easy to overlook the strict standards applied by the United States immigration authorities to all persons entering the United States.

This publication will be especially helpful to business persons and investors, as well as their advisors, to whom immigration concerns may be secondary to other strategic business planning. It will also be useful to other foreign persons, whether they are students or immediate relatives of U.S. citizens or permanent resident aliens. It is not the author's purpose to encourage nor discourage immigration or the transfer of capital to the United States. Rather, the book is offered in the context of certain political, economic, and sociological factors over which the author has no control or ability to affect. These factors can be summarized as follows:

1. **The relative ease of international transportation and communication.** This phenomenon has created the illusion that political and national boundaries are of less importance now than in the past. The mass media as a result of technological advances during the past few decades has projected the United States culture and way of life to the most remote parts of the world. Thus, many persons in foreign countries may be already familiar with certain cultural characteristics of the United States and may want to participate in our life style.

2. **The interdependence of national economies.** As a result of some of the technological advances already mentioned, the community of nations' business and commerce is more interrelated and interdependent. This often requires the transfer of business personnel to the United States. This, of course, is often a bilateral process with many expansive U.S. firms transferring their U.S. employees to other parts of the world as well. The world economy often pays little heed to national boundaries, and companies and individuals are often substantially affected by the

events or predictions of financial centers far removed from their home offices.

There is a growing body of opinion that there is one global economy and financial market, with three regional centers: Tokyo, New York, and London; and that these centers are so interrelated that the cause and effect sequence as to their individual influence on the world economy is academic since each center is so closely dependent upon and influential of the others that their combined effect on the world's economy is a constant force.

3. **The relative strength and adaptability of the U.S. economy.** This reality makes the United States an attractive market for foreign investment, both on a large and small scale. The entrepreneurial spirit reacts much the same way to this fact, whether it is that of a large multinational firm or of a smaller business whose owners are very often also its key employees. This fact coupled with the recent weakening of the U.S. dollar makes business acquisitions in the United States very attractive—especially real estate.

4. **The political stability of the United States.** In addition to being politically stable, the United States has a history of relative tolerance for immigrants from foreign countries—especially for those immigrants who share an affinity for the capitalist ideology. There are pockets of ethnic communities throughout the U.S. where a foreign person of a particular ethnic background can feel secure and find the familiar cultural characteristics of home. The United States is a geographically diverse country with regions resembling those of other countries. Furthermore, various geographic areas of the United States offer pleasant climates as well as attractive and modern urban, suburban and agricultural areas. There is a place for everyone.

5. **The United States nurtures personal freedoms.** In the United States personal and political freedoms such as the right of free speech, right of assembly, freedom of the press, freedom of

physical movement, etc., are jealously protected. U.S. residents have the right to succeed and enjoy the fruits of their labors and are expected to bear the risk of failure as well.

As a result of the above factors, there is a tremendous worldwide demand for both permanent and temporary visas to the United States.

There are counter-currents, however, to a liberal immigration policy. These are illustrated by the following:

1. **The increase in overall U.S. population and its effects:** This worldwide phenomenon and its local effects have caused U.S. political leaders to take the position that further population growth is generally negative. Indeed, the increasing population places strains on public services in general as well as on the natural environment.

2. **Differences in the ethnic and cultural make-up of current immigrants:** This is a more subtly expressed objection, but many Americans seem to resent the changing ethnic makeup of their communities. Statistics verify that the largest percentage of immigration to the United States during the last twenty years or so have come from Asia and Latin America.

3. **The social cost of the presence of large numbers of illegal aliens:** Americans resent their government's inability to deter the thousands of foreign persons who enter the country unlawfully and then remain permanently or for extended periods of time. Insofar as most of these illegal immigrants are poor and uneducated they require the expenditures of public funds to provide for them. In addition to certain welfare costs, statistics reflect that a relatively high percentage of jailed inmates are illegal aliens. In addition, the proliferation of fraudulent immigration documents and the perceived abuse of the asylum procedures has further eroded the traditional welcoming mentality of the U.S. people and many of their political leaders.

4. **The political rationalization of immigration as the cause of various social ills.** Since non U.S. citizens are not permitted to vote, it has become politically irresistible to blame immigration for many of the country's ills. It has become expedient for many United States politicians to take up the issue of immigration as a political rallying point for the benefit of their own campaigns and careers.

The above are some of the motivations that have resulted in an increase in the control of the quality, quantity, and character of inward migration. However, the convergence of these two drives causes many personal and business problems, many of which can be avoided or minimized through proper planning.

The author's intention is to explain the major visa considerations that a prospective immigrant or temporary visitor must understand in order to logically and intelligently plan an entry into the United States. Additionally, this edition of the book also suggests certain long term strategies in order to avoid the loss of the U.S. visa. This work may be criticized by certain members of the immigration legal community for being too simplistic and not providing enough detail on certain intricacies of the administrative and legal processes involved in the procurement of visas for foreign persons. I accept such anticipated criticism by stating that I do not intend this book to replace the services of competent professional guidance. Indeed, the book recognizes that professional assistance, not just in the field of law, but also in the disciplines of accounting, marketing, finance, etc., is very often critical in making successful long-term decisions respecting business/visa matters.

The purpose of the book is to prepare and educate individuals (or their employees) so they or their professional consultants may comply with the requirements of the United States immigration regimen. It is my purpose to describe the methodology and bureaucratic psychology of the U.S. Immigration regimen, since an understanding of these principles will enable a person or company to adapt to the overall situation as it otherwise applies to him.

Some may criticize the inclusion of more detail than the average person is willing to know. My response is, with all respect, that this book is not written for the average person. It is written for that special person who, in search of economic and personal improvement, desires to expand personal and business activities beyond the borders of home by transferring some or all of those activities into the most dynamic society on this planet: the United States of America.

ACKNOWLEDGMENT

I wish to express my sincere gratitude to Steve Rushing for his insightful and yet very human cartoons; Virginia Kohl for the excellent editing work that she did on the manuscript; my assistant Paula Harshberger for her patience and originality in solving many of the format challenges that this book presented; my daughter Andrea M. Carrion for her assistance in making the editorial changes; and finally Mark Warda for his encouragement to write this book in the first place.

Using Self-Help
Law Books

Whenever you shop for a product or service, you are faced with various levels of quality and price. In deciding what product or service to buy, you make a cost/value analysis on the basis of your willingness to pay and the quality you desire.

When buying a car, you decide whether you want transportation, comfort, status, or sex appeal. Accordingly, you decide among such choices as a Neon, a Lincoln, a Rolls Royce, or a Porsche. Before making a decision, you usually weigh the merits of each option against the cost.

When you get a headache, you can take a pain reliever (such as aspirin) or visit a medical specialist for a neurological examination. Given this choice, most people, of course, take a pain reliever, since it costs only pennies, whereas a medical examination costs hundreds of dollars and takes a lot of time. This is usually a logical choice because rarely is anything more than a pain reliever needed for a headache. But in some cases, a headache may indicate a brain tumor, and failing to see a specialist right away can result in complications. Should everyone with a headache go to a specialist? Of course not, but people treating their own illnesses must realize that they are betting on the basis of their cost/value analysis of the situation, they are taking the most logical option.

The same cost/value analysis must be made in deciding to do one's own legal work. Many legal situations are very straight forward, requiring a simple form and no complicated analysis. Anyone with a little intelligence and a book of instructions can handle the matter without outside help.

But there is always the chance that complications are involved that only an attorney would notice. To simplify the law into a book like this, several legal cases often must be condensed into a single sentence or paragraph. Otherwise, the book would be several hundred pages long and too complicated for most people. However, this simplification necessarily leaves out many details and nuances that would apply to special or unusual situations. Also, there are many ways to interpret most legal questions. Your case may come before a judge who disagrees with the analysis of our authors.

Therefore, in deciding to use a self-help law book and to do your own legal work, you must realize that you are making a cost/value analysis and deciding that the chance your case will not turn out to your satisfaction is outweighed by the money you will save in doing it yourself. Most people handling their own simple legal matters never have a problem, but occasionally people find that it ended up costing them more to have an attorney straighten out the situation than it would have if they had hired an attorney in the beginning. Keep this in mind while handling your case, and be sure to consult an attorney if you feel you might need further guidance.

INTRODUCTION

It is an understatement to say that much has changed in the world since the first edition of this book was published in 1989. Yet, there is no better way of putting this work into perspective than to recount some of those changes, since directly or indirectly, they affect the purpose and scope of this book.

First and foremost, the U.S. Congress enacted in September of 1996 the Illegal Immigration Reform and Immigrant Responsibility Act (IIRAIRA). This law, which took effect in April of 1997, imposed a complicated series of punitive measures against a number of typical visa violations and created some new violations. This act contrasts with the Immigration and Naturalization Act of 1990 (IMMACT90), which established the basic substantive law establishing the requirements for legal immigration. There is no reason to doubt that there will be further major changes in the immigration regimen of the United States in the near future. Indeed, the pace of change of U.S. immigration law seems to mirror the pace of change in other current world economic and political institutions. This book attempts to explain the law in a manner that will be understandable to the lay public, especially to foreign persons, whatever their occupations and/or stations in life may be. The book will discuss those features of the law that are likely to apply to most persons seeking entry to the United States. It will not attempt to be the definitive scholarly or technical work in this area, for even as I write, the government is drafting administrative rules and regulations that will implement and further interpret the law.

The rest of the world also has changed. The "Cold War" between the Communist East and the Capitalist West is over. Germany has been reunited. The former Warsaw Pact countries have abandoned the traditional Marxist/Leninist school of communism and have adopted, or are trying to adopt, more traditional market-based economies and similarly have adopted political institutions which more closely resemble Western-style democracies.

The Union of Soviet Socialist Republics no longer exists. The era of Gorbachev has come and gone in a whirlwind of events that has staggered the imaginations of even the most eclectic of political analysts. In place of the former U.S.S.R., a group of distinct and independent republics has reemerged and it remains to be seen if there will be again in our time an effective confederation of the former Soviet republics. We now speak of Georgians, Ukrainians, Russians and have dropped the word "soviets" from our language. New international conflagrations have either erupted or threaten to erupt with potentially devastating effects which reach far beyond the confines of the battlefield jurisdiction. Nationalism and other cultural conflicts have replaced the East/West ideological differences as the primary catalyst for armed conflict and genocide.

In the first few months of 1991 the United States under the authority of the United Nations, carried out an intense and technologically impressive military campaign against the country of Iraq. This event resulted in the "liberation" of Kuwait and the reestablishment of the primacy of United States military prowess, but did not eliminate the basic power arrangements in the Middle East.

At the same time that it has demonstrated its military abilities, the United States has experienced an economic renaissance which has both revealed the ultimate strength and resilience of the U.S. economy while also demonstrating that it too is dependent on global economic conditions. Compared to the almost total collapse of the economy of the former U.S.S.R., the resilience of the U.S. economy demonstrates its fundamental strengths. Significantly, Japan and China have emerged as economic "super powers" with the ability to influence global economic events and conditions without the necessity of aggressively projecting any significant military capability.

Finally, the pace of the technological revolution continues unabated and creates many paradoxes as the rules of the past conflict with the harsh realities of the present and future. Many of the U.S. immigration law provisions were formulated in another time when only the poor and the downtrodden sought admission to the United States. Now, it is the needs of international commerce and business as well as the desire to share in the knowledge of the new technology which fuel much of the motivation for long-term visas. The immigration regimen has great difficulty in dealing with the changing character of "employment" both as to its content and its legal definition. Jobs can now be effectively exercised by computer and certainly in the service industries it is sometimes difficult to identify the exact location where the services are rendered. Our government blames the loss of jobs to foreign sites while making it difficult to import highly trained workers from abroad who are capable of enhancing U.S. domestic industrial competitiveness. Indeed the pace of change may be beyond the ability of governments to control.

Perhaps all these events manifest the unfolding of a new era in which the phrase "it's a small world" will have a more poignant and relevant meaning to all of us.

THE VISA SYSTEM IN GENERAL 1

Every time foreigners come to the border of the United States seeking entry, even if only for a holiday visit, they confront the formidable immigration regimen of the United States. The term *immigration* in the context of this book means every entry or attempted entry into the territory of the United States.

The immigration system of the United States is the product of unique historical and political forces which produce some seemingly incongruous policies. Immigration has created a procedural system that is so complex and obscure that it almost creates the opportunity for a foreign person to unintentionally violate the law and then provides almost no methodology for a foreign person to correct the violation. It is a system which requires the foreign person to know in advance of any filing or application what the applicable law is, since the immigration system often does not provide an applicant an opportunity to modify his or her approach in order to comply with the law. For this reason it is imperative that foreign persons and their advisors understand the special meaning given to many terms which are routinely used in business and in normal conversation.

Brief Legal/Historical Context

The United States was founded by immigrants, that is, by people who were not originally from the nation. Yet, the Constitution of the United States, the organic document which established the unique political existence of this nation is almost silent on the entire question of immigration. There is only a fleeting mention of this subject in that document and it does not contain a political or philosophical articulation of a policy or system of immigration. In very concise language, the Constitution simply authorizes the U.S. Congress to make the laws concerning immigration. There is no statement of policy or principle manifested in the Constitution concerning the subject of immigration.

History reveals that during the first 150 years, the motivating force for immigration to the United States was privation and persecution abroad. People came to the United States to escape negative forces in their home countries. They came to this country fully expecting to experience personal sacrifice in exchange for political, economic, and religious freedom. Until the end of the 19th Century there was basically no control or limitation on immigration to the United States. However, since 1882, a series of general immigration statutes have been enacted in response to the type and numbers of people who had previously entered. From that year forward, the United States embarked on a series of restrictions on immigration. Thus, specific national origins quotas were imposed from time to time which were ethnically and racially discriminatory. Quantitative restrictions were introduced into the immigration regimen in 1921 with the passage of the first quota system applicable to designated nationalities.

Immigration has come to the United States in waves of specific nationalities to escape adverse conditions such as drought, famine, depression, religious persecution, etc. in their countries of origin. While that is still the case today for many persons, many others now seek to come to the United States for temporary periods of time in order to accomplish specific business, cultural, or other personal goals. These include education, tourism and business investment and entrepreneurial exploitation. While the deprivation of the crowded steamship has been replaced by the comfort of the jet airliner, the administrative problem at the immigration counter has not changed very much.

With the passage of the McCarran-Walter Act in 1952, the legislation that molded the basic structure of the immigration law as we know it today, a new phenomenon began to emerge. The U.S. immigration system began to partake of a more democratic character as the law attempted to apply admissions policies without direct regard to national and racial origins. The last trace of racial or ethnic discrimination was removed with the abolition of the separate quota for Western Hemisphere aliens in 1978.

As a result of the passage of the Immigration Act of 1990, the immigration regimen with respect to permanent visas now emphasizes the policy of attracting persons who possess desirable occupational skills or economic resources. The law still provides for the unification of families and close relatives of U.S. citizens and, to a lesser extent, of permanent residents. The law, now for the first time, establishes a category for the issuance of permanent visas to investors who establish or invest in new, job creating enterprises. There have also been some substantial changes with respect to the issuance of temporary visas to the United States. One reality is constant and indisputable: there is a higher demand for visas, permanent and temporary, to the United States than there is supply and perceived need. With this general background, let us look more closely at the United States visa system.

In September of 1996, the President of the United States signed into law the latest modification of the visa system of the United States. It is known as the Illegal Immigration Reform and Immigrant Responsibility Act (IIRAIRA). This law while designed to stem the flow of illegal immigration to the United States also harbored some mean spirited provisions which can be dangerous to both U.S. citizens and foreign persons alike. This law contains certain retroactive provisions which render persons deportable who in some cases have been long term abiding citizens of the United States. It also makes deportable dependents such as spouses and children of foreign persons who may have inadvertently exceeded or violated their status.

The United States federal government has jurisdiction over all visa and immigration matters. The individual state and local governments have only a limited role in this field, such as the initial processing of labor certification applications. As an illustration of this point, I would emphasize that the quality and strength of the alien's connection with state and local governmental and business institutions are of very limited help in qualifying for a long-term visa. This elementary fact is very often overlooked by foreign persons who do not understand the nature of the federal system of government in the United States. In fact, the programs and policies of a state concerning a particular subject can be different from those of the federal government on the same subject. Unfortunately, if the subject matter in question is one which the Constitution of the United States assigns to the federal government, then the federal law takes precedence over the state law. This is the reality with matters concerning United States immigration policy.

Failure to fulfill the detailed requirements of the United States visa system can often result in a denial or delay in the issuance of a visa petition even if the local or state authorities welcome individuals and their investments. In short, neither the Immigration and Naturalization Service nor the U.S. Consul abroad depends upon the recommendations of the local or state government or of the local Chambers of Commerce, community service organizations, etc. The alien entering the United States must comply with the formal requirements of a federal bureaucratic system that is largely insulated from "outside" interests.

U.S. Consulates Abroad

Outside of the United States, aliens deal almost exclusively with the United States Consulate or Embassy in their home country. The U.S. consul has, within the confines of the law, almost complete discretion as to whom and under what circumstances a visa to the United States will be granted. Furthermore, there is no appeal from a denial of a visa by the U.S. consul other than for interpretations of law. This means that an alien should have a complete understanding of the law, and should be thoroughly prepared and documented to comply with the law before the alien first approaches the U.S. consul on any visa question. The U.S. Department of State, acting through its U.S. consulates abroad, does not view itself as a counseling agency for individuals who seek to immigrate to the United States. Please read this paragraph again and accept it as a fundamental principal in dealing with the host country United States consulate with respect to visa matters.

In addition, the local U.S. Consul abroad probably has an in-depth understanding of political and economic conditions of that country and is able to apply that knowledge and experience in adjudicating the intentions and motivations of individual applications of host country citizens who seek visas to the United States.

Immigration and Naturalization Service

An alien who is already in the United States must deal with the Immigration and Naturalization Service (INS). This agency is a division of the Office of the United States Attorney General and operates through various regional and subregional offices throughout the United States. A list of these offices is found in appendix A of this book.

Once aliens are already in the United States, they enjoy slightly more procedural rights than would be the case if they were outside the United States.

Certain visa petitions such as the Form I-129 (used for the L-1 visa) must be filed within the United States at a regional office of the Immigration and Naturalization Service. Other visa petitions such as for the B-1 visa must be filed abroad at the local U.S. Consulate. Some visa applications may be filed either in the United States or the U.S. Consulate abroad. Often the choice of where to file a petition can be either a strategic or tactical decision depending upon many factors, including the prevailing and often divergent attitudes of these two U.S. agencies. There are four Regional Service Centers within the United States and forming part of the Immigration and Naturalization Service to which individual petitions are sent for adjudication. There is a trend toward centralizing this approach so as to ensure uniformity and efficiency. As a result of this trend, it is clear that the INS is developing a cadre of officers who are knowledgeable about current business practices as well as current legal and social trends in the United States. This is often lacking in certain U.S. Consular posts abroad since often the adjudicating officers have received little training and are rotated frequently. The regional service centers are essentially "think tanks," to which access from the public, including even immigration attorneys, is limited. The philosophy of utilizing these regional service centers is to ensure that visa petitions will be adjudicated in an objective manner.

Regardless of how foreign persons may have entered the United States, after their entry they are under the jurisdiction of the INS.

INSPECTION, EXCLUSION, AND REMOVAL (DEPORTATION)

Every independent nation has complete discretion as to whom it will admit within its borders. When aliens appear at the U.S. border or other port of entry, they are subject to the power of inspection and removal by the immigration inspector. The purpose of the inspection is to determine whether or not the foreign person is admissible to the United

States. Inspectors of the U.S. Immigration and Naturalization Service (INS) have the right to examine the alien's passport and visa to ensure that the physical person in front of them is the person identified in the travel documents. Additionally, the officer is authorized, by interrogation and physical inspection of luggage and of the person, determine whether the person is entitled to enter the United States in the visa category requested and for how long a duration. Lately, the duration of stay under particular visa categories has been established by regulation, so that in most instances the immigration inspector is bound by the term established in the applicable regulation or operating instruction. Normally, the actual inspection time takes only a few minutes unless the inspecting officer suspects an irregularity.

Upon inspection and in accordance with law, U. S. immigration officers may exclude an alien from entering the United States, if they find the alien ineligible to enter the U.S. This power to exclude is the primary obstacle to an alien entering the United States. It should be noted that many foreign persons complain of rudeness on the part of the INS inspectors at the ports of entry. Unfortunately, one's experience with the inspection process depends upon many factors, not the least of which is the inspector's personality. As in all areas of human interaction the vagaries of chance and happenstance as well as the facts surrounding the alien will determine whether the experience is forgettable or otherwise. INS inspectors often view themselves as police officials trying to prevent illegal entry into the United States rather than as good will emissaries of the United States. This unfortunate attitude is reinforced by the strong demands for visas to the United States and by continuous attempts by certain aliens to circumvent the law and attempt to enter the United States illegally. I can only warn alien readers of this fact, so that they will not be overly intimidated by the occasional unfriendly reception they may receive at the point of entry. If the foreign person reads this book and understands how the immigration system functions, he or she will get through the border with the least amount of upset and inconvenience.

One of the most controversial changes wrought by IIRAIRA is the power given to immigration inspectors to exclude a person from entry to the U.S. on an expedited basis and without appeal of any kind whatsoever. In effect, the inspector becomes judge and executioner. Even a person with a valid visa may be excluded or admitted provisionally on parole or under a process called *deferred inspection* at the border, if the immigration official determines or suspects that the alien is not entitled to use the visa in his passport. Indeed, the law provides that a person who attempts to enter the United States with a visa which is inappropriate for the alien's intended or perceived purpose can be summarily removed on the basis of fraud and become permanently ineligible to enter the United States.

"I BELIEVE YOU ARE WHO YOU SAY YOU ARE LORD BELLYWOO, BUT REGULATIONS REQUIRE ME TO INSPECT YOUR HAIRPIECE."

GENERAL GROUNDS OF INADMISSIBILITY

IIRAIRA enacted broad and profound changes with respect to the grounds for the removal of aliens to the United States. Among the many changes created by IIRAIRA is the power of expedited removal given to the immigration inspector coupled with the elimination of all appeals from the inspector's decision. Aliens encounter the concept of exclusion or removal when they appear at the U.S. consulate and apply for a visa and, again, when at the border attempting to enter the United States.

Thus, an alien might have the visa petition denied by the U.S. consular office because the consular office believes that one or more grounds of exclusion may apply to the particular alien. Decisions made by consular officers are difficult to reverse since they are granted broad discretion in interpreting the factual circumstances surrounding any particular alien petitioner.

If aliens already have a visa in their possession, the Immigration and Naturalization inspector at the border may deny them entry to the United States on the basis that one or more of the following grounds of ineligibility for admission might apply. With respect to certain of the grounds for inadmissibility, the law provides "waivers" or exemptions which may, nonetheless, permit a foreign person to enter the United States even though one or more grounds for inadmissibility may apply. When the term "waiver" is used in the context of inadmissibility it refers to an exception or a pardon of the grounds for inadmissibility.

HEALTH-
RELATED
GROUNDS

These primary grounds would apply to any foreign person found by the Department of Health and Human Services to have a communicable disease of public health significance. This would include, for instance, any person who has been diagnosed as HIV positive. This category of inadmissibility would also apply to any other form of communicable disease such as Tuberculosis.

In addition, the law now requires that a foreign person seeking admission as an immigrant (permanent resident) provide documentation of having received vaccination against a myriad of vaccine-preventable diseases such as, mumps, measles, rubella, polio, tetanus influenza type B and hepatitis B and any other vaccination against vaccine-preventable diseases recommended by the Advisory Committee for Immunization Practices. There are waivers available for this requirement if it can be documented that it would be medically dangerous for the person to receive the vaccination or if there is proof that the person was previously vaccinated.

This ground of inadmissibility would apply to any foreign person determined by the Department of Health and Human Services to have a physical or mental disorder or to manifest any behavior that could or that has in the past posed a threat to others. The determination that a particular person has a physical or mental disorder will be made on a case-by-case basis because this is essentially a new provision. How the method and scope of enforcement of the new law will differ from the prior law is not clear.

If the Department of Health and Human Services determines that the alien is a drug abuser or a drug addict, the alien could be rendered inadmissible from entry. This ground of inadmissibility is separate from the provision which would bar any person from entering the United States who has been convicted of any criminal offense involving drug use. Apparently, experimentation alone will not render a foreign person inadmissible but it is not clear what conduct would be included in the exception of mere "experimentation." The law also provides grounds for discretionary relief against inadmissibility if the foreign person has necessary family ties and otherwise proves mitigating circumstances which would move the Immigration and Naturalization Service to waive this ground of inadmissibility and permit the alien to enter the United States in spite of being found to be a drug abuser or addict. The purpose for the waiver provision is to keep families together and to prevent a hardship where a proper family environment would mitigate any danger to the public. The law also provides that grounds for exclusion on this basis may be waived if a bond is provided.

CRIMINAL GROUNDS

There are essentially five grounds of inadmissibility on the basis of criminal conduct:

1. Conviction or admission of a crime of moral turpitude or a crime involving a drug offense. It is important to understand the concept of crimes of "moral turpitude." This designation refers to those crimes that are indicative of bad moral character, such as crimes of theft, assault and battery, murder, rape, and the like. There are limited waivers (dispensations) to exclusion for

persons convicted of any of these offenses. A waiver is available for conviction of minor offenses, which are defined as offenses for which the sentence imposed is less than six months. A waiver is possible if the crime was committed by an alien who was under the age of eighteen at the time of the crime, and the crime was committed more than five years before the date of application for the visa. Another exception to excludability applies to crimes for which the maximum possible penalty does not exceed one year, and, if the alien was actually convicted of the crime, where the alien was not in fact sentenced to a term of imprisonment in excess of six months.

2. Conviction of two or more crimes if the combined custodial sentence imposed is for five years or longer regardless of whether or not the crime arose from a single stream of events or whether or not the crimes were of moral turpitude.

3. When the consular or immigration officer knows or has reason to believe that the alien is or was a drug trafficker or was a person who aided, abetted or conspired in drug trafficking.

4. Any alien who was involved in prostitution or is coming to the United States to engage in any other unlawful commercialized vice.

5. Aliens involved in serious criminal activity who have asserted immunity from prosecution and departed. This would apply, for instance, to persons who committed crimes or committed acts which could have been crimes, but who asserted diplomatic immunity.

Waivers of inadmissibility on the above grounds may be available under section 212(h) of the Immigration and Nationality Act for non-drug-related crimes, for prostitution or for conviction of a single offense of possession of thirty grams or less of marijuana. The waiver is available upon the passage either of fifteen years from the disqualifying event coupled with proof of the alien's rehabilitation, or in the event of extreme hardship to designated U.S. citizens or permanent resident relatives, i.e., spouse, parent, son, or daughter. This waiver is not available to aliens who have already been admitted to the U.S. as permanent residents if since the date of their admissions they have been convicted of an aggravated felony or the alien has not resided continuously in the U.S. for at least seven years before the date removal proceedings are begun. No court has jurisdiction to review a decision of the INS to grant or deny this waiver.

SECURITY AND
RELATED
GROUNDS

This category of inadmissibility would apply to:

1. Any person who, in the opinion of the U.S. Consular Officer, entered the United States to engage in prejudicial and unlawful activities which would include espionage, sabotage, and violation or evasion of laws concerning the prohibition of export from the United States of goods, technology or other sensitive information. There is a waiver possible for anyone who violates the provision concerning the export of technology, if the person seeks to re-enter the United States solely as a non-immigrant.

2. Anyone who is engaged in terrorist activity and who is an active member of the PLO. Terrorist activity is defined to encompass active support for terrorist organizations through a variety of activities, including fund-raising. The Secretary of State can also designate the organizations which are considered to be "terrorist" organization. Terrorist activity in this case is defined to apply immediately to a person who is an officer, official, representative or spokesman of the Palestinian Liberation Organization. (This is one questionably discriminatory section of the statute which I believe will be subject to judicial scrutiny.) Terrorist activity also includes, of course, highjacking or sabotage of any vehicle or conveyance which includes aircraft and seagoing vessels; killing, detaining or threatening to kill or injure another individual in order to compel a third person to act or abstain from acting as an explicit condition for the release of the individual, as well as a

violent attack upon an internationally protected person. To engage in terrorist activity also is defined to include:

an act which the actor knows or reasonably should know affords material support to any individual, organization or government in conducting a terrorist activity at any time, including any of the following acts:

Providing any type of material support, including a safe house, transportation, communications, funds, false identification, weapons, explosives, training through any individual the actor knows or has reason to believe has committed, or plans to commit, an act of terrorist activity, or anyone who solicits funds or other things of value for terrorist activities or terrorist organizations.

3. Anyone whose entry would have a foreign policy consequence seriously adverse to the interests of the United States. This is a general exclusionary right given the U.S. Consulate. Exceptions to exclusion on these grounds are made for foreign government officials and politicians in cases in which their exclusion would be based upon speech or association which would have been lawful in the United States.

4. Other individuals who are not foreign government officials who intend to engage in speech or association which also would be lawful in the U.S. This is also subject to veto by personal determination of the Secretary of State based upon a compelling U.S. foreign policy interest.

5. An alien who seeks to apply for immigrant status and who was a member or is actively a member of a communist or totalitarian party. An exception to excludability on this basis is available for those persons who were members of the Communist party on an involuntary basis or who were members when they were under the age of sixteen. An additional exception to excludability is available to persons whose membership terminated two years

before the visa application was made. If the totalitarian party still controls the alien's country, then an exception can be made for former Communist party members only if their membership terminated at least five years previous to application for entry.

Waivers or exceptions to these grounds of excludability are available for any of the above aliens who are immediate and dependent family relatives of U.S. citizens if they are otherwise not a threat to U.S. security.

7. Anyone who participated in the NAZI persecution of World War II or in genocide. There is an exception to this exclusionary grounds for those persons who are seeking to enter the United States only as diplomatic representatives.

PERSONS LIKELY
TO BECOME A
PUBLIC CHARGE

This category of inadmissibility applies to persons who are or are likely to become a public charge, meaning they cannot support themselves. In determining whether an alien is excludable as likely to become a public charge, the government official must take into account the alien's age, health, family status, assets, resources, and financial status as well as an Affidavit of Support.

The Affidavit of Support: The law now requires every alien seeking admission as a family-sponsored immigrant or, in certain cases, as an employment-based alien, to provide a legally enforceable financial guarantee by a U.S. sponsor, the sponsor must document sufficient income to provide the alien with an income level which is 125% of the poverty level as established by the Director of the Office of Management and Budget. If the U.S. sponsor does not have sufficient income to meet this requirement, the law allows the use of assets (including those of the alien) which are readily convertible to cash to substitute for income, as long as the assets have a value five times the amount of income which is being substituted. Sponsored aliens can contribute their own income if they have been living with the U.S. sponsor for at least six months.

The law provides that the U.S. sponsor shall remain liable to the government for any means-based governmental economic benefits which the alien receives until the alien either becomes a citizen or has worked a total of forty qualifying quarters of time. This is the equivalent of ten years of employment. A divorce will not terminate the financial and legal obligation of a sponsoring U.S. spouse and the law allows the federal and state governments as well as the sponsored alien the right to file a legal claim against the U.S. sponsor in order to enforce this provision. The Affidavit of Support (included as appendix E) now creates legal and financial consequences for the sponsor and alien which require some analysis based upon the particular personal and financial circumstances of the parties.

PROTECTION OF THE U.S. LABOR MARKET

This category of inadmissibility applies to persons who are entering the United States seeking to engage in gainful employment. Anyone who seeks to enter the United States to work and who does not have a Labor Certification from the United States Department of Labor is inadmissible. In this regard, please refer to page 41 of this book for a discussion of employment-based permanent residency visa preferences which require a labor certification.

Professional athletes are permitted to move from team to team after admission to the U.S. if the new team is in the same sport as the previous team and the league in which the teams play has a combined total revenue of at least $10,000,000.00.

PHYSICIANS

Also inadmissible under this designation would be those physicians who are unqualified to practice medicine in the United States. In order for physicians to enter the United States, they must have passed an English proficiency test and must have taken one of two national medical exams.

UNCERTIFIED FOREIGN HEALTH-CARE WORKERS

Any person seeking to immigrate as a permanent resident for the purpose of performing labor as a healthcare worker, other than as a physician, is inadmissible unless the alien presents a certificate from the Commission on Graduates of Foreign Nursing Schools or from an equivalent independent credentialing organization which confirms 1) that the alien's education, training, license, and experience is equivalent to that of a similar U.S. worker; 2) that the alien is sufficiently competent in the English language' and 3) that the alien has passed any test which is recognized by a majority of States as predicting success on the profession's licensing and certification examination. The validity of the above tests is to be determined solely by the Secretary of Health and Human Services and are not subject to further administrative or judicial review.

ILLEGAL ENTRY INTO THE UNITED STATES

This category includes: An alien present in the U.S. without being admitted or paroled, or who arrives in the U.S. at any time or place other than as designated by the INS is inadmissible. There is an exception for certain "battered women and children" as long as they can establish that their illegal presence is caused by the battery or extreme mental cruelty. The concept of "battered women and children" is discussed on page 70 of this book.

In addition, any alien who without reasonable cause fails to attend a removal proceeding and who then seeks admission to the United States within five years of the alien's departure or removal is inadmissible.

Persons guilty of material misrepresentation of any petition or other document with respect to a visa. This provision bars foreign persons from entering the United States who seek or have sought to obtain a visa, documentation, entry or other immigration benefit by committing fraud or otherwise willfully misrepresenting material facts. There is a waiver for this exclusion ground for those persons who are immediate relatives of United States citizens or of permanent resident aliens or for cases where the fraud occurred at least ten years before entry. These grounds of waiver of excludability apply only to persons seeking to enter the United States as immigrants.

Any alien who falsely represents, or has falsely represented himself or herself to be a citizen of the United States for any purpose or benefit under the immigration law or under any other federal or State is also inadmissible.

Also, any lien who was admitted as a non-immigrant and who has obtained any governmental benefits for which the alien was ineligible, through fraud or misrepresentation, under federal law is excludable for a period of five years from the date of the alien's departure from the United States.

Also included are stowaways and smugglers of aliens. Waivers of excludability are available to aliens guilty of smuggling their immediate family members. This section, however, would not apply to anyone engaged in the smuggling of a person into the United States for profit.

Finally, violators include student visa abusers. An alien who obtains a student visa (F-1) and who violates a term or condition of such status by either attending a public school for longer than permitted or by transferring to a public school from a private school shall be excludable until the alien has been outside the U.S. for a continuous period of five years after the date of the violation. Presumably this exclusion grounds would apply even to a child and even if the violation were attributable solely to his or her parents or guardians.

ENTERING WITHOUT PROPER DOCUMENTS

Grounds of inadmissibility apply to aliens who do not have a valid visa or entry document or who do not have the required documents in support of their immigration status upon entry.

There are general waiver provisions applicable to the above grounds of inadmissibility.

PERSONS INELIGIBLE FOR CITIZENSHIP

This category of inadmissibility applies to persons who are ineligible for citizenship because of violating U.S. military service requirements and who are draft evaders.

ALIENS PREVIOUSLY REMOVED

Any alien who has been ordered removed and who again seeks admission within five years of the date of removal at the point of entry (or within twenty years in the case of a second or subsequent removal or at any time in the case of an alien convicted of an aggravated felony) is inadmissible.

Any other alien who is removed from the U.S. after entry is barred from entering the U.S. for a period of ten years from the date of the departure or removal (or for a period of twenty years in the case of second or subsequent removal or at any time in the case of an alien convicted of an aggravated felony).

Bar to entry based upon prior unlawful presence: Any alien (other than an alien lawfully admitted for permanent residence) who was unlawfully present in the United States for a period of more than 180 days but less than one year, voluntarily departed the United States prior to the commencement of removal proceedings is barred from re-entering the U.S. for a period of three years from the date of such alien's departure or removal.

Any alien who has been unlawfully present in the United States for one year or more, is barred from entering the United States for a period of ten years from the date of such alien's departure or removal from the United States.

The term *unlawfully present* generally means the overstay by a foreign person of the time authorized by the INS, and as usually noted on the ARRIVAL-DEPARTURE RECORD (Form I-94), for a person to remain in the United States. It also includes the time after the INS or the immigration court has determined that a person has violated the conditions of admission. It is important to bear in mind that the definition of unlawful presence is a dynamic one and as of the date of the publication of this book, the INS was interpreting this term to include the time that a foreign person is required to remain in the U.S. while in formal removal proceedings.

The bar may be waived by the INS in its sole discretion if the alien can establish that its imposition would create an extreme hardship on a U.S. citizen or permanent resident spouse or child.

In addition the bars to re-entry based upon unlawful presence do not apply to any period of time in which an alien:

☞ was under the age of eighteen years,

☞ had a "bona fide" asylum application pending,

☞ was the beneficiary of a family unity protection application, or

☞ was a "battered woman or child."

The time in which an alien who has been lawfully admitted to the U.S. has pending a non frivolous bona fide application to change or extend status is not counted as unlawful presence for a maximum period of 120 days provided the alien has not worked without authorization.

An alien who has been unlawfully present in the U.S. for a period of one year or who has been previously removed from the U.S. and who then seeks to enter the United States at a place other than a lawful entry point is permanently inadmissible. This permanent bar can be waived by the INS if the alien's attempted re-entry is at least ten years after the date of the alien's last departure from the U.S., if prior to the alien's reembarkation at a place outside the U.S. the INS has consented to the alien's reapplication for admission.

POLYGAMY

It is against the public policy of the United States for a person to have more than one spouse.

ALIEN GUARDIANS ACCOMPANYING HELPLESS ALIENS

An alien who is accompanying another alien who is inadmissible and who is certified to be helpless from sickness, mental or physical disability, or infancy and whose protection or guardianship is determined to be required by the inadmissible alien is inadmissible.

INTERNATIONAL CHILD ABDUCTORS

This ground applies to an alien who may be involved in a domestic (family) dispute involving child custody. During these emotional controversies, aliens may be tempted to simply remove themselves and their children from the United States to their country of origin and thus thwart the possibility of the United States citizen acquiring child custody rights. Under U.S. and international law, such conduct is improper and amounts to domestic abduction. An alien who is found to be an international child abductor is excludable without relief. There are no waivers available for such a person.

UNLAWFUL VOTERS

Any alien who has voted in violation of any federal, State, or local constitutional provision, statute, ordinance, or regulation is excludable.

FORMER CITIZENS WHO RENOUNCED CITIZENSHIP TO AVOID TAXATION

Any alien who is a former citizen of the U.S. who officially renounces U.S. citizenship and who is determined by the Attorney General to have renounced U.S. citizenship for the purpose of avoiding taxation by the U.S. is excludable.

If any of the above categories of inadmissibility apply, the alien who is considering making a visa application to the United States should consult a qualified U.S. immigration attorney before submitting the application. The above categories can also be grounds for deportation in the event the alien enters the country by misrepresentation or omission of information.

Removal is the term for the official removal of aliens who have either already entered the United States or who seek admission at a port of entry. This book deals with the concept of removal as excludability from entry and not with the concept of removal as applicable to a person who has already entered the United States and is being removed for violations of law or regulation after lawful admissibility.

DISTINCTION BETWEEN IMMIGRANT AND NON-IMMIGRANT VISAS

There are generally two types of visas available to foreign persons seeking to enter the United States. The first is a permanent residency or immigrant visa (also known as a *green card*), and the other is a non-immigrant visa, or temporary visa.

There is only one type of permanent residency visa, and once that is obtained, there are no special subclassifications or conditions attached to that visa—except as to the two-year condition placed on aliens who have obtained "conditional residence" based upon either an employment creation petition or a spousal petition based upon marriage to a U.S. citizen. Permanent Residency card (Form I-551) is also called the *green card* even though the card is no longer green in color. Regardless of how a person obtained a green card—whether as a result of marriage to a U.S. citizen, or as a result of a labor certification or by other family relationship to a U.S. citizen—the resulting permanent residency visa consequences are the same in every case. Permanent residency visas enable foreign persons to live and work wherever they choose without distinction as to how the permanent residency visa was obtained.

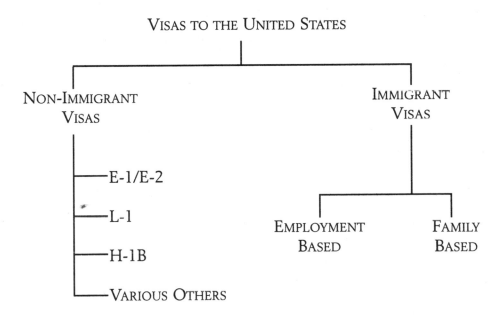

There are, however, many different types of temporary visas and each visa has its own set of qualifications and conditions, both as to their duration and as to the activities the alien may lawfully undertake in the United States in accordance with the visa. The above diagram illustrates this fundamental but very important point.

Chapter 1 of this book will discuss the permanent visas and chapter 2 will discuss some of the most important temporary visas for most people. Which category of visa, i.e., permanent or temporary, is the most appropriate for a foreign person depends upon many factors deserving of study and consideration, not the least of which is the alien's own intention.

The Problem of Intent

Probably the most important concept to be understood by any foreign person is the importance attached by the immigration authorities to the alien's intention as to duration of stay and purpose in the U.S. An example: A permanent residency visa is given only to a qualified person who intends to remain living in the United States permanently, while a temporary (non-immigrant) visa is issued only to a qualified person who intends to stay in the United States for a temporary period and then depart. In the latter case, if the alien's immediate intention is to remain permanently in the United States, then the only type of visa for which he can qualify is the immigrant visa. Looking at it in reverse, the alien would not be qualified for a temporary visa if he has an immediate intention to remain in the United States permanently, even though he might be otherwise qualified to obtain that temporary visa.

There are exceptions to this rule, but in general, an alien who meets the objective qualifications for a non-immigrant visa will be denied that visa or entry to the United States under that visa if the U.S. Consul abroad or the INS examining officer at the border feels that the alien's true intention is to remain in the U.S. permanently. Furthermore, all aliens entering the United States are presumed to be immigrants (and thus excludable) unless they can demonstrate that they have a valid non-immigrant visa in their possession and are entitled to enter the United States under that visa.

In the event the immigration border inspector determines that a foreign person is not entitled to enter the United States, he can deny to that foreign person the right to enter and require that person to return to his country of origin. In some limited cases, however, the immigration officer may permit the foreign person to enter the United States on "parole" and then schedule a formal hearing at the local office of the Immigration and Naturalization Service to determine whether or not the person should be "removed" or admitted to the United States.

Thus, instead of a "welcome," there is a "keep out" attitude framed in the law. This has two possible practical consequences. First, U.S. consular officers in the foreign country will only grant a non-immigrant visa if they are satisfied that the person will return to his home country. If U.S. consuls are not so convinced, then they may deny issuance of the visa, regardless of whether the alien meets the other objective qualifications for the issuance of the visa. Secondly, aliens may be excluded or "removed" at the border if the immigration officer is convinced that their intentions for entering the U.S. are different from those required by the visas in their passports, or they are otherwise not entitled to enter the United States. The above four paragraphs should be reread and thoroughly understood.

An example of the first situation can be illustrated by the problem many Iranians encountered after the Iranian revolution, when they tried to obtain visas to the United States as visitors (tourists). Even though many of the applicants were well-respected business people with homes and property in Iran, experience taught the U.S. consuls that most people leaving Iran would never return, regardless of the cost to them of their abandoned property. The same problem exists for persons coming from other troubled spots in the world. Thus, the question of intention is absolutely critical in many cases and is subject to the discretion of the U.S. consul abroad. This statement is not meant to be a criticism of the State Department practice; it merely reflects reality.

During the Lebanese civil war in the late 1970s and early 1980s, a young Lebanese man who was married to a U.S. citizen and was himself a permanent resident alien wanted to bring his parents who were Lebanese citizens to visit with him in the United States. He sought my assistance because his parents' application for visitors' visas (B-2) had been denied by various U.S. consuls in Europe. His parents had left Lebanon and were in Europe trying to obtain U.S. visitors' visas. I explained that B-2 visas are issued abroad and that there was little that I could do for them here in the United States other than to suggest some documentation that they should present to the U.S. Consul. Nonetheless, I telephoned various U.S. Consuls in Europe to see if I could help. I was told by all of them that based upon their experience most business people leaving war-torn Lebanon were doing so with the intention of never returning.

I suggested to the young man that he might offer to provide a cash bond guaranteeing to the U.S. Consul where his parents were located that his parents would depart the United States at the conclusion of their visit. After speaking with the United States consul in a particular European country, I suggested that the young man travel to that U.S. consul and plead his case directly. The young man noted all that I told him and left. Some months later while I was shopping in a local department store this same young fellow approached me and identified himself to me as the person in this story. I asked him about his parents. He told me that he had traveled to the United States consular post in Europe, had convinced the consul his parents would return to Lebanon after their visit, and that his parents then obtained their visitors' visas. I congratulated him on his fine efforts and asked him how his parents enjoyed their visit to the United States. He then told me that his parents, after spending some time in the United States, decided that they were not returning to their home country. Since he had recently become a United States citizen, he was filing an immediate relative petition to obtain their permanent residency for them. This was precisely what the U.S. Consul with whom I had spoken on the telephone predicted would happen. Under these circumstances one can hardly blame United States Consular officials for being skeptical of a person's spoken motivations or intentions.

As stated previously, obtaining a non-immigrant visa abroad is no guarantee that the alien will be admitted to the United States. An example of this is the story of the European young person with a valid non-immigrant visa who was turned away at the border because of his idle and nervous chatter with the immigration officer. The person emphasized his happiness at finally being in the United States, and his unwillingness to ever return to his cold and inhospitable country again. Whether or not the story's details have been exaggerated is not important. The important point to note is that upon arrival at the border foreign persons must prove that their intent coincides with the visas in their passports or else the immigration inspector can remove the foreign person on an expedited basis, without hearing or appeal.

The question of intent arises when a person who has a permanent visa leaves the United States for an extended period of time. The law presumes that if permanent resident aliens remain outside the United States for one year or more, this absence from the United States can be considered an abandonment of their visa. Persons who remain outside the United States for periods of six months or longer are subject to inspection and admission. They do not lose their permanent residency status based upon a six month departure but are subject to establishing that they are otherwise admissible. Permanent resident aliens contemplating a long but temporary stay outside the United States should, therefore, make that fact known to the immigration authorities before departure to obtain a re-entry permit that will permit return to the United States even after the extended absence. Permanent residents will retain the permanent residency visa if the reason for the extended stay abroad is for valid reasons beyond their control.

The question of intent also arises within the context of different types of *non-immigrant* visas. For example, if a person enters the United States as a tourist with a B-2 visa and then shortly after entry applies for a change to a different type of visa, the Immigration and Naturalization authorities will require an explanation as to why the individual did not originally apply in his home country for the visa which he now seeks by way of change. If the Immigration and Naturalization Service officials do not receive a satisfactory explanation they may deny the change of status based upon a form of fraud known as *preconceived intent*. The Immigration and Naturalization Service will infer that the alien gained entry to the United States by way of the tourist visa with a preconceived intent of applying for a different visa status shortly after arrival.

We will treat the question of intention throughout this book, and discuss its consequences in various circumstances. Thus, foreign persons must accept that their intentions will be under scrutiny by the U.S. immigration and consular authorities when they apply for any type of visa.

Unauthorized Employment

The United States government is attempting to stifle illegal immigration by enforcing its laws against unauthorized employment by aliens. It seeks to accomplish this goal by imposing civil and criminal penalties on United States employers who hire aliens who are not legally authorized to work. This law renders it difficult for aliens who are not authorized to work to engage in meaningful employment since it exposes their employers to legal sanctions. The employer, thus, becomes part of the enforcement apparatus as a result of self interest in avoiding the civil and criminal sanctions imposed by the law. The employer is required to file a form (I-9) which establishes the documentation that the alien presented to the employer to verify the alien's authorization to work. In addition to the employer sanctions, aliens are still subject to removal if they are found to be engaged in unauthorized employment.

The law provides for the grant of work authorization to certain aliens in the United States who might not otherwise be eligible to work. Thus, aliens for whom an immigrant visa is immediately available, such as immediate relatives of U.S. citizens, may obtain work authorization. In most cases, an identity card, known as an EAD (Employment Authorization Document) with a photograph of the alien is issued as documentation of this status. Included in appendix B is the instruction sheet for Form I-765 which defines the basis for the issuance of work authorization.

PERMANENT IMMIGRANT VISAS FOR PREFERENCE CATEGORIES

2

The United States establishes two general categories of persons who may immigrate permanently to the United States. One of these categories is composed of persons who are subject to an annual worldwide numerical limit. The other category is composed of those persons who may immigrate at any time regardless of the worldwide demand for immigrant visas. The first group of persons is subject to a system of categories or *preferences* which determines the priority of immigration classifications based on the annual quota. The annual quota is 675,000 persons. This is known as the preference system for permanent visas.

There is another group of persons who are not subject to the preference system and who, when qualified, may enter the United States regardless of the annual numerical quota system. This classification is known as *non-preference* immigrants. This category includes refugees (who have their own quota), and immediate relatives of United States citizens and children born to a permanent resident during a temporary visit outside the United States. Most persons entering the United States as non-preference immigrants are immediate relatives of United States citizens. In this book we will characterize immigrant visas by the terms preference visas and non-preference visas.

The United States preference system for immigrant visas is sometimes called a "numbers game." That is because the law establishes the total number of foreign persons who will be admitted annually to the United States as permanent residents. In order to understand the system of immigrant visas, it is important to understand how the "numbers game" works.

Of the total annual quota of immigrant visas, every nation is limited to an annual maximum number of permanent visas for family-sponsored and employment-related permanent residency visas which cannot exceed seven percent of the total annual number of available visas. Dependent areas such as St. Kitts, Nevis, etc. are limited to two percent of the yearly quota.

Hong Kong is treated separately under the current law and is considered an independent country for permanent visa allocation.

Generally, the birth place of the alien determines the country to which they will be charged for immigration and visa purposes. There are, however, special rules which allow the immigrant authorities the right to charge the aliens' spouse's or child's home country with the immigration number rather than the principal alien's country in order to provide for a family unity.

One way to visualize the worldwide numerical limitations quota is to imagine a long line of persons attempting to enter the Unites States. In order to get to the immigration counter to have one's visa application considered on its merits, each person has to take a number and wait in line. In our metaphor, the "number" on the line is the priority date. That is the date on which the alien's visa petition or application was accepted as complete. When the alien's priority date is reached, his immigrant petition will be considered on its merits. It is this waiting period that we refer to when we speak of the backlog, or delay, in the annual numerical limitations quota. For instance, a three-year backlog for persons coming to perform labor means that only persons who filed petitions or labor certifications three years earlier would be eligible for admission to the United States.

In addition, persons from certain countries may have an even longer waiting list because their home countries may have already exceeded their annual limitation. At the time of the writing of this book, those countries with priority dates (waiting lists) longer than the worldwide quota include: the Philippines, Mexico, India, China, the Dominican Republic, and dependent areas such as Hong Kong, St. Kitts, Nevis and Antigua.

Of course, not everyone who desires to immigrate to the United States is eligible to receive a permanent residency visa. The law establishes certain categories ("preferences") of persons who may enter the United States by way of this annual worldwide limitations quota and establishes other categories of persons who may enter without regard to the numerical limitations quota. Entry to the United States is based upon qualitative and quantitative restrictions, all of which are scrupulously regulated by the immigration authorities.

THE NUMERICAL PREFERENCE/QUOTA SYSTEM

As stated in the beginning of this chapter, most foreign persons seeking to enter the United States as permanent residents or immigrants are subject to a worldwide annual quota of 675,000 persons unless they are also in one of those special categories previously discussed in the last chapter.

The law establishes four preferences of family-sponsored immigrants and five preferences of employment-related immigrants. The following table illustrates this system.

SCHEDULE OF PREFERENCE CATEGORIES
OF IMMIGRANT VISAS

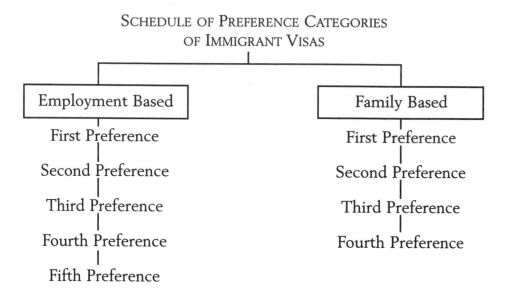

Employment Based	Family Based
First Preference	First Preference
Second Preference	Second Preference
Third Preference	Third Preference
Fourth Preference	Fourth Preference
Fifth Preference	

The annual numerical limitation or quota for family-sponsored immigration is 460,000. Of this number, the law establishes that a minimum of 226,000 visas is reserved for distribution among the four preference categories which will be discussed below. The annual limitation or quota for employment related visas is 140,000. These numbers are subject to change depending upon the political vagaries of the U.S. Congress. The following sections discuss the principal qualifications and conditions of each of these preferences.

FAMILY SPONSORED IMMIGRANTS

The law establishes four preferences for persons who are eligible for permanent immigrant visas to the U.S. based upon family relationships. The total number of visas under this category is 480,000 visas. These annual numerical limitations represent the total number of visas issued to all immigrants based upon family relationships, including immediate relatives of United States citizens. Remember that immediate relatives of U.S. citizens are not counted under the family-sponsored preference category. The number of family-sponsored preference visas is set at a minimum of 226,000. So, in fact, the total number of family-sponsored preference visas could rise above the 226,000 minimum if a large number of immediate relative petitions were filed in any given year. The formula for determining the exact number of family-sponsored preference visas is somewhat complex, but for purposes of this book it is sufficient to know that the total number of family-sponsored preference visas is now considerably higher than it was previously.

FIRST
PREFERENCE

Unmarried sons and daughter of U.S. citizens. The first preference comprises persons who are the unmarried sons and daughters of U.S. citizens. This preference is allotted 23,000 visas annually and includes adult, divorced sons and daughters of U.S. citizens. An unmarried son or daughter is defined differently under the law than a "child," since a "child" is defined as an unmarried person under the age of twenty-one years. A "child," as opposed to a "son or daughter," of a U.S. citizen is under the age of twenty-one years and is unmarried and is entitled to enter the U.S. without regard to the numerical limitations formula.

The first family based preference is a category of limited application and of limited demand and, as a result, is not backlogged on the worldwide quota. In the language of the immigration regimen, this preference is considered "current," and anyone who qualifies may make an immediate application for an immigrant visa.

SECOND
PREFERENCE

Spouse and unmarried sons and daughters of lawful permanent resident aliens. This preference pertains to spouses and unmarried sons and daughters of lawful permanent resident aliens. This preference is different from the first preference described above because the second preference benefits certain relatives of permanent residents as opposed to U.S. citizens. Please note that the term "unmarried son or daughter" is different from the definition of child and in order to comply under this preference, the son or daughter must be unmarried at the time of the application for the visa, though the person may be of any age. This preference is allotted a minimum total of 114,200 visas. This preference is subdivided so that at least seventy-seven percent of such visas are to be allocated to spouses and children of permanent residents. The other twenty-three percent of the total number of visas under this preference is allocated to the unmarried sons or daughters of permanent residents. A divorced son or daughter of a permanent resident will qualify under this preference.

When a permanent resident alien of the United States marries a foreign person, then the U.S. resident's foreign spouse does not receive their immigrant visa and is not permitted to enter the United States until his or her visa priority dates is current. Thus, after the marriage takes place, the permanent resident alien may file an immigration petition for the foreign spouse, but the foreign spouse is required to remain abroad until his or her priority date becomes current. If the foreign spouse were already in the U.S. at the time the permanent residency petition is filed, there is no assurance that the Immigration and Naturalization Service would permit the spouse to remain in the U.S. until the priority date became current. On the contrary, if a foreign spouse of a United States permanent resident (not a U.S. citizen) remains unlawfully present in the United States for a period in excess of 180 days (as of January 14, 1998 and thereafter), then he or she will be required to depart the United States in order to process the permanent residency visa. The departure from the U.S. will then trigger either the three or the ten year bar against re-entry to the United States. The only waiver to the three or ten year bar is for situations in which the U.S. or permanent resident spouse or child can establish, in the sole discretion of the INS, that it would be an "extreme hardship" to the U.S. citizen or permanent resident to enforce the bars. Unless there is a change in the law, the above provision places severe strains on families when one of the petitioning spouses is a permanent resident as opposed to a U.S. citizen.

This category is currently backlogged for a number of years and will remain so indefinitely.

THIRD
PREFERENCE

Married sons and daughters of United States citizens. This preference provides for a total of 23,400 visas, plus any visas that have not been used by the first two family-sponsored preference groups. The third preference benefits qualified persons who are the married sons or daughters of U.S. citizens. This preference should be distinguished from the first family-based preference which, as already explained, applies to unmarried adult sons and daughters of United States citizens. As with the family-sponsored second preference, a divorced person qualifies as a beneficiary of this category. This preference, as of the writing of this book, was also backlogged and is expected to remain so in the foreseeable future.

FOURTH
PREFERENCE

Brothers and sisters of United States citizens. The fourth preference provides for a total of 65,000 visas, or twenty-four percent of the worldwide annual quota plus any visas that have not been utilized by the first three family-sponsored preference groups and benefits qualified persons who are the siblings (brothers and sisters) of United States citizens. The United States citizen petitioner must be at least twenty-one years of age in order to file a petition on behalf of the sibling. Half brothers and half sisters are entitled to the benefits of this preference, as long as the sibling relationship was created before both of the siblings were twenty-one years of age.

As a result of the relatively wide spread eligibility standard of this visa, there is a long waiting list for this visa preference. In the language of immigration law it is heavily "oversubscribed." In fact, it is so oversubscribed that the actual waiting list for a new petitioner based upon the current rate of advancement of this preference is probably more than fifteen years. This is because advancement of the priority date does not coincide with the normal advancement of the calendar. Over the last few years, the priority date for this preference has advanced at a rate of approximately one week per actual calendar month.

Many United States citizens, in order to benefit their brothers and sisters, might almost routinely file an immigrant visa petition for their foreign siblings, on the basis that at some unspecified future time their brothers or sisters may wish to immigrate permanently to the United States. This action can result in an unfortunate trap, since the foreign sibling may be unable to obtain a temporary nonimmigrant visa to the United States as a result of the filing of the family-sponsored third preference petition by the sibling in the United States. This is because the filing of the immigrant visa petition establishes that the foreign person has an intention to reside in the United States on a permanent basis and this intention, of course, conflicts with the temporary intent required for any one of the various nonimmigrant visas, even the B-2 visitor visa.

When the foreign sibling is a business person who may need to come to the United States on temporary business and does not already have a B-1/B-2 visa, it is probably better to avoid filing the fourth preference petition unless the foreign person already has a valid B-1/B-2 visa in his passport. Otherwise the foreign sibling may have (as a condition to obtaining his B-1/B-2 visa) to convince the U.S. consul in the home country that he or she intends to return to the foreign country after each visit to the United States and presently has the intent of visiting the United States only on a temporary basis. This is especially true in the case of persons who are nationals of developing countries or of countries from which there is a history of visa fraud.

While it may seem logical that foreign persons who have a fourth preference petition filed on their behalf, which has at least a seven or eight year waiting period, would still have an intent to return to their home country after a short visit to the United States, the United States consular authorities may require some special proof or documentation before granting a temporary visa to the foreign person.

Note: It is important to bear in mind that all of above family-based beneficiaries (foreign persons for whose benefit the petition was filed) are subject to the three and ten year bars against re-entry to the United States if they are unlawfully present in the United States for a period of 180 days or more.

EMPLOYMENT-BASED IMMIGRANTS

Whereas the above described Family Sponsored Preferences provide for family unity and are premised upon familial relationships, the following Employment-Based Preferences—with the exception of the new *employment creation* visa—are intended to benefit qualified U.S. employers who need certain qualified workers. Unless a foreign person is fortunate to have an immediate relative who is either a citizen or permanent resident of the United States, or unless the foreigner qualifies as a refugee or an asylee, the employment-based preferences are the only avenues of obtaining a permanent residency visa. The law establishes five main categories of employment-based immigrants. The total number of employment-based immigrant visas is 140,000 annually, plus any unused family-sponsored immigrant visas during the previous fiscal year. The table illustrating the employment-based categories follows:

IMMIGRANT VISAS

Employment Based

- •EB <u>First</u> Preference
  - — (Nobel Prize, Lee Iacocca)
  - — (Researchers, Scientists, Jonas Salk)
  - — International Executives
- •EB <u>Second</u> Preference (Masters + Degree Professionals)
- •EB <u>Third</u> Preference
  - — Professional with Baccalaureate Degree
  - — Two year training or experience
  - — General or unskilled labor
- •EB <u>Fourth</u> Preference
  - — Certain juveniles
  - — Ministers of religion
  - — Retired former employees of U.S. Government abroad
- •EB <u>Fifth</u> Preference
  - — Employment creation investors

**FIRST
PREFERENCE**

Priority workers. There are 40,000 visas annually available under this category. This preference category encompasses three subcategories of immigrants:

☞ Persons of extraordinary ability in the arts and sciences, in the field of education, business, or athletics.

☞ Outstanding professors and researchers.

☞ Multinational executives or managers who will work in the United States for the same multinational employer for whom they were employed abroad for one out of the last three years in an executive or managerial capacity.

The most distinguishing characteristic of this visa preference aside from its high level of achievement is the fact that a labor certification from the U.S. Department of Labor is not required as a prerequisite to obtaining this visa. In fact, the alien does not need to be "sponsored" by a U.S. employer. Qualified Employment-based first preference immigrant may petition themselves.

Aliens of extraordinary ability. The high level of achievement that is required by this preference category is demonstrated by sustained national or international acclaim which must be extensively documented. The alien must be seeking to enter the United States to continue work in the field of endeavor which is the subject of the acclaim and the alien's presence and activities must be of benefit to the United States. These requirements must be established with documentary evidence of a highly reliable nature.

The required high level of achievement can be demonstrated by receipt of a major internationally recognized award such as the Nobel Prize or the Academy Award for motion pictures. Alternatively, the alien must provide at least three of the following types of evidence:

☞ Receipt of a lesser national or international prize or award for excellence in the particular field of endeavor.

- ☞ Membership in associations which require outstanding achievements of their members, as judged by nationally or internationally recognized experts in the particular field.

- ☞ Published material in professional journals, major trade publications or the major media about the alien's accomplishments in the field of endeavor. These items must include title, date, author and must be translated into English.

- ☞ Participated on a panel or individually as a judge of the work of others in the same or allied field of endeavor.

- ☞ Original scientific, scholarly, or artistic contributions of major significance in the field of endeavor.

- ☞ Authorship of scholarly articles in the field, in professional journals or other major media (national newspapers, magazines, etc.).

- ☞ Display of his/her work at artistic exhibitions in more than one country.

- ☞ Performance in a lead, starring or critical role for organizations or establishments with distinguished reputations.

- ☞ Commanding a high salary or other significantly high remuneration for services in relation to others.

- ☞ Commercial success in the performing arts, as shown by box office receipts; or record, cassette, compact disk, or video sales.

- ☞ Other comparable evidence if the above types of evidence do not readily apply to the alien's occupation.

The INS has ruled that notwithstanding the furnishing of the minimum amount of documentation requested by the foreign person, there is no assurance that the petition will be approved unless from the totality of the evidence, the INS is convinced that the foreign person has satisfied the qualitative condition of "extraordinary ability." There is absolutely no substitute in this area for the assistance of an experienced and competent immigration attorney in the preparation of the documentation required to fulfill the requirements of this visa preference.

Outstanding professor or researcher. Aliens qualify as an outstanding professor or researcher if they have received international acclaim in a particular academic field, have had at least three years of experience in teaching or research in the field, and seek to enter the United States for a tenured or tenure-track teaching or research position. The position can be for a university or other educational institution or for a private employer so long as the employer has at least three other persons employed in full-time research.

Evidence that the professor/researcher is recognized internationally requires at least two of the following:

- ☛ Receipt of major international prizes or awards for outstanding achievement in the academic field.

- ☛ Membership in academic associations requiring outstanding achievement.

- ☛ Published materials and professional publications written by others about the alien's work.

- ☛ Participation on a panel, or as an individual judging work of others.

- ☛ Original scientific/scholarly research contribution.

- ☛ Authorship of scholarly books or articles

Multinational executive or manager. In order to qualify as a multinational executive or manager under this preference, aliens, during the three years preceding the application, must have been employed for at least one year by the same multinational firm or other business entity which employs them in the United States. Furthermore, the alien must seek to continue rendering services to the same employer in a managerial or executive capacity. The definition of "executive" and "manager" is identical with the definition of those terms under the L-1 visa rules.

This preference category represents an excellent planning opportunity for individuals who also qualify for the L-1 nonimmigrant visa which is discussed in more detail later in this book. There is no specific requirement as to the size of the petitioning company or its gross business volume but the company (employer) must have been in business in the United States for at least one year prior to the filing of the immigrant visa petition (Form I-140).

The law establishes the definition of the terms "managerial capacity" and "executive capacity" and they are identical for both this immigrant visa category as well as the nonimmigrant L-1 intracompany transferee visa (chapter 4). In order to be qualified as a manager, a person must:

☞ Manage a corporation, department, subdivision, or function.

☞ Supervise and control the work of other supervisory, professional, or managerial employees, or else manage an "essential function."

☞ Have the authority to make personnel decisions as to hiring and termination, or else function at a "senior level."

☞ Exercise discretion over the day to day operations of the activity or function for which he or she has authority. Please note that first-line supervisors are excluded from the statutory definition of a manager "unless the employees supervised are professional."

Thus, a manager includes persons who manage a function as well as other people. The term *executive capacity* is also redefined as follows:

☞ The person must manage an organization or major component or function.

☞ Has the authority to establish goals and policies.

☞ Has wide latitude and discretionary decision making authority.

☞ Receives only general supervision from higher executives, board of directors, or stockholders.

The above definitions encompass executives who also perform tasks necessary to produce the product or provide the service offered by the organization if the executive is also a professional, such as an engineer or architect. This subcategory would permit an owner of a business enterprise to immigrate to the United States so long as he could otherwise satisfy the substantive eligibility requirements described above. In a situation in which the prospective employee was also an owner of the enterprise which would hire him, the Immigration and Naturalization Service will scrutinize the petition very closely to discourage fraud. A specific job offer is not required for issuance of this visa, even though it is contemplated that the alien is coming to perform valuable services for a business entity. This subcategory is very advantageous and is therefore closely scrutinized by the INS in order to ensure that it is not abused.

This category represents an important alternative to the Employment Creation Visa discussed on page 50, since proper planning by a qualified investor can result in issuance of a Permanent Residency visa without the necessity of investing one million dollars in a new enterprise that creates a large number of jobs.

SECOND
PREFERENCE

Aliens of exceptional ability. This preference benefits aliens who have:

☞ Advanced degrees or their equivalent in professional fields.

☞ Exceptional ability in the sciences, arts, or business.

In order to establish the first status described above, the alien must submit the official academic record showing a United States advanced degree or a foreign equivalent degree, or an official academic record showing that the alien has a United States baccalaureate degree or a foreign equivalent degree and evidence in the form of letters from current or former employers stating that the alien has at least five years of progressive post-baccalaureate experience in the specialty.

In order to establish exceptional ability in the sciences, arts, or business (the second status mentioned above), the alien must document at least three of the following:

☞ An official academic record showing that the alien has a degree, diploma, certificate, or similar award from a college, university, school, or other institution of learning relating to the area of exceptional ability.

☞ Evidence in the form of letter(s) from current or former employer(s) showing that the alien has at least ten years of full-time experience in the occupation.

☞ A license to practice the profession or certification for a particular profession or occupation.

☞ Evidence that the alien has commanded a salary or other remuneration for services which demonstrate exceptional ability.

☞ Evidence of membership in a professional association.

☞ Evidence of recognition for achievements and significant contributions to the industry or field by peers, governmental entities or professional or business organizations.

The INS has indicated that it will consider comparable evidence that is appropriate to the alien's application in the event the alien cannot provide the type of documentation listed above.

The law allows a person to have the equivalent of an advanced degree if that person has at least five years' progressive experience in the profession beyond the Bachelor's degree. Persons who have exceptional ability in business, however, will still be required to obtain a labor certification. It is important to note that the possession of a degree, diploma, certificate or similar award from a college, university, school, or other institution is not sufficient evidence of exceptional ability by itself. Thus, there must be something beyond the basic qualification in a field of endeavor in order for a person to qualify as having exceptional ability.

The National Interest Waiver. For this preference category, a job offer and labor certification from the Department of Labor is required unless the INS waives that requirement in the national interest. Since the labor certification requirement is such a difficult and expensive process, the alien or the employer should consider whether or not a case can be made that the particular job benefits the national interest.

A series of administrative law decisions has defined the government's policy with respect to establishing the requirements for the "national interest waiver" of the labor certification. The range of cases and decisions indicates that the government requires a fairly direct benefit to the community-at-large before it will agree that a job is in the national interest. A job, for instance, that consists of basic research in attempting to find a cure for the AIDS virus will satisfy this requirement. A job that results in the rescue of a company from bankruptcy and that saves dozens of other jobs will also meet this burden. As a matter of strategy, it is imperative to identify an issue of substantial national interest and then demonstrate how the job in question benefits that national interest in order to prevail on this issue. It is normally necessary to obtain the written opinion of an objective expert in order to prove that a particular job satisfies the national interest. I do not recommend that a person attempt to obtain the national interest waiver without the assistance of a competent and experienced immigration law consultant.

THIRD PREFERENCE

Skilled and unskilled workers. This preference is a general category that includes all other aliens who attempt to obtain permanent residency in the United States based upon an offer of employment. This category also has 40,000 visas annually plus any of the unused visas from the first two employment-based preferences. A job offer from an employer as well as a labor certification from the U.S. Department of Labor are required. The subject of labor certification is discussed later on in this chapter. The employment-based third preference contains three sub-categories:

☞ skilled workers, defined as aliens capable of performing a job requiring at least two years of training or experience,

☞ professionals with a Bachelor's degree (only), and

☞ other workers, also referred to as unskilled workers, who are capable of filling positions requiring less than two years of training or experience.

The first two subcategories share 30,000 of the 40,000 visas allotted to the Third Preference. Only 10,000 of the 40,000 annual visas in the Third Preference are available to unskilled workers and as a result of this limitation, I predict that the backlog or waiting time for this category will be substantial. The present immigration law is obviously geared toward bringing in skilled workers for the economy and is skewed against bringing in unskilled workers.

The segregation of the unskilled workers from the other two above mentioned skilled and professional categories will prevent these from becoming as heavily oversubscribed and backlogged as is the category for unskilled workers. The category for unskilled workers is presently experiencing a six-and-a-half-year delay and is practically unavailable.

FOURTH
PREFERENCE

Special immigrants. This preference category is allocated 10,000 visas annually plus any left over visas from the higher employment-based categories.

Ministers of religion. In order to qualify for this category, the religious worker must have been a member of and working for the religious organization for at least two years and be seeking to enter the United States as a minister of religion. This visa preference expires in November of the year 2000 but probably will be extended in some form after that date.

Former employees of U.S. government abroad. This special visa category is reserved for former employees of the U.S. government abroad who have provided at least fifteen years of faithful service. This category also includes certain employees of the Panama Canal Company as well as former employees of international organizations who have resided in the United States for a period of totaling at least one-half of the seven years before the date of application for a visa or for adjustment of status.

Certain juveniles. A third sub-group of special immigrants is aliens who have been declared dependent on a juvenile court and for whom a court has decided that it is not in their best interest to be returned to their homeland. The natural parents of such aliens are unable to derive any immigration benefits simply because their child has gained special immigrant status.

FIFTH
PREFERENCE

Investors/employment creation. This employment-based preference category contains 10,000 visas per year for foreign persons who invest a minimum amount of capital in a new enterprise that creates employment. The 10,000 annual visas are a fixed number and does not benefit from any unused visas in any of the other employment-based preferences. The amount of the required investment ranges from a low of $500,000.00 for "targeted employment areas" up to a high of $3,000,000.00 for an enterprise located in a region deemed to be of low unemployment. The alien must have invested the capital after November 29, 1990 or be in the active process of investing the capital.

The standard investment must be of $1,000,000.00 and must create at least ten full time jobs for U.S. citizens, permanent resident aliens, or other immigrants lawfully authorized to be employed in the United States. This group of ten workers provided for by the law cannot include the investor or the investor's immediate family.

Targeted employment areas. The law encourages investment in areas of high unemployment or other areas known as "targeted employment areas" and those areas are defined as rural areas or areas having an unemployment rate at least $1^1/_2$ times the national average. A total of ten jobs still need be created and the required investment is reduced to $500,000.00. A total of 3,000 of the 10,000 annual visas in this preference category are reserved for this level of investment. A *rural* area is defined as an area outside of metropolitan statistical area or a municipality with a population of less than 21,000 people.

In order to implement the application of the $500,000.00 amount, it is necessary for the individual states to designate, subject to federal government approval, the state authority which will determine the geographic areas or political subdivisions which are identified as rural or targeted employment areas.

The administrative regulations published by the Immigration and Naturalization Service provide that a qualified investment includes the purchase of an existing business so long as the enterprise's net worth, after the completion of the sale, is at least 140% of the value of the enterprise prior to the date of the acquisition or that there is a forty percent increase in the level of employment. This requirement will preclude an investor from merely purchasing an ongoing business without causing any substantive improvement in the capital or employment levels of the enterprise.

In addition, the regulations provide for the purchase and overhaul of a troubled or undercapitalized business enterprise by a foreign person so long as the acquisition will save jobs. A troubled business is defined as one that has been in existence for at least two years and has experienced a twenty percent diminution of its net worth during the last two years. In any event, a total of $1,000,000.00 (or $500,000.00 if applicable) must be invested and ten jobs must have been created or preserved.

The ability to reorganize an existing business in compliance with this visa category feature is very interesting because business consultants agree that in most instances it is preferable to purchase an ongoing business enterprise rather than for a person to attempt the development of a business from the beginning—especially, in the case of a foreign person. Since there is a highly developed industry in the United States for the acquisition and sale of existing commercial enterprises, it is advisable for a prospective foreign investor to utilize the services of these professionals in the identification of a suitable acquisition. The occupations of business brokers and mergers and acquisitions consultants is explained in more depth in chapter 6 of this book.

This visa requires that the investor manage the business personally and does not anticipate that the investor be merely a passive financier. There is an exception to this rule in the case of a limited partner of a limited partnership formed in accordance with the requirements of a certain uniform limited partnership law. The provision for the limited partner is contradictory to the requirement that the investor directly manage and/or supervise the investment. This is because the limited partnership act referred to, by its very terms, defines the limited partner as a passive investor. Since a limited partnership interest is a security and will support an employment creation investor visa, one wonders why the INS regulations do not also permit other types of securities or passive investment arrangements to warrant a permanent visa as long as the requisite level of employment is created.

The law provides a number of measures to discourage fraud by immigrant investors by providing for fines of up to $250,000.00 and jail for up to five years. In addition, the law makes the grant of permanent residence to immigrant investors conditional and has established a two-year trial period. During this two-year period, by rule and regulation, the Immigration and Naturalization Service will determine whether the enterprise was in fact established, whether or not the capital was in fact invested, and whether the alien did sustain the enterprise. During a ninety day period prior to the end of the two-year period, the investor must file an additional petition with the Immigration and Naturalization Service requesting that the conditional status of residence be removed.

Conditional grant of visa. This visa will be issued initially for a period of two years after which time, if the investment is still in place, the visa will be permanent and no longer subject to the investor's continued personal involvement in the enterprise. In order to remove the two-year condition and grant the alien permanent residence, the alien must file a form I-829 together with appropriate documentation.

The petition for removal of conditions must be accompanied by the following evidence:

1. documentary evidence that a commercial enterprise was established by the alien,

2. evidence that the alien invested or was actively in the process of investing the requisite capital,

3. evidence that the alien has, in good faith, substantially met the required capital investment and continuously maintained his or her capital investment over the two years of conditional residence, and

4. evidence that the alien created or can be expected to create within a reasonable time ten full-time jobs for qualifying employees. In the case of a "troubled business" as defined above, the alien entrepreneur must submit evidence that the commercial enterprise maintained the number of existing employees at no less than the pre-investment level for the period following his or her admission as a conditional permanent resident.

If the alien investor fails to file Form I-829 within the ninety-day period immediately preceding the second anniversary of the date the alien obtained lawful permanent residence on a conditional basis, then the alien's permanent resident status shall be terminated and removal proceedings will be started.

If an entrepreneur dies during the prescribed two-year period of conditional permanent residence, the spouse and children of the entrepreneur will be eligible for removal of conditions if it can be demonstrated that all the conditions of the investment have been met.

This immigrant visa category is quite appropriate for the acquisition of hotel/motel properties, especially in resort or tourist areas where the real estate (*propiedad inmueble*) can be expected to retain its value. It is the author's personal view that foreign persons should favor the more conservative approach to investment in the United States until they have developed insight into the economy and business customs of the location in which they are investing. Real estate enterprises, including hotels and motels, and other franchised enterprises are good candidates for this level of investment so long as they are sufficiently labor intensive to satisfy the above described job creation requirements.

Remember that by becoming permanent residents of the United States, foreign persons become United States taxpayers and thus, subject their worldwide income to taxation. Proper pre-investment planning is absolutely essential in order to avoid fiscal disasters, and a foreign investor should consult a number of consultants, both abroad as well as in the United States to assist in the various phases of the investment. In this regard the reader is invited to peruse the section on taxation starting on page 198 of this book.

THE LABOR CERTIFICATION PROCESS

The second, third, and fourth employment based preferences require as a precondition that the prospective employer receive a *labor certification* from the U.S. Department of Labor. The labor certification is a finding that there are not enough qualified workers in the U.S. location where the foreign person will perform the job or services, and that the employment of the alien will not adversely affect the U.S. labor market. In practical terms, this means that an employer will offer a position to a foreign person and will employ that foreign person if the Department of Labor approves the employment.

It is difficult to obtain a labor certification from the Department of Labor. First, the processing time for the labor certification, which is a prerequisite to filing the second and third employment-based visa petitions, can be one year or more in length. In addition to the job certification delay, the alien must still wait for the "priority date" to become current for the visa itself. The prospective employee receives his priority date on the day that his labor certification request (the Form ETA 750) is accepted for processing by the U.S. Department of Labor.

The prospective employee cannot file the immigrant visa petition until the labor certification has been issued. In addition to the delay in obtaining the labor certification, there is also a delay in visa availability. The backlog in the priority dates for visas for unskilled workers has been, as of the writing of this book, about four-and-a-half years. This means that an unskilled worker will not be eligible to receive a permanent residency visa for about ten years, since the priority dates advance about one week per actual calendar month in this category.

The application for job certification is filed on a form known as Form ETA 750 which is comprised of two parts, A and B. Part A is filled out by the employer and lists the employer's requirements, while Part B is filled out by the employee and lists the employee's qualifications.

The process is initiated when the employer offers the alien a job and then files an application for a labor certification with the U.S. Department of Labor. The form is filed with the local state labor office which then processes and transmits the form, together with its recommendations, to the regional U.S. Department of Labor office.

In order to obtain a labor certification, the employer must prove to the Department of Labor that:

- ☞ the job being offered to the alien is available and is otherwise open to persons in the United States,

- ☞ there are no unreasonable or unnecessary conditions placed on the position, and

- ☞ the wage offered is at least the prevailing wage in the community.

In the United States, a job requirement that a person must speak a particular foreign language is considered prima facie unreasonable and can only be overcome by proof that knowledge of a foreign language is essential to the proper performance of the job. The employer must also prove that it has made a reasonable effort to fill that position with U.S. citizens or permanent residents. The employer is required to advertise the position in a newspaper of general circulation, (sometimes in a professional or trade journal), and must post in his place of employment information concerning the availability of that position.

In order to fully appreciate the philosophy of the Department of Labor and the Immigration and Naturalization Service with respect to the issuance of labor certification(s), the following quotation from the Federal Register concerning the employment based second and third preferences is instructive:

The labor certification process briefly described: Generally, an individual labor certification from the department is required for employers wishing to employ an alien under preference groups 2 and 3. In issuing such certifications, the Department of Labor applies two basic standards to exclude an alien: (1) if U.S. workers are able, willing, qualified, and available for the position; and/or (2) if the employment of an alien will adversely affect the wages or working conditions of U.S. workers similarly employed.

In brief, the current process for obtaining a labor certification requires employers to actively recruit U.S. workers in good faith for a period of at least thirty days for the job openings for which aliens are sought. The employers' job requirements must be reasonable and realistic, and employers must offer prevailing wages and working conditions for the occupation. The employers may not favor aliens or tailor the job requirements to the aliens' qualifications.

During the thirty-day recruitment period, employers are required to place a three-day, help-wanted advertisement in a newspaper of general circulation, or a one-day advertisement in a professional, trade or business journal, or ethnic publication. Employers are also required to place a thirty-day job order with the local office of the state employment service. If employers believe they have already conducted adequate recruitment, they may ask the Department of Labor to waive the mandatory, thirty-day recruitment. If the employer does not request a waiver of recruitment or if the waiver request is denied, the help-wanted advertisements that are placed in conjunction with the mandatory thirty-day recruitment will direct the job applicants to either report in person to the employment service or to submit resumés to the employment service.

The job applicants are then referred to the employer or their resumés are sent. The employer then has forty-five days to report to the employment service the job-related reasons for not hiring any United States workers referred. If the employer hires a United States worker for the job opening, the process stops at that point, unless the employer has more than one opening. If, however, the employer believes that qualified, willing and able United States workers are not available to take the job, the application, together with the documentation of the recruitment results and prevailing wage information are sent to the regional office of the Department of Labor. There, it is reviewed and a determination is made as to whether or not to issue the labor certification.

In practical application, the above explanation means that the Department of Labor will deny the labor certification if the employer requires special conditions that only a foreign person can or is willing to fulfill, unless those conditions are essential to his business. Therefore a requirement that the person holding the job speak a foreign language will disqualify the labor certification unless the employer can prove that the foreign language requirement is an essential part of the job. Mere convenience or slight competitive advantage to an employer is not sufficient. Also, the employer must offer the prevailing wage for that job that is paid in the community and must not impose higher than normal educational or experiential requirements for the position.

Obviously, the Department of Labor wants to ensure that an employer does not bypass available United States workers so that the employer can give the job to an alien of his choice. The labor certification process can be long and arduous and very often places considerable administrative burdens on the employer as well as personal and financial strains and risks on the employee. The employer is not permitted to hire a foreign person in preference to a U.S. worker merely because the foreign worker is better qualified than the United States worker. This means that the U.S. employer is required to hire the United States worker who satisfies the minimum recognized requirements for the particular job.

Thus, there are two impediments to the obtainment of permanent residency based upon the issuance of a labor certification. The first is the requirement that the job be qualified as a "skilled" job; that is, the job must have a training or learning component of at least two years. If the job can be learned in less than two years then it will not qualify as a "skilled" job. This is important because if a job is considered "unskilled" a visa will not be available at all within the reasonable future. It is important to remember that it is not the industry or character of the company that is relevant, rather it is the job itself. Thus, an "unskilled" job (customer service representative, receptionist, salesperson, etc.) for a high-tech firm or even a highly remunerative "unskilled" job (salesperson for a luxury automobile dealer like Mercedes Benz or Lexus) will not qualify for an EB-3rd Preference Permanent Residency application.

The second component of risk is that even if the job itself qualifies as a "skilled" job, there may be U.S. persons in the local labor markets who are qualified to perform the job. If a qualified U.S. person applies for the job, the employer must either hire the U.S. person or withdraw the job offer on behalf of the alien.

It is important to remember that the U.S. employer does not have the right to offer the job (on the basis of a labor certification) to the foreign person simply because the U.S. worker is not equally skilled. The U.S. employer can only offer the job to the foreign person if the U.S. worker candidate does not meet the minimum qualifications for the job. The Department of Labor establishes these minimum qualifications and they are all listed in a publication entitled the "Dictionary of Occupational Titles" (DOT).

While the conditions of the local job market will determine the possibility of obtaining a labor certification, certain trends are obvious.

First, as a matter of practical reality, immigrant visas are only available for persons whose jobs require a minimum of two years or more of training and experience in order to perform the job. This is caused by the long backlog in the category of "other workers" for the third employment based preference. It is so long (about six years as of the date of this book) that most job offers will not survive the long delay—neither may the U.S. job sponsor or the beneficiary. Second, the job market will militate, as it normally does, against offers for jobs for which there is an abundance in the particular area. As an example, it may be very difficult to prove that there is a job shortage for hotel managers in a resort area such as Miami, Florida, or San Francisco, California because these jobs and geographical areas attract many qualified U.S. candidates.

Secondly, the economy and the law favor foreign persons who have particular job capabilities and skills that are not readily obtainable in the U.S. labor market. For example, an employer who wishes to hire a foreign person who possesses only general administrative and sales skills will find it very difficult to obtain the labor certification. It is always advisable to consult with a qualified immigration attorney who is familiar with the job market in the area of intended employment.

In certain cases, it may be possible to avoid the labor certification by proving to the Department of Labor that the employer has, during a period of at least six months, attempted to fill the position with normal and customary efforts and has failed to find qualified workers. Under these circumstances it may be possible to have the Department of Labor agree that there is no need for a labor certification application since the employer has already without success made reasonable and good faith efforts to fill the position. If the employer can document these good faith efforts over a sustained period of time, it will request permission for a "Reduction in Recruitment" certification which will accept the employer's efforts as dispositive of the labor market test.

Obviously, this is an area of practice which strongly suggests professional assistance.

Problem of intent (again). As a result of filing the immigrant visa petition, an alien may find that the ability to travel to the U.S. can be curtailed. This could happen in at least two typical circumstances: First, the U.S. Consulate in the foreign country may not grant a temporary visa to the alien; or secondly, if the alien already has a valid temporary visa to the U.S., the alien's right to enter the U.S. under the temporary visa may be challenged by the immigration inspector at the port of entry. In this latter case, the INS may interview to determine whether use of the temporary visa for entry to the United States is entitled. In some extreme cases, the INS may not allow the person to enter the United States at all and thus, may turn the person away at the border.

The above problem is caused by the requirement of the law that the alien's intent as to duration of stay as well as to the alien's deemed activities in the U.S. be consistent with the visa the alien holds. If the alien has filed a petition for permanent residency, the intent is to remain in the United States on a permanent basis. Thus, the INS may decide that the alien is ineligible to receive or use a nonimmigrant (temporary) visa since these visas require that the alien have an intention to remain in the U.S. for a temporary period only. This problem of intent can present a most unfortunate surprise. So, an alien who wishes to travel to the United States on a temporary visit should not file the petition for permanent residency until his temporary visit has been concluded.

If aliens are already in the U.S., the filing of permanent visa petitions may disqualify them from extending or renewing their temporary visas, or the duration of stay under the temporary visas. These problems do not apply to persons who are attempting to obtain L-1 or H-1B visas.

SPECIAL PROBLEMS

LIVE-IN
DOMESTIC
WORKERS

The United States does not look kindly upon live-in domestic workers. First, since domestic workers are considered "unskilled" workers, there are no visas available for this category of worker for at least ten years. Second, even though the Department of Labor acknowledges there is a shortage of live-in domestic workers, it discourages the employment of live-in workers in favor of live-out domestic workers. It is a characteristic of U.S. society that domestic workers generally are not willing to live in the household of their employers, at least not without requiring a premium in wages.

In order to obtain an immigrant visa as a live-in domestic worker the alien must prove by documentation twelve months of paid experience in the capacity of a domestic worker abroad. However, the most difficult part of a live-in domestic worker application is the requirement that the employer prove there is an absolute "business necessity" for employing a live-in domestic. Normally, an employer must show there are no adults at home that could take care of either the young children or the adult who may require constant attention. Employers must prove that their job occupation requires frequent travel away from the home and that there is no practical alternative to a live-in worker. The Department of Labor will go to great lengths to suggest alternatives to employers as to how they could rearrange their lives, so as not to require a live-in domestic worker.

The difficulty in obtaining the labor certification, together with the over burdened third preference for unskilled workers, results in the practical elimination of visas based upon employment as a live-in domestic worker. Currently, waiting period (priority date backlog) is approximately ten years. This long delay makes it virtually impossible to obtain a job offer and enter the United States as an immigrant on this basis. Some enterprising households have sought to get around this problem by claiming that they need a well-trained child monitor or nurse or specialty cook (kosher) for the household. Obviously, the government does not look sympathetically at these types of applications.

INVESTORS

(*Note:* This section does not apply to investors who qualify for the new employment creation visa.) Business entrepreneurs could technically qualify under a second or third employment based preference visa, except that they must be entering the United States as employees. The obvious suggestion comes to mind that perhaps the investors could form companies in the United States that would hire them. While this is technically possible, in the practical world, it is very difficult to achieve.

Investors must compete with U.S. job seekers for the positions they seek to fill themselves. The Department of Labor has a negative attitude about permitting an investor to evaluate applicants who are competing with the investor for the position. The United States Department of Labor is obviously concerned that the investor may not be objective in an analysis. The Department of Labor will require that the investor prove that the labor certification selection process is conducted by objective persons, independent from the influence of the investor. If the Department of Labor determines that the employee for whom the labor certification is sought is the principal or is one of the principal investors in a company, it will routinely deny the labor certification. As a result, the investor has the burden of establishing the objectivity of the selection process. Under the circumstances described this would be an almost impossible burden. There have been instances in which an investor holding a small minority of stock, generally no more than five percent, has been certified for the position sought. These circumstances are rare, however, and I would advise such applicants not to invest in the company in which they are seeking employment. It would be preferable to obtain an option to purchase stock in the future based upon job performance rather than proving to the Department of Labor that the investor, as a result of minority ownership of stock, will not be in a position to unduly influence the selection process of workers for the position which he also is seeking.

OCCUPATIONS FOR WHICH LABOR CERTIFICATION IS NOT REQUIRED

The law identifies a group of occupations that are presumed to be in demand in the United States and for which no labor certification is required. These occupations are designated under "Schedule A" of the Department of Labor regulations: there are two groups of persons who, upon proof of their qualifications, do not need to obtain a labor certification before applying for an immigrant visa. These groups are as follows:

GROUP ONE Physical therapists, and professional nurses. Physical therapist is defined in the law as follows:

> A person who applies the art and science of physical therapy to the treatment of patients' disability disorders and injuries to relieve pain, develop or restore function, and maintain performance, using physical means such as exercise, massage, heat, water, light, and electricity as prescribed by a physician (or surgeon). (20 CFR 656.10a4 I)

> To prove eligibility for this group, the alien must have all the qualifications necessary to take the licensing examination in the state in which he intends to practice physical therapy. Thus, the alien must file, together with his application, a letter or statement signed by an authorized licensing official in the state of intended employment stating that the alien is qualified to take the state's licensing examination for physical therapists. (20 CFR 656.22 C)

Professional nurses are also exempt from the labor certification requirement and these are defined as follows:

> Persons who apply the art and science of nursing, which reflects comprehension of principles derived from the

physical, biological, and behavioral sciences. Professional nursing generally includes the making of judgments concerning the observation, caring, and counsel of persons requiring nursing care; and administering of medicines and treatments prescribed by the physician or dentist; the participation in activities for the promotion of health and the prevention of illness in others. A program of study for professional nurses generally includes theory and practice in clinical areas such as: obstetrics, surgery, pediatrics, psychiatry, and medicine. (20 CFR 656.50)

In addition to the above, the nurse alien must pass a special test approved by the Commission on Graduates of Foreign Nursing Schools Examination, as well as hold a full and unrestricted license to practice professional nursing in the state of intended employment.

GROUP TWO   Persons of "exceptional ability in the sciences or arts, including college and university teachers who have been practicing their science or art during the year before the application." The Department of Labor takes the position that the term "exceptional ability" means international renown.

> Such aliens should be so far above the average members of their fields that they will clearly be an asset to the United States. (Federal Register, Number 5, 1976)

In order to qualify for this category of skilled worker which will eliminate the requirement of a labor certification application, aliens must file a considerable amount of documentary evidence establishing their international renown and recognition by recognized experts in the field. The documentation may include the following: documentation of internationally recognized prizes or awards, of membership in international associations which require outstanding achievement of members; published treatises and materials and professional publication, evidence of the alien's participation on panels or as a judge of the work of others in the same or similar field; scholarly research contributions of major significance; evidence of the alien's scholarship and published scientific or scholarly articles; international professional journals, and evidence of the display of the alien's work at artistic exhibitions in more than one country. It must be emphasized that documentation is critical and any alien who feels qualified for admission to the U.S. under this exception must accumulate as much detailed documentation as is possible. It is doubtful that such an application could be presented properly without the assistance of an attorney who specializes in immigration law.

DIVERSITY IMMIGRANTS

Starting October 1, 1994 in addition to immigrants entering the United States based upon marital or family relationships and employment-sponsored visas, a third category will be called *diversity* immigrants. 55,000 visas per year will be made available for diversity immigrants and their family members on a lottery-type basis.

These diversity immigrant visas will be made available to persons who are nationals of "low admission" countries. The prospective immigrant must have at least a high school education or equivalent, or have worked at least two years in an occupation that requires two years of training or experience. The law (IMMACT90) divides the world into six regions and then establishes a formula for determining which region and which state qualifies as high admission or low admission. In the recent past, the greatest number of immigrants to the United States have come from Asia and Latin America, with a smaller number coming from Europe and Africa. The purpose of the diversity immigrant visa is to provide a separate entry basis for those persons who come from low admission regions and states.

It is beyond the scope of this book to go into the details of the mathematical formula which is utilized to determine low admission as opposed to high admission areas. While the number of these regions and states will vary from year to year, it is safe to assume that those countries that presently have high admissions into the United States will continue to be, at least for the near term, high admission countries in the future, and thus, the nationals of those countries would be excluded from participating in the diversity program. The high admission countries which would probably be excluded from this visa program are as follows:

Canada	Colombia	Dominican Republic
El Salvador	Haiti	India
Jamaica	Korea	Mexico
Philippines	Taiwan	United Kingdom
Peoples Republic of China		

There is a growing amount of criticism concerning this program since it prefers to issue visas to persons on the basis of luck alone and not on the basis of benefit to the country or for any other traditionally recognized purpose.

The U. S. State Department is charged with the responsibility of operating the diversity immigrant program and it designates the period during which diversity visa petitions or applications must be filed for the next fiscal year. At this time, the State Department regulations have not been issued which would otherwise specify the information which must be included in the petition as well as the supporting documentation. These specific rules will probably change year-by-year as circumstances warrant.

Each diversity visa applicant can submit only one application in a given year and there will be some form of control so that if more than one visa application is received from one applicant, it will void all of the applications. It is probable that the diversity visa program will operate similar to a lottery, with a system of random selection of all eligible entries.

PERMANENT IMMIGRANT VISAS FOR NON-PREFERENCE CATEGORIES

3

PERSONS ELIGIBLE TO IMMIGRATE TO THE U.S. WITHOUT REGARD TO THE QUOTA SYSTEM

IMMEDIATE
RELATIVES OF
U.S. CITIZENS

The law provides that certain immediate relatives of U.S. citizens may receive permanent visas without regard to the system of numerical limitations. The categories for which this chapter applies are the parents, spouse, or child of a United States citizen. The philosophy behind this, as well as other categories of immigration systems is to provide for the maintenance of the unity of the family. It is important to understand, however, that it is the United States citizen who has the right to make a petition to the United States Government requesting that the beneficiary receive a permanent visa. Understanding this simple concept can very often avoid unfortunate consequences, especially to the spouse of a U.S. citizen.

Spouse of a U.S. citizen. A United States citizen may petition either the Department of Naturalization and Immigration Service or the U.S. Consul abroad for a permanent visa for the alien spouse. The foremost prerequisite under the law for this category is the existence of a valid and subsisting marriage between the parties and official recognizance of the marriage in the jurisdiction in which the marriage took place. The law does not recognize polygamous marriages nor proxy marriages, unless, in the latter case, the marriage has been consummated.

The law also does not recognize sham marriages or marriages where the primary purpose is to obtain immigration benefits and where the parties never intended to live together as husband and wife. In addition, however, to the fact that sham or fraudulent marriages are not recognized for the purpose of conferring immigration benefits on the alien spouse, the use of a sham marriage to apply for visas is against the law and subjects both parties as well as any other person involved in procuring the visa under these fraudulent conditions to criminal prosecution.

"I STILL NEED TO SEE YOUR MARRIAGE LICENSE"

Conditional residence for marriages under two years: Under the terms of current law, if a marriage is of less than two years duration at the time the petition for the permanent visa is filed, the alien spouse of a U.S. citizen receives only "conditional" permanent resident status. Upon the second anniversary of the granting of the original conditional permanent resident status, the alien may remove the condition and achieve the permanent resident status. The temporary resident status automatically terminates within two years except that the alien and spouse jointly must submit a petition within ninety days prior to the end of the twenty-four month period requesting the removal of the conditional grant of resident status. This is accomplished by filing a documented Form I-751. This form either confirms that the parties are still married and living together, or, in the event the marriage has been terminated, provides an opportunity for the alien spouse to prove that the marriage at inception was entered into in good faith.

After the filing of the Form I-751 the parties may also be interviewed again by an immigration officer. If the foreign person fails to file the required form on time together with supporting documentation, the conditional permanent resident status will be terminated and the foreign person becomes immediately deportable. Late filing of this form will be accepted only upon proof of good cause and extenuating circumstances justifying the late filing. In addition, the conditional status or temporary resident status will be terminated by the attorney general within two years if any of the following apply:

☞ the qualifying marriage was entered into for the purpose of obtaining the alien's entry as an immigrant,

☞ the qualifying marriage has been annulled or terminated, other than through the death of the spouse, or

☞ a fee or other consideration was given for the filing of the petition (other than attorneys fees for assistance in preparing petitions).

The major cause for concern by an alien spouse is the second condition which states that the attorney general is authorized to terminate the visa if the marriage has been terminated other than through death. In the event of a termination of a marriage prior to the expiration of the two-year period, it is possible that an alien may obtain a waiver with respect to the consequences imposed by the fact that the marriage was terminated, only if the alien can demonstrate that:

☞ Circumstances arose during the period of the conditional permanent residence which would cause extreme hardship if he or she were deported.

☞ The qualifying marriage was entered into in good faith but was terminated for good cause and that the alien was not at fault in failing to meet the requirements ordinarily prescribed for the removal of the condition period. It is this provision that allows most aliens who divorce their U.S. citizen spouses to remain as U.S. permanent residents. The key is to document the existence of a normal and good faith marriage at the inception.

☞ The alien spouse or his/her child has been physically battered or subject to extreme mental cruelty by the U.S. citizen spouse. The requirements for proving that the spouse is a "battered spouse" have been liberalized somewhat so that the government will consider any and all relevant and reliable evidence to establish this ground. Typical evidence consists of reports from police authorities, physicians, mental health and marriage counselors, letters and affidavits from clergy and direct witnesses, and any official court records. If an alien spouse feels that he or she cannot continue in the marriage because of physical battery, he or she should consult an immigration attorney as well as a qualified matrimonial lawyer in order to document the battery properly.

Related to the above provisions is a requirement that an alien who obtained lawful permanent residence status as the spouse of a U.S. citizen or of a permanent resident alien is also precluded for a period of five years from obtaining approval of a visa petition seeking a second preference status on behalf of another spouse acquired after termination (other than by death) of the marriage which formed the basis for the grant of the original permanent residence to himself/herself. This restriction may be waived if the alien can establish, by clearing and convincing evidence, that the prior marriage was not entered into for the purpose of evading the provision of the immigration laws.

Widows and widowers of U.S. citizens. A widow or widower of a U.S. citizen may apply for an immigrant visa as an immediate relative so long as he or she had been married to the United States citizen for a period of two years prior to the U.S. spouse's death. It is necessary that the decedent have been a U.S. citizen for at least two years prior to his/her death and that the petition be filed by no later than two years following the death of the U.S. citizen. It is also required that the widow/widower not have been legally separated from the United States citizen at the time of the citizen's death.

It is difficult to imagine how this requirement will be implemented in the case of those persons who live in states where there is no legal status known as "legally separated." In the state of Florida, for example, a marital separation exists when the parties physically or even sexually separate and there is no particular legal process to determine when the parties have done so. This is one of the peculiarities of the U.S. immigration regimen in that it attempts to establish a defined legal status even though the particular state may not use the same nomenclature or even agree to implement the public policy that motivates the immigration law or regulation.

Also, the widow/widower must not have remarried at the time of the petition. It is unclear as to the policy reason for this rule.

Note: Normally, an alien does not have a vested right to immigrant status based upon marriage to a U.S. citizen. If the marriage should terminate, whether by divorce or death, prior to the granting of the visa the alien will have no right to apply for an immigrant visa, except as noted above, regardless of how long he or she has lived in the United States or how otherwise deserving the alien may be of obtaining the visa.

Thus, an alien should require that his or her U.S. citizen spouse file the petition on their behalf as soon as possible after the marriage unless the marriage will soon reach the second anniversary, in which case it is advisable to wait until then in order to avoid the conditional two year visa. All of this discussion presumes that the alien is already in the United States at the time of the marriage.

If the parties are outside of the United States at the time of the marriage, then the alien will not be permitted to enter the United States until the visa petition has been approved at the U.S. consulate abroad. This process may take as long as four months! Therefore, it is advisable to plan the marriage and/or the entry to the U.S. accordingly. Also, if the parties were married in the United States, the alien spouse should not depart the United States until such time as the alien's status has been adjusted to that of a permanent resident alien (immigrant). Again, the mere fact that an alien is married to a U.S. citizen does not convey on the alien the right to enter or remain in the United States prior to having received an immigrant visa. This simple statement should be thoroughly understood by both the U.S. citizen and alien spouse.

If either spouse has been previously married, it will be necessary to prove the valid termination of the prior marriage(s).

Child of a United States citizen. The law permits unlimited immigrant visas to persons who qualify as the "child" of United States citizens. *Child* as defined under the law means an unmarried person under the age of twenty-one years of age. If an alien does not qualify under this category as a result of age or marital status, the alien may still qualify for an immigrant visa under the first or fourth preferences, both of which are covered in this book.

A stepchild is also included within the scope of "child" if the marriage between the natural parent and the stepparent occurred prior to the stepchild's eighteenth birthday.

The benefits of the law apply only to legitimate children unless the child was legitimated according to the law and/or recognized custom of the child's birthplace, or unless the mother of the illegitimate child is a U.S. citizen. In the case of children who are nationals of countries which have eliminated the distinction between legitimate and illegitimate children, the law requires evidence by the U.S. father (normally) that a normal parent-child relationship was established and maintained before the child turned twenty-one years of age.

An adopted child is also recognized under the law for immediate relative status if the adoption occurred prior to the child's sixteenth birthday and the child has resided with the adopting parents for a minimum period of two years.

An orphan also qualifies under the law if the child was orphaned before attaining sixteen years of age and has been either adopted by the U.S. parents, or single parent who has attained the minimum age of twenty-five years; or if the U.S. parents or parent, as the case may be, have satisfied the U.S. immigration authorities of their intention to adopt the orphan in the United States and that they have qualified for the adoption under law of the state where they intend to live.

Parents of a U.S. citizen. The third category of the "immediate relative" category, which enables an alien to enter the United States without regard to the numerical quota, benefits the parents of United States citizens. The U.S. citizen, however, must be at least twenty-one years of age in order to give the parent the right of entry under the immigrant visa. The two chief requirements under this section are that the relationship of "parent" and "child" as defined by law must have been established at the time the family relationship was created. Thus, if an alien adopts a United States person over the age of twenty-one, the alien will not gain immigration benefits. This is because at the time of the adoption the person adopted was not a "child" as defined under the law. The adopted person was an adult and thus the parent is not the parent of a United States "child."

If the U.S. citizen was a "child" at the time of the adoption but is an adult at the time of the filing of the petition, the parent may still obtain the benefits of this section since the legal immigration definition of "parent" and "child" were satisfied when the civil relationship was created. Under all of the previous three sections with respect to the immediate relative status, the U.S. citizen must file a Form I-130 (a *preliminary petition*) on behalf of the alien. This form is readily available at all U.S. Consulates abroad and all INS offices in the United States.

OTHER PERSONS NOT SUBJECT TO THE QUOTA SYSTEM

In addition to the immediate relatives of a U.S. citizen, there are other persons who may enter the United States for permanent residency without the requirement of conforming with the worldwide numerical quota. The first of these, of course, is the permanent resident alien who is returning to the United States from a temporary visit abroad. Thus, the alien must have already been lawfully admitted for permanent residence, and the visit abroad must have been temporary without an intention to abandon the immigrant status in the United States. Usually the immigrant visa (*green card*) itself is sufficient documentation to enable an alien who has been temporarily abroad to return to the United States.

An alien planning to remain outside the United States for a period of six months or more should obtain permission (Re-Entry Permit) from the United States Immigration and Naturalization Service to do so, and this is obtained by filling out Form I-131. This form, when approved by the Immigration and Naturalization Service, establishes that the alien is not abandoning permanent residency in the United States even though the alien may be outside the country for a period of more than one year. This permit is usually valid for a period not to exceed two years. Other persons who have special status are (certain) foreign medical school graduates who obtained (certain) H or J Visas before January 10, 1978, remained in the United States and were licensed to practice medicine in the United States on or before January 9, 1978.

ACCOMPANYING FAMILY MEMBERS

The spouse and child(ren) of the petitioning alien receive a derivative visa which permits them to enter the United States together with the petitioning alien. In immigrant cases, this provision of law regards the spouse or child(ren) as accompanying the principal if they receive immigrant visas within four months after the principal obtains an immigrant visa or adjustment of status within the United States, or within four months after the principal departs from the home country. In fact, if the principal's family members as defined by law "follow to join" the principal they would be entitled to derivative status at any time after the principal acquires an immigrant visa.

Also, beneficiaries of an immediate relative petition cannot bestow permanent residency on their other immediate family members. Thus, if a foreign person becomes a U.S. citizen and obtains a permanent residency petition for his or her parents, the other children of the parents do not automatically receive permanent residency.

If the relationship of spouse or child is created after the principal has obtained a visa, then the family members would not be entitled to the derived permanent visa status. This would be the case if the principal were to marry after acquisition of an immigrant visa. Also, an accompanying relative may not precede the principal alien to the United States. In either of the above cases, the family members would be required to file a separate immigrant visa petition and would be subject to the worldwide numerical limitations quota.

ADJUSTMENT OF STATUS

Normally, the permanent visa is issued at a U.S. Consulate abroad. The U.S. Congress has long recognized that for many people who are already in the United States, the necessity of a trip abroad for final processing is both inconvenient and expensive. As a result, a procedure entitled *Adjustment of Status* enables a person in the United States to receive the permanent visa from within the United States. The alien person must be eligible to receive a permanent visa immediately. Thus, a person who is the beneficiary of a Preference Petition which is presently backlogged is ineligible for "adjustment." As an example, the priority date for the unskilled category under the third employment-related preference is presently six-and-a-half years in arrears. Thus, a person who is in the United States and who has an approved employment third preference petition would be ineligible to file for Adjustment of Status until the priority date is current.

Many of the prior conditions to this procedure have been eliminated and the government now essentially encourages a person to adjust his status within the United States rather than to travel to a U.S. Consulate abroad to make the application for the permanent residency visa.

Except for certain persons who filed visa petitions by January 14, 1998, the only persons who now have the option of filing for adjustment of status are the following:

☛ immediate relatives of U.S. citizens, and

☛ persons on whose behalf a petition based upon employment (including an application for labor certification) has been filed, provided the total time in which they have been in unlawful status does not exceed 180 days.

Adjustment of Status is essentially a procedural privilege. Ineligibility for privilege does not affect eligibility for permanent residency status. It does mean that persons will have to invest in an airplane ticket to the U.S. Consulate of their country of origin or in certain cases to a friendly U.S. Consulate in a third country in order to obtain their permanent residency visa.

REFUGEES

This section deals with an immigration status which differs from all of the others described in this book. In order to take advantage of the benefits of the law with respect to either refugee or asylee designations, aliens must establish certain proof which relates to political, ideological or sociological conditions in their home country which adversely and personally affect them. This proof involves issues which affect certain specific foreign policy interests of the United States and for these reasons this category has been treated separately in this book.

This area of law invites much litigation and discussion in the United States and is subject to changes both in interpretation of the law and in U.S. political inclination, depending upon world events. Certain political conditions may cause the United States to assume that a member of a particular group qualifies as a refugee or asylee while denying that status to other groups similarly situated.

DEFINITION   The law defines a refugee as follows:

> (42) The term 'refugee' means (A) any person who outside any country of such person's nationality or, in the case of a person having no nationality, is outside any country in which such person last habitually resided and who is unable or unwilling to return to, and is unable or unwilling to avail himself or herself of the protection of that country because of persecution or a well-founded fear of persecution on account of race, religion, nationality, membership in particular social group, or political opinion, or (B) in such special circumstances as the President, after appropriate consultation (as defined in section 207 (e) of the Act) may specify, any person who is within the country of such person's nationality or, in the case of a person having no nationality within the country in which such person is habitually residing, and who is persecuted or who has a well-founded fear of persecution on account of race, religion, nationality, membership in a particular social group, or political opinion. The term 'refugee' does not include any person who ordered, incited, assisted, or otherwise participated in the persecution of any person on account of race, religion, nationality, membership in particular social group, or political opinion.

One of the purposes of the above law was to adopt the major provisions of the United Nations Protocol Relating to the Status of Refugees to which the United States is a signatory. Also, the law attempts to establish a permanent and consistent method of admitting refugees and asylees to the United States. The following sections discuss and explain the principal features of the law.

NUMERICAL
LIMITATIONS

The law provides for a separate system of numerical limitations for refugees than that which is applicable to persons seeking permanent residence in the United States under the preference system described in this book.

The refugee section of the immigration regimen of the United States establishes a mechanism by which the President of the United States (with the advice and consent of the Congress) establishes the total number of refugees which will be admitted in a given year as well as the numerical limit applicable to individual countries or sections of the world. The law provides for the exercise of executive discretion in the designation of those countries or sections of the world and thus the availability of refugee admissions may vary from year to year. U.S. foreign policy and the political conditions in other parts of the world may very well influence the President's decision to implement the refugee program in any given year.

INDIVIDUAL
ELIGIBILITY

A refugee as defined by the law is a person who is physically outside the United States. If a person is physically within or at the borders of the United States, then application for asylum will be considered subject to the eligibility requirements of that status as discussed in the following chapter.

The key provision in the refugee section as to eligibility is the requirement that the person be unwilling or unable to return to his home or other country either because of persecution or a well-founded fear of persecution on account of race, religion, nationality, membership in a particular social group, or political opinion.

The law does not discriminate between socialist or capitalist nations, except in the case of Cuba, nor does it require that the person have actually fled from his home country. Obviously, persons who claim persecution by a country whose government or foreign policy is hostile to the United States have a much better chance of being adjudged refugees than persons who come from countries that are friendly to the United States.

In order to prove that a person is subject to the conditions underlined above, a person must prove first that the government is oppressive and tyrannical and for that reason denies to the applicant the protection otherwise afforded to nationals of that country through the legal or political institutions of that country. Second, the person must prove individual persecution or a well-founded fear of persecution.

The first requirement, i.e., proof as to the general oppressive nature of the foreign regime, is easier to provide than the second requirement, i.e., proof as to the persecution of the alien. Usually there will be more documentation available about the regime's behavior as to human rights, and in certain instances the United States may already recognize the oppressive nature of the foreign government. There are various documentary sources and human rights organizations which maintain information as to the human rights environment in certain countries and these can be made available to an applicant for refugee status. The refugee applicant must prove that the home country's institutions and/or policies are not available for individual protection. The Department of State of the United States does not always agree with an applicant's assertion of the home country's despotic nature in which case the applicant bears a heavy burden of persuasion.

The second requirement as outlined above is very often the greatest obstruction to a finding of refugee status when it is asserted by an individual who is not a member of a group that has been recognized as such by the Department of State. The applicant must present documented evidence that individually or as a member of a group, the alien will be subject to persecution. For obvious reasons, the Immigration and

Naturalization Service will not always accept the mere self-serving statements of the applicants regarding persecution. The law provides that the burden of proof may be established solely by the testimony of the refugee or asylee but this is not easy to accomplish.

Unless the individual is a member of a group of persons whom the United States government accepts as a persecuted group in a foreign country, the individual must provide documentary proof as to personal exposure. As a matter of experience, this requirement presents a greater burden to an applicant for asylum, since by definition that person is already outside of the home country and probably within the national borders of the United States. Thus, it is difficult, if not impossible, to obtain and present the type of documentary proof which the INS requires.

In addition to the above two requirements for eligibility, the alien applicant also must be innocent of any acts of persecution, and must otherwise be a person of good moral character.

THE
APPLICATION
PROCESS

The applicant has the burden of providing eligibility for the designation of refugee. The application is completed by the filing of Form I-590, biographic information on a Form G-325 and a fingerprint card for each person over the age of fourteen years. In the event of a successful refugee application, the spouse and children accompanying or coming to join the principal alien are entitled to derivative refugee status unless they have engaged in acts of persecution themselves.

The application process is conducted abroad either by the Immigration and Naturalization Service in those countries where it maintains offices or at certain designated U.S. Consular posts abroad. In every case the applicant is subject to customary investigation for security and police purposes and is required to present a series of personal documents for verification. In addition, the applicant is subject to medical examination to rule out certain communicable diseases.

If the application is approved, the refugee is authorized to enter the United States and is authorized to work and otherwise receive wages.

After a period of one year from the date of entry, the alien is permitted to file an application for Adjustment of Status to that of a permanent resident alien. Before an alien may enter the United States there must be proof of sponsorship for employment, a residence in the United States and that the person will not become a public charge. It is for this purpose that many volunteer and philanthropic agencies become active in the resettlement of aliens, even though the same purpose may be achieved by an individual, as is so often the case with respect to relatives or other members of a closely knit religious or ethnic group.

If an alien has been firmly settled in another country then eligibility is denied for refugee status to the United States. The criteria for being firmly settled depends upon many factors, such as the type of legal status the person has been granted, as well as the nature of any restrictions that may have been imposed which may limit the alien's ability to adapt reasonably to the new country.

Asylum

If a foreign person is already in the United States and reasonably fears persecution abroad based upon race, religion, nationality, membership in a particular social group, or political opinion, then the individual may petition for asylum to the United States. The standard is essentially the same as that for achieving refugee status.

The law provides as follows with respect to asylum:

> Sec. 208(a) Any alien who is physically present in the United States or who arrives in the United States (whether or not at a designated port of arrival and including an alien who is brought to the United States after having been interdicted in international or United States waters), irrespective of such alien's status, may apply for asylum in accordance with; this section or, where applicable, section 235 (b).

The principal difference between the Asylum and Refugee categories is that the former applies to those aliens who are already in the United States while the latter applies to persons outside the United States. The law provides for a procedure by which an asylee who has been admitted into the United States may have a spouse and child(ren) join him in the United States upon proof of the familial relationship.

The grant of asylum status is discretionary. The Attorney General acting through his representatives in the Department of Immigration and Naturalization may withhold the granting of asylum for good cause. Thus, if an alien were to secretly enter the United States and bypass the normal refugee process which was otherwise available to him, the grant of asylum could be denied on that basis.

The following categories of persons are not eligible to file for asylum in the United States:

- ☞ an alien who may be removed, pursuant to a bilateral or multi-lateral agreement, to a third country in which the alien would have access to a full and fair procedure for determining a claim to asylum or equivalent temporary, protection, unless the INS finds that it is in the public interest for the alien to receive asylum in the United States.

- ☞ an alien who files his or her application later than one year after entry, unless the person can demonstrate to the satisfaction of the INS that changed country conditions have caused the delay in filing. This would apply to an individual who entered the United States in some non-immigrant status and then because of changes in the home country cannot now return without being subject to persecution.

- ☞ an alien who has previously applied for asylum and has had such application denied.

The law does not allow an alien to appeal the decision of the INS to any court with respect to a decision on any of the above points.

Even though the INS will prepare regulations that will define the requirements and procedures for these applications, asylum is not available to an alien if the INS determines that:

1. the alien ordered, incited, assisted, or otherwise participated in the persecution of any person on account of race, religion, nationality, membership in a particular social group, or political opinion;

2. the alien, having been convicted by a final judgment of a particularly serious crime, constitutes a danger to the community of the United States;

3. there are serious reasons for believing that the alien has committed a serious nonpolitical crime outside the United States prior to the arrival in the United States;

4. there are reasonable grounds for regarding the alien as a danger to the security of the United States;

5. the alien is inadmissible as a terrorist or as a member of a terrorist organization. The Palestinian Liberation Organization is at the time of this book an organization engaged in terrorist activity, or is removable for having engaged in terrorist activity after admission to the U.S., unless, in the case only of an alien inadmissible the Attorney General determines that there are not reasonable grounds for regarding the alien as a danger to the security of the United States; or

6. the alien was firmly resettled in another country prior to arriving in the United States.

Also, an alien who has been convicted of an aggravated felony shall be considered to have been convicted of a particularly serious crime and thus not eligible for asylum. The law also gives the INS the authority to create new conditions under which an alien will be ineligible for asylum. This is unusual under U.S. law in that an administrative body is generally not given the power to create additional conditions for ineligibility under the law. Nonetheless, this is the law as it stands now.

Aliens rarely have the evidence at hand to document that they would be the subject of persecution in the foreign land. Nonetheless, the alien has the burden of proving to the Immigration and Naturalization Service that he or she would be subject to persecution abroad. The sole testimony of the alien is seldom sufficient without some outside evidence, documentary or otherwise.

There are various organizations in the United States that compile dossiers of documentary evidence about the human rights violations of countries and these may be helpful in a particular case. The organization—Amnesty International, 705 G Street, S.E. Washington, D.C. 20003—would be an excellent starting point for anyone who felt that he or she was eligible for a grant of political asylum. In addition, the Internet has ample resources to develop these secondary sources of country conditions.

As a result of the recent changes in the law governing asylum both as to procedure as well as substance, a prospective asylee is well served to seek competent legal assistance in the preparation of an asylum petition.

TEMPORARY NON-IMMIGRANT VISAS

In this section we shall discuss the most important and common non-immigrant visas. With the exception of the H-1B visa, there is no annual quota on the number of non-immigrant visas that may be issued. The United States issues many more non-immigrant than immigrant visas.

Typically, a person will apply for a U.S. non-immigrant visa abroad at the U.S. Consulate within the country of residence. If the visa is issued, it is prima facie evidence of the person's eligibility to enter the United States. Foreign persons will first use the visa when they show the visa to the international carrier's airline or ship representative as a precondition to boarding the airplane or vessel.

Upon arrival at the United States border, the foreign person is inspected by a U.S. immigration inspector. If the foreign person is admitted into the United States, a small white card or piece of paper known as a Form I-94 is issued, which is the official entry document. This form proves that the person has lawfully entered the United States and also establishes the visa category of admission as well as the designated duration of stay. The Form I-94 should be kept in the passport and physically carried by the foreign person at all times. Few people are aware of this requirement and INS officers often chastise the alien for not having the passport and form I-94 immediately available. While this is an archaic requirement, it is still the law.

The length of time that the foreign person may remain in the United States is determined in the Form I-94 and not by the terminology of the visa that is stamped in the passport. Thus the legend on the B-1/B-2 visa which states that the bearer is entitled to unlimited entries to the United States, does not mean that the person may remain in the United States for an indefinite period of time, nor that re-entry may be made into the United States as the individual wishes. It simply means that the person does not need to reapply for another visa within any particular time period. The duration of time for remaining in the United States is limited to the date indicated in the Form I-94.

There are several characteristics of non-immigrant visas that set them apart from the immigrant visas discussed in the previous chapters.

First, the non-immigrant visa grants the foreign person the privilege of entering the United States for only a temporary and defined period of time. This of course requires that the alien's intention as to intended duration of stay must also be temporary. There are many types of non-immigrant visas which will not be discussed in this book because they pertain to a very limited class of persons and are very specialized in their application. Examples of these visas are the NATO visa for NATO officials, the A-1 visa for diplomatic personnel and the I visa for news media reporters and representatives.

Second, each particular visa imposes certain restrictions and conditions on the activities that the alien may engage in while in the United States. In other words, there are different visas for different activities to be conducted in the United States. Thus, the tourist or visitor visa does not authorize employment, the student visa authorizes study at only a certain institution, the treaty investor visa authorizes employment only in a defined enterprise and so forth.

Very often a non-immigrant visa is more aptly suited to the needs of a foreign person than the immigrant visa, especially for investors, business visitors, and professionals. The non-immigrant visa can be obtained in much less time than an immigrant visa. Since most non-immigrant visas are much more readily obtainable than immigrant visas, some foreign persons attempt to use the non-immigrant visa as a substitute for the immigrant visa. This is often viewed as fraud by both the U.S. Consular officials and the Immigration and Naturalization Service. One of the most peculiar characteristics of bureaucratic action is an almost total lack of flexibility. Once an individual demonstrates an intention to accomplish a particular end, a governmental official will often find it outside his or her point of reference to imagine that an applicant can sincerely modify his or her goals so as to remain in conformity with the law.

For all of the above factors there has been an increase in the demand for the non-immigrant visa. This demand for non-immigrant visas has, in turn, resulted in an increased scrutiny of non-immigrant petitions (applications) by the U.S. immigration authorities. Therefore, a thorough understanding of the limits, conditions, and purposes of the various non-immigrant visas to the U.S. is essential for proper planning by the foreign person or entity. I cannot overemphasize the importance of advanced and thorough planning by the foreign person. It may very well mean the difference between denial or approval of the visa petition by the visa officer.

TOURIST/BUSINESS VISITOR (B-1/B-2)

The B-1/B-2 visa is by far the most common visa issued by the United States Consular authorities for entry to the United States. For most foreign persons, this is the easiest of all the non-immigrant visas to obtain. The B-1 visa is used for specific categories of business in the United States, while the B-2 visa is issued to tourists or visitors for pleasure. In neither case, however, may the holder of the visa engage in activities which will result in financial compensation such as wages, tips, fees, commissions, etc. The "business" contemplated by the B-1 visa does not include the active management of a business or commercial enterprise in the United States. A B-1 visa holder may properly attend business meetings, court hearings, etc., and may engage in professional or commercial undertakings so long as any compensation is earned and paid from abroad. The B-2 visa holders, as already indicated, are limited to non-business, visitor activities.

In order to qualify for the B-1/B-2 visa the foreign person must hold a valid passport or other travel document and must establish to the satisfaction of the U.S. visa officer the following:

☛ He or she has a permanent domicile outside of the United States which he or she has no intention of abandoning.

☛ He or she has the necessary financial capacity to conduct a business or pleasure trip in the United States and has a round trip ticket from the transportation carrier.

☛ He or she is not otherwise disqualified (excludable) from entering the United States for reasons such as having a criminal record, etc.

While the documentary and qualitative requirements are fairly simple to meet, persons from developing countries may find it difficult to obtain this visa. In every case a foreign person must establish a personal motivation to depart the United States within the time period established by the immigration officer at the border.

The United States Consular officers very often use "profiles" to determine whether a person might be a poor risk for receiving a B-1 or B-2 visas. As an example, a young, unmarried person without a job or other visible means of support would probably be denied a B-1/2 visa because there would be insufficient motivation for that person to return to the country of origin. The situation would be worsened if, in addition to the above, the young person has close relatives in the United States and comes from an underdeveloped country.

In a situation in which one or more of the above factors may be present, I recommend that the visa applicant prepare for the Consular officer's inquiry by organizing documentary proof that there exists a strong motivation to depart the United States at the conclusion of the visit. This might entail proof of a good job in the home country, the ownership of valuable property, as well as the existence of other strong economic, emotional and cultural ties to the home country. Remember, the presumption is that the visa applicant is not entitled to the visa until proven otherwise to the satisfaction of the Consular visa officer. In any event it is advisable to have all the evidence properly organized before approaching the United States Consulate for the visa.

The B-1/B-2 visa is obtained at a U.S. Consular post abroad and is valid for an initial entry of up to six months. This period may be extended for good cause for an additional period of six months but extensions beyond that are very difficult to obtain. Occasionally I am asked by foreign visitors if these time limitations can be legally avoided by merely taking short trips out of the United States shortly before the expiration of stay which is listed in the Form I-94. My answer is to remind my client that the border inspection officer has the right to deny entry to a foreign person if the border officer is convinced that the person is living in the United States permanently or is otherwise acting out of status. The officer is able to assume that someone who has spent the majority of time (perhaps the last sixteen months) over a lengthy period (perhaps the last eighteen months or so) of time in the United States is probably a *de facto* immigrant, that is, an intending immigrant without a proper visa, and is therefore, removable.

Canadians especially should be aware of this fact. Canadian citizens do not need visas to enter the United States *if they enter as visitors*. The border crossing formalities are minimal for Canadians—so long as they are entering as visitors. Many Canadians forget that all the other immigration law restrictions still apply to them. Thus, if a Canadian citizen attempts to cross the land border towing a trailer loaded with personal effects and furniture, the U.S. immigration border will probably deny entry on the basis that the person is not entering as a visitor. A Canadian citizen who tries to board an airliner destined to the U.S. at the Toronto International Airport while carrying a one-way ticket may be denied entry on the suspicion that he or she is not a bona fide visitor. Remember, the inspector does not have to prove that the foreign person is not a bona fide visitor. It is the foreign person who has the burden of proving his visitor status to the satisfaction of the immigration inspector.

EXTENSION OF STAY

The duration of stay under the B-1/B-2 visa may be extended. A first extension of stay is possible but it is not automatic. The visitor must prove possession of a return transportation ticket and must prove financial means of supporting oneself and timely activities while in the United States. The INS will carefully scrutinize the reason for the extension and if the foreign person fits the profile of a risk for absconding or of otherwise violating the B-visa status, the extension will be denied. I recommend that an extension request be taken seriously and that a competent immigration lawyer be consulted to prepare the extension request. Regardless of how strong the foreign person's relationship is with the visa officer in the U.S. Consulate of his home country, it counts for very little while the foreign person is in the United States. A second extension is almost unobtainable.

The Immigration Reform and Control Act of 1986 established a Visa Waiver Pilot Program which provides that aliens from designated countries can enter the United States as visitors for a period of up to three months without a visa. The program was initially limited to visitors from the United Kingdom. Visitors from the United Kingdom are defined to be persons who have the right of permanent abode there and are unrestricted in their travel within the United Kingdom. The Visa Waiver Pilot Program now includes the following countries (and others may be added):

Andorra	Austria	Belgium
Brunei	Denmark	Finland
France	Germany	Iceland
Ireland	Italy	Japan

Liechtenstein	Luxembourg	Monaco
The Netherlands	New Zealand	Norway
San Marino	Spain	Sweden
Switzerland	United Kingdom	

Visitors from the above countries who enter on the basis of the Visa Waiver program are subject to certain restrictions, such as the inability to extend their stay, change their non-immigrant status or adjust to permanent residence. The alien may still be barred from entering the United States at the border if unable, for any reason, to substantiate that the purpose of entry to the United States is as a visitor. Under all circumstances, it is essential that anyone entering the United States, even under this visa waiver pilot program, be able to substantiate and support all the requirements for entrance under the B-visa.

I do not recommend that a prospective business investor or executive utilize this program for preparatory or research visits to the United States unless the person is certain that an extended stay or change of status to the visa category will not be necessary. This is because of the inflexibility of the program which prohibits extensions of stay or change of status.

Treaty Trader/Investor (E-1/E-2)

This is one of the most important non-immigrant visas to the United States. The United States has signed treaties of navigation and commerce with certain other nations which provide among other things that nationals of those countries may enter and work in the United States under certain defined conditions. If the treaty trader or treaty investor is a company, then the employee in the United States must have the same nationality as the company. The employee must usually perform managerial or executive functions, although if the employee possesses some specialized skill not otherwise obtainable in the United

States, then a purely staff or labor position could support the E visa. The visa authorizes an initial duration of stay of up to two years and there is no limit to the total time period that the employee may remain in the United States with proper extensions, provided a continued employment which originally supported the visa. The E visa holder's spouse and minor dependents are also accorded the same visa. Another advantage of the E visa is that it is unnecessary to establish that the visa holder continues to maintain a home in the foreign country to which the intention is to return.

The two types of activities and their corresponding visas that are contemplated are as follows:

E-1 VISA   The E-1 visa is known as the treaty trader visa and benefits nationals of the treaty partner who are engaged in a "substantial" volume or trade with the United States. While it is not possible to define precisely what the term "substantial" means, it requires a volume of trade that is sufficient to at least support the employee in the United States. The trade transactions do not have to be individually large as long as they are numerous and the total percentage volume of trade must be at least fifty-one percent by and between the United States and the treaty country.

The term *trade* includes "the exchange, purchase, or sale of goods and/or services."

Goods are tangible commodities of merchandise having intrinsic value, excluding money, securities and negotiable instruments. Services are economic activities whose outputs are other than tangible goods. Such activities include, but are not limited to, banking, insurance, transportation, communications and data processing, advertising, accounting, design and engineering, management consulting and tourism. This new definition greatly expands the applicability of the treaty/trader provisions since the government now accepts the modern reality that much of international trade has to do with the movement of services rather than goods and commodities. This new interpretation permits the utilization of this visa for many types of businesses that are not capital intensive.

There is a disadvantage of this visa compared to the E-2 visa. The E-1 requires that the trade continue principally between the U.S. and the foreign treaty country during the life of the visa. It is possible for an otherwise successful entrepreneur to become disqualified from the visa if the majority of trade volume shifts from the treaty trader country to that of a third country. This is indeed an anomaly that is possible and of which the wise entrepreneur should be aware. The INS regulations suggest that if this occurred the alien would not become disqualified from the visa, but there is no explicit acceptance of this contingency. One way of avoiding this problem would be for the entrepreneur to create another company in which trade to other countries would be channeled. Another method would be to utilize, if possible, the treaty trader country as a purchase and distribution center so that all invoices and payments are channeled between the United States and the treaty country. If at all possible, utilize the E-2 visa instead of the E-1.

The countries which have E-1 treaty privileges include:

Argentina	Austria	Belgium
Bolivia	Brunei (Borneo)	Bulgaria
China	Colombia	Costa Rica
Denmark	Estonia	Ethiopia
Finland	France	Germany
Greece	Honduras	Iran
Ireland	Israel	Italy
Japan	Korea	Latvia
Liberia	Luxembourg	The Netherlands
Nicaragua	Norway	Pakistan
Paraguay	The Philippines	Spain
Sultanate of Muscat and Oman		Switzerland
Thailand	Togo	The United Kingdom
Vietnam	Yugoslavia	

E-2 VISA   The E-2 visa is known as the treaty investor visa and is issued to an alien who is a national of a treaty country and who is entering the United States to develop and manage a business enterprise into which he or she has invested or is committed to invest a substantial amount of capital and which investment is not marginal.

The United States has signed treaties of friendship and commerce providing for E-2 treaty investor benefits with the following countries:

Argentina	Austria	Australia
Belgium	Bulgaria	China
Colombia	The Czech Republic	Costa Rica
Ethiopia	France	Germany
Honduras	Iran	Ireland
Italy	Japan	Korea
Liberia	Luxembourg	The Netherlands
Norway	Oman	Pakistan
Paraguay	The Philippines	Slovakia
Spain	Sweden	Switzerland
Suriname	Thailand	Togo
The United Kingdom	Vietnam	Yugoslavia

Eligibility. The investment must be of a "substantial" nature and must not be "marginal." The law does not establish a particular amount of money to fulfill the requirement of "substantial," nor is the term "substantial" defined clearly nor is there a mathematical formula that can be used to discover this meaning. In addition, the term "substantial" is subject to varying interpretation in different consular posts, and indeed, perhaps between different consular officers in the same post.

> ## E-2 TREATY INVESTOR
>
> ★ Treaty nationals only
> ★ Substantial investment
> ★ Active (entrepreneurial) risk
> ★ Direct and manage
>   -or-
>   supervisory/executive employee
> ★ Cannot be marginal, must create
>   jobs
>   -or-
>   profit
> ★ Investment must be committed

With respect to the start up of a new enterprise which is being originally developed by the investor, whether or not a particular amount of capital is considered substantial is very often determined by a comparison of the size of other similar types of businesses. In addition to the overall size of the business, the number of employees contemplated is also very important in predicting the success of the visa application. The more employees there are, the less emphasis there will be on the question of whether or not the investment is substantial.

In start up enterprises, there is usually less of a problem in establishing to the satisfaction of the U.S. Consul that the investment is committed, as a precondition to the issuance of the visa. Since there was no pre-existing business structure in place prior to the foreign person's investment, it is not logical to expect the business to function before the visa is issued to the alien. The foreign investor must establish that he or she is past the point where liability can be escaped by failing or refusing to complete this transaction. The details of this item of evidence will vary from case to case. Newly developed business enterprises present other problems, however, all of which will be covered in the section on Franchises and Business Opportunities.

The investor is at greater business risk in a newly developed enterprise than would be the case where the investor is purchasing an existing business. Most business consultants would agree that, all else being equal, it is preferable to acquire either an existing, ongoing business enterprise or a franchised business opportunity. The United States has a relatively free economy which, while providing the freedom to succeed, also provides the environment to fail.

The statistics kept by the Small Business Administration of the U.S. Department of Commerce indicate that the majority of new enterprises fail within the first two years of existence. One can only deduce that for foreign persons who do not have very much insight into the norms and customs of the commercial community into which they venture, the risk of failure is at least as high as it is for United States residents. I suspect that the percentage of failure by foreign investors with respect to "start up" enterprises is higher than it is for United States residents.

Because of these realities, most foreign individuals would rather invest in an enterprise that is already in existence and is already functioning. Enter the world of immigration. The rules and regulations require that a foreign person invest a relatively high percentage of the price of the business opportunity. Indeed, much higher than sellers require of U.S. resident purchasers. My "rule of thumb" for determining what is substantial with respect to the purchase of an existing business is that the investor should purchase the largest business possible with a direct investment of at least fifty percent of the price of the business.

Substantiality. There is no mathematical formula or fixed minimum amount for determining "substantial." The newly enacted regulations of the Department of State articulate the question of substantial as follows:

> Substantial amount of capital. A substantial amount of capital constitutes that amount that is:
>
> (1)(i) Substantial in the proportional sense, i.e., in relationship to the total cost of either purchasing an

established enterprise or creating the type of enterprise under consideration;

(ii) Sufficient to ensure the treaty investor's financial commitment to the successful operation of the enterprise; and

(iii) Of a magnitude to support the likelihood that the treaty investor will successfully develop and direct the enterprise.

(2) Whether an amount of capital is substantial in the proportionality sense is understood in terms of an inverted sliding scale; i.e., the lower the total cost of the enterprise, the higher, proportionately, the investment must be to meet these criteria.

Substantiality is very often determined by the use of a *proportionality* or *relative* test. There are two methods:

1. In the case of the acquisition of an existing business enterprise, the capital invested by the alien must be proportional to the total value or cost of the particular business enterprise as follows:

   ☞ If the cost of acquisition is $100,000.00 or less the required percentage of capital investment should be between 90-100%.

   ☞ If the cost of acquisition is between $100,000.00 to $500,000.00, the required percentage of capital investment should be between 60-75%.

   ☞ If the cost of acquisition is between $500,000.00 and $3,000,000.00 the required percentage of capital investment should be over 50%.

   ☞ If the amount invested is over $1,000,000.00 the investment will probably be considered substantial per se.

2. In the case of the creation of a new business by the foreign person, the capital invested must be an amount normally considered necessary to establish a viable business enterprise of the type contemplated.

As a general guideline, the minimum amount of cash required to meet the test of substantiality is $100,000 U.S., as long as that amount is proportional to the cost of acquisition. In certain U.S. Consulates abroad, $100,000 would be considered minimal; thus, this figure must be considered only as a "rule-of-thumb" and must be analyzed in light of the type of business, the investment, the proportion of capital to acquisition cost, the rate of return, and all of the other factors described in this section. Nonetheless, an investment of less than this sum might seem to many U.S. consuls as insubstantial, unless one could establish that the business does not require more capital than that invested and that the sum invested represents all or almost all of the price of acquisition.

If the business enterprise by its nature does not require a high capital cost (such as a service business) then a relatively small amount of capital, say $50,000.00 might be considered substantial. This would be especially true where the investor possesses special and unique skills and talent such as an artist or architect. As an example, in the case of an architect, engineer, or other designer who purchases and installs state-of-the-art computers, software and printers containing advanced "computer aided design" (CAD) features, the office headquarters might not require much more than standard office furniture in order to be a complete and properly functioning enterprise.

The above proposed proportionality tests are not mandatory and may be modified in individual cases, but I fear that the bureaucratic tendency is to use these guidelines as "white line" tests and that if a particular investment does not fall within the proportions outlined, there will be a presumption of ineligibility. This is especially unfortunate since often the foreign person may be very experienced and knowledgeable in business while the examining consular officer who has the authority to issue or deny the visa may be lacking in business experience and intellect. In my home state of Florida, businesses are usually purchased for considerably less than the amounts required by these regulations.

One technique that may avoid the economic problem inherent in the proportionality test is to subdivide the transaction so that the foreigner's capital is proportionately invested in the purchase of key assets or components of the business; other assets could be purchased later in a related, though separate, transaction. There are many variations of this technique that may be applicable in particular circumstances and it is imperative that proper planning be conducted prior to the execution of any documents for the acquisition of the business enterprise. The employment of a competent immigration attorney and knowledgeable business consultant is essential in this type of situation.

With an investment of a large sum of capital in the amount of $1,000,000.00 or more, "substantiality" will be presumed as a result of its sheer size, even though it may not approximate the recommended percentages. In most instances, the concept of "substantiality" is dependent upon the type of business that is being developed as well as the proportion of equity invested by the alien.

The investment cannot be "marginal" and very often the concepts of "substantial" and "marginal" are interrelated. The concept of "marginality" will be explained in greater detail further on in this chapter. The following is an example of the "substantiality" concept.

An investment in a heavy marine construction firm would obviously require millions of dollars, since each individual piece of equipment is quite costly; i.e., the cost of barges, cranes, tug boats, and additional equipment. Compare this type of investment with an investment in a wholesale distribution business for which the only capital investment required other than the wholesale inventory would be warehouse space, office furniture, perhaps the purchase of certain intangible assets, such as contract rights, etc. This business could be sufficiently capitalized with, let us say, $75,000.00. In the warehouse business, it is very likely that the Immigration and Naturalization Service or the U.S. Consul abroad will require an investment of at least ninety percent of the total amount required for the business; whereas, for the first company in our example, a lesser percentage is probably acceptable if the investment were large and if the investor were still directing the enterprise.

Investor's own funds. The U.S. Consul abroad will usually require documentary proof that the funds invested are the investor's own funds. Any person interested in this visa should begin to gather documentation to trace the funds from the account in the home country into the United States. The U.S. Consul will want documentary proof as to the origin and/or ownership of the funds and will usually not settle for anything less than this. This may be a problem for certain investors who live in countries where there is a restriction on the conversion of local funds into foreign currency or that may have various restrictions on the expatriation of capital.

It is not uncommon for persons of means in these countries to move certain amounts of their funds to a third country and to use various legal and accounting maneuvers to isolate these funds from themselves. Thus, it may be excessive for that person to reveal actual ownership of funds which the individual now seeks to move into the United States. Even though this may be a common practice in a particular country, the U.S. Consul will still require documentary proof that funds brought into the United States belong to the investor. Where an individual secretly takes large amounts of cash out of one's country and appears at the U.S. border and files the appropriate customs declarations with respect to the funds that the individual is bringing into the United States, the U.S. Consul or Immigration and Naturalization Service, for purposes of complying with the E-2 requirements, may still require that the foreign investor prove that the cash funds transported to and declared at the U.S. border are in fact his or her funds.

While the rules and regulations require that the foreign investor utilize one's own funds, loans that are guaranteed by the personal credit of the investor will suffice to meet the standard of "substantiality" as long as the loan is not also collateralized by the acquired assets. Loan proceeds that are collateralized by the assets that are being acquired by the foreign investor do not count as part of the foreign person's capital requirement for E-2 visa purposes.

The investor is not limited to a capital investment of cash only into the enterprise. Equipment, fixtures, inventory, and other valuable tangible assets are also valid assets for investment. Even intangibles such as patent rights, royalty, or other contract rights can be used in the valuation of the alien's investments as long as they can be objectively appraised.

Investor to direct and manage. It is imperative that the alien prove that he is entering the United States to direct and manage the investment/enterprise. This requirement is dependent upon proof that the investor owns and/or controls the enterprise that is the subject of the visa application. While ordinarily the alien must establish ownership of at least fifty percent of the equity in the enterprise, it may be possible to demonstrate control by contracts or other agreements that essentially place the management and control of the enterprise in the hands of the alien.

Logic alone would indicate that if the alien is not in control of the investment and does not need to be present in the United States in order to manage it, the visa would be unnecessary.

Active enterprise. The rules and regulations also require that the investment be an active enterprise as opposed to a passive investment. Investments in vacant land or in stocks, bonds, mutual funds, etc., will not qualify the investor for an E-2 visa, regardless of the amount involved. The E-2 visa was created to bring key individuals into the United States whose presence is required to direct and manage a business enterprise. Obviously, if the investment is one that does not require the personal involvement of the investor, the E-2 visa would not be appropriate for that person. Of course this is a generality, and there may be some rare exceptions which will require close analysis if the line between a passive and an active enterprise is not clear. An example is someone who invests in the business of land or home development. While the ownership of land per se is insufficient as an entrepreneurial investment, someone who assumes the active entrepreneurial risk of developing land for commercial purposes could be an investor for E-2 designation.

The points discussed above may be difficult to rationalize in certain cases. I remember specifically a situation some years ago when a prominent real estate broker brought two wealthy European investors to my office. These gentlemen were about to purchase a large tract of orange groves, already under lease to an orange grove operator. The investors would not be involved at all in the orange grove business and sought to make their profit by re-selling the grove in the future. The foreign individuals were about to invest more than a million dollars, U.S. cash, for the property, since it provided a favorable rate of return and was fairly secure. The investors, however, had one condition on their investment: that they obtain an E visa, so they could enter the U.S. and spend extended periods of time here at will. After analyzing the investment and their participation in the investment, I came to the conclusion that the investment would clearly not qualify for the E-2 visa. The investors were disappointed that the large investment that they were willing to make would not entitle them to the visa but were happy to find this out prior to making the commitment to complete the transaction. Had they purchased the investment on the understanding that they would qualify for this visa, they would have been disappointed later.

Marginality. The newly issued INS regulations state the following as to the question of marginality:

> For purposes of this section, an enterprise may not be marginal. A marginal enterprise is an enterprise that does not have the present or future capacity to generate more than enough income to provide a minimal living for the treaty investor and his or her family. An enterprise that does not have the capacity to generate such income, but that has a present or future capacity to make a significant

economic contribution is not a marginal enterprise. The projected future income-generating capacity should generally be realizable within 5 years from the date the alien commences the normal business activity of the enterprise.

The terminology of the above regulation is full of legal significance and must be carefully considered. First of all, the meaning of a "minimal living" is not clear. This term is very often defined by the treaty visa officer abroad in the context of the usually expensive cost of living in the principal city where most U.S. Consulates are located. Thus, what may be a minimal living for a person residing within commuting distance of the city of London may be a comfortable living for someone who resides in a rural community in the United States. Second, there is no definition of "significant economic contribution." Thus, it is not clear if this terminology permits the creation of an enterprise in which just low skilled jobs are created is sufficient. It is not entirely clear whether an enterprise which currently is or promises in the future to be highly profitable but which creates little or no employment is satisfactory. How about a business that doesn't provide high direct employment, but does provide much indirect employment, as would be the case of a company such as a building constructor in which most of the labor is provided by independent contractors? These are all dynamic concepts which require interpretation based upon all of the above factors, not the least of which is the particular U.S. Consulate involved.

It is also obvious that most E-2 investor applications should be augmented by a comprehensive business plan, which should be written in clear and simple language so that a person who has little or no training in business matters can understand it.

The concept of marginality is a difficult concept for the foreign person to grasp because it is a negative concept; that is, in order to be successful in a visa application the investor must prove that the proposed investment does not have the characteristic of *marginality*.

A component of *substantial economic contribution* is whether or not the investment will provide employment for U.S. citizens and/or residents. If the proposed business investment will provide for employment of other persons, it is less likely the investment will be found to be marginal. Thus, if the business will only support the investor and one or two other subsidiary employees, an investment may not support an E-2 visa unless the other factors described are present in a substantial degree. If the nature of the business is such that large numbers of employees are not normally necessary, such as would be the case if the alien investor were a commercial artist, then the employment requirement can be relaxed. This is because the nature of the business or endeavor, i.e., the creation of art, depends upon the unique and particular talent of the investor, whose efforts cannot be delegated to other employees. However, the business must still justify that it makes a "significant economic contribution." It is clear that the focus is on the purely economic benefits of an enterprise rather than its other possible non-economic benefits.

The more U.S. persons that will be employed by the business, the less attention or importance will be placed on the profitability of the business. The requirements described above are all interrelated and are somewhat interdependent.

Let us examine the following example:

A restaurant is offered for sale by a U.S. seller at a price of $175,000. The transaction requires a total cash investment of only $75,000 since the present U.S. owner is willing to finance the balance ($100,000.00) of the purchase price. Indeed, this is a debt to equity ratio that would be customary in many areas in the United States. Furthermore, let us assume in our hypothetical transaction that the alien investor reasonably expects to derive a salary of $25,000 per annum and does not have income from any other source for support. The INS and/or the Department of State (U.S. Consulate abroad) will probably decide that a $75,000 investment is not in and of itself substantial under these circumstances. Secondly, they will decide that a $25,000 return, where there is no other income from any other sources indicates that the investment is one that will merely provide this person with a minimum salary. Thus, this investment will probably fail for lack of substantiality and for being marginal in nature. If, on the other hand, the investor could show rehabilitation of a troubled business and thereby saving the jobs and—better yet—if the foreign investor could show an increase in the number of employees, the investment might be approved, especially if the investor could show that the amount invested was more than the norm or more than what would typically be required to establish or purchase a similar restaurant in the area. One cannot overemphasize the importance of documentary evidence to establish the accuracy of all assertions concerning the concept of "substantial" investment and the required lack of "marginality."

As stated previously, the Department of State and the INS are wary of alleged investments that may be nothing more than an attempt to immigrate to the United States in circumvention of the normal immigrant visa process. Consequently, these authorities look for evidence of immigrant intent in non-immigrant visa applications. In my judgment, the purchase by an investor of a home in the United States before issuance of the non-immigrant visa can be a tactical error.

In the case of an E-2 visa applicant for instance, the money invested in a private dwelling (house or condominium apartment, for example) is basically wasted as it reduces the amount of capital available to satisfy the substantiality requirement of the law. This is especially true when the proportion of cash investment in the home exceeds that in the business. It does seem in these instances that the cart is before the horse. In my geographic area in particular, the lovely State of Florida, most prospective foreign investors with whom I speak are either planning to or have already acquired an expensive home, sometimes for cash. I generally advise my clients that, unless they are sufficiently wealthy, the purchase of the home should represent an insignificant economic undertaking and should be deferred until their investment is firmly rooted. I have spoken to foreign persons who erroneously believed they met the substantiality requirement by acquiring an expensive home for cash and then investing a small percentage of cash in the business enterprise.

In certain instances the purchase of a personal residence at the inception of a business investment can be objectively justified—but generally I do not believe it prudent to impose that additional burden on the application. It is better to approach the situation conservatively and patiently by concentrating on the business first and then personal accommodations. The law now does not require the alien to maintain a home abroad nor does it require specific evidence of the alien's intent to return to the country of origin. Nonetheless, it is an excellent technique, especially in investment applications based upon a modest investment, to be able to demonstrate voluntarily that the alien does in fact maintain a foreign residence and that the alien's interest in acquiring or developing the U.S. enterprise is purely financial.

ADVANTAGES OF
THE E-2 VISA

The E-2 visa may be renewed indefinitely so long as the investment originally supporting the E-visa continues in existence, although the visa is initially granted for up to five years at most United States Consuls. The duration of the initial E-2 visa is reciprocally dependent upon the duration of similar visas extended to U.S. investors by the other signatory country. Also the E-2 visa investor does not need to maintain a foreign domicile to which his intent is to return. Thus, the expense of maintaining two residences can be avoided. However, as a result of the attitude and working philosophy of the U.S. consulate, I still recommend to my clients, at least during the application period, they have maintained a foreign domicile as well as other close contacts with the home country in order to establish the temporary intent that is still required of an E-2 visa applicant.

Additionally, employment by family members is not normally viewed as a violation of status even though the rules do not specifically sanction such employment. However, under the terms of the Immigration Reform and Control Act of 1986, it is doubtful whether a family member would be employable in the United States as employers now face criminal and civil sanctions for employing a person who is not otherwise authorized to work.

The E-2 visa is flexible. There is no requirement for the foreign person to have previously conducted business in a particular legal entity in the home country. Unlike the situation with the L-1 Visa, individuals (by investing the funds) can qualify for the E-2 visa even if they have operated in the past and intend to operate in the future as a sole proprietor. Additionally, the investors do not need to prove that they are an executive or manager, etc., but merely prove that they are in a position to direct and manage the enterprise. This has been interpreted by rule and regulation in case law to mean that they must be in control of the enterprise. This distinction eliminates many of the technical problems involved in proving the status of executive or manager as indicated previously.

Procedure. It is preferable to process this visa application at the U.S. Consulate abroad even though the INS has recently adopted the policy of *dual intent*. The acknowledgment of dual intent enables foreign persons to apply for the E-2 visa in the United States even if they have had a petition for permanent residence filed on their behalf.

The E-2 visa application may be filed in the United States if the foreign person is already in the United States in a valid non-immigrant visa status. After the change of status is granted by the INS the alien can remain in the United States and start working in the investment. If the alien departs the United States then, in order to re-enter, he must apply for and obtain from a U.S. consulate an E-2 visa. Often the United States consulate will require an entirely new E-2 visa application and will reserve the right to adjudicate it anew. As a result of the obvious inconvenience and risk inherent in this situation, an entrepreneur should plan so as to minimize the problem of visa issuance—especially since in this situation the enterprise has already commenced.

There is another variation of the intent problem already discussed in previous chapters which may affect holders of non-immigrant visas.

Since it is often easier to obtain one particular visa as opposed to another (for example, the B-2 visitor visa) an alien might be tempted to enter the United States on one visa and then once in the United States, file an application for a change to a different visa. There is nothing wrong with this procedure if the change of intent is genuine. However, if the INS believes that the alien entered the United States with a pre-conceived intent to apply for a change of visa after arrival, then the requested visa may be denied just for that reason. Furthermore, even if the INS approves the change of status, this is no guarantee that the U.S. Consulate abroad will issue the visa in the event the foreign person is required to travel outside the United States. The U.S. Consulate may deny issuance of the E-2 visa even if the foreign person has commenced business operations in the United States under the authority of the INS. The rationale is that the Department of State is required by law to exercise its own independent judgment with respect to visa issuance.

Be advised that the Department of State jealously guards its prerogatives and one sure way to earn the animosity of the treaty visa officer is to indicate by word or deed that one is merely seeking to have the visa stamped into the passport.

Each U.S. Consulate has developed a method for processing E-visa applications even though most of them use the same form (OF-156 with E Supplement). Every consul will require proof of all the elements outlined in this chapter so an individual applying for an E-visa should have all of the requirements thoroughly documented. Even though not required, it is strongly recommended that an individual applying for this visa, as well as certain other temporary visas, utilize the services of an experienced immigration professional for assistance in organizing the evidence required and to answer any of the questions of the U.S. consul. There is a saying that there is no second chance to make a favorable first impression and it would be imprudent to submit an E visa application that did not evidence care and consideration. In many cases, a consul will appreciate having a professional handling the application because many problems can be avoided.

In addition, as a result of the passage of the North American Free Trade Act, both Canadian and Mexican citizens are now eligible to obtain the E visas.

EMPLOYEES OF E-VISA TRADERS OR INVESTORS

If the E-Visa applicant is not the Trader or Investor principal, then the applicant's job must be of either executive and supervisory in nature or must have "special qualifications." The regulations state that the following requirements for E-2 employee:

> Executive and supervisory character. The applicant's position must be principally and primarily, as opposed to incidentally or collaterally, executive or supervisory in nature. Executive and supervisory duties are those which provide the employee ultimate control and responsibility for the enterprise's overall operation or a major component thereof. In determining whether the applicant has established possession of the requisite control and responsibility, a Service officer shall consider, where applicable:
>
> (i) That an executive position is one which provides the employee with great authority to determine the policy of, and the direction for, the enterprise;
>
> (ii) That a position primarily of supervisory character provides the employee supervisory responsibility for a significant proportion of an enterprise's operations and does not generally involve the direct supervision of low-level employees, and;
>
> (iii) Whether the applicant possesses executive and supervisory skills and experience; a salary and position title commensurate with executive or supervisory employment; recognition or indicia of the position as one of authority and responsibility in the overall organizational structure; responsibility for making discretionary decisions, setting policies, directing and managing business operations, supervising other professional and

supervisory personnel; and that, if the position requires some routine work usually performed by a staff employee, such functions may only be of an incidental nature.

(18) Special qualifications. Special qualifications are those skills and/or aptitudes tat an employee in a lesser capacity brings to a position or role that are essential to the successful or efficient operation of the treaty enterprise. In determining whether the skills possessed by the alien are essential to the operation of the employing treaty enterprise, a Service officer must consider, where applicable:

(i) The degree of proven expertise of the alien in the area of operations involved; whether others possess the applicant's specific skill or aptitude; the length of the applicant's experience and/or training with the treaty enterprise; the period of training or other experience necessary to perform effectively the projected duties; the relationship of the skill or knowledge to the enterprise's specific processes or applications, and the salary the special qualifications can command; that knowledge of a foreign language and culture does not, by itself, meet the special qualifications requirement, and;

(ii) Whether the skills and qualifications are readily available in the United States. In all cases, in determining whether the applicant possesses special qualifications which are essential to the treaty enterprise, a Service officer must take into account all the particular facts presented. A skill that is essential at one point in time may become commonplace at a later date. Skills that are needed to start up an enterprise may no longer be essential after initial operations are complete and running smoothly. Some skills are essential only in the short-term for the training of locally hired employees. Under certain circumstances, an applicant may be able to establish his or her essentiality to the treaty enterprise for a longer period of time, such as, in connection with activities in the areas of product improvement, quality control, or the provision of a service not yet generally available in the United States. Where the treaty enterprise's need for the applicant's special qualifications, and therefore, the applicant's essentiality, is time-limited, Service officers may request that the applicant provide evidence of the period for which skills will be needed and a reasonable projected date for completion of start-up or replacement of the essential skilled workers.

Planning tip. From a discussion of the above requirements of documentation and proof it should be apparent that it is much easier to establish whether or not a given business investment satisfies the "substantiality" requirement if the business is acquired rather than developed from the very beginning. The price established between two independent parties is accepted by the government as the "going" or market value for that particular business enterprise. If the business must be developed from the very beginning, then the government can, and frequently does, require independent proof that the investment is substantial for that particular type of business. This can require a written opinion from an independent expert as well as an audited financial statement from a Certified Public Accountant. It must be remembered that the immigration authorities do not generally have personnel who are competent or otherwise trained in business matters. The prospective investor must therefore generally prove and document to a non-business person what to the investor may be obvious.

BILATERAL INVESTMENT TREATIES
The United States has ratified a series of bilateral accords known as *Bilateral Investment Treaties* (BIT) with the following countries:

Albania   Argentina   Armenia
Azerbaijan   Bangladesh   Belarus

111

Bulgaria	Cameroon	Congo
Croatia	Czech Republic	Ecuador
Egypt	Estonia	Finland
Georgia	Grenada	Ireland
Jamaica	Jordan	Kazakhstan
Kyrgyzstan	Latvia	Moldova
Mongolia	Morocco	Panama
Romania	Russia	Senegal
Slovak Republic	Sri Lanka	Trinidad
Tobago	Turkey	Tunisia
Ukraine	Zaire	

Nationals of these countries are also eligible to apply for E-2 treaty investor visas.

CANADA AND CANADIANS: SPECIAL ADVANTAGES

Canada has traditionally been treated in a special and generally preferred manner by the immigration regimen of the United States. Canadians (together with certain classes of Mexican citizens) do not needed visas to enter the United States. Of course, this does not mean that the immigration law does not apply to Canadians; rather that Canadians entering the United States merely have to demonstrate to the officer at the border that they were otherwise qualified to enter in whatever visa category applied.

On January 2, 1988, the President of the United States and the Prime Minister of Canada signed a bilateral accord known as the Free Trade Agreement (FTA). This agreement was superseded by the North American Free Trade Act which was passed by the U.S. Congress in 1994. NAFTA addresses primarily topics such as trade, commerce, and tariffs but in order to facilitate the overall trade purposes of the act, also made some major sweeping changes in the immigration procedures of both countries. The immigration provisions do not replace the existing substantive immigration law, but rather modify the existing law. The immigration provisions of NAFTA present very favorable changes for both Canadian and Mexican business persons/investors.

As an example, the legislation and administration Rules and Regulations makes the Treaty/Trader Investor visa (E-1, E-2) classification available to Canadian and Mexican citizens. All of the provisions and requirements as described in this book, that apply to E Treaty applicants, now apply to Canadian and Mexican citizens. Canadian citizens applying for an E visa in the Western Hemisphere do not need to possess a passport and may have their visa issued on a separate document (Form OF-232).

Unlike Canadians, Mexican citizens applying for an E visa must have a passport.

The provisions of NAFTA apply only to citizens of Canada and Mexico. Canadian Landed Immigrants are not benefited. In order to qualify under the appropriate division of NAFTA, an individual must fit within the prerequisite definition of a "business person:" someone who is engaged in the trade of goods or services or investment activities. "Temporary entry" is defined as "entry without the intent to establish permanent residence." With respect to the latter requirement, all of the previous discussion on intention applies.

There are four groups of non-immigrants covered by NAFTA. They are as follows:

BUSINESS VISITORS

Business visitors may come temporarily to the United States for research and design, growth, manufacture and production, marketing, sales, distribution, after-sales service and general service. An alien who qualifies under this provision is not entitled to receive salary or remuneration from a United States source. However, a business visitor may receive incidental expenses from a United States source.

The initial entry period is for one year and the rules state that the extension may be granted in six-month increments. At the date of the publication of this book, the limit on the duration of stay under this category was unclear but it would seem there is no precise limitation as to how many extensions may be granted even after the original one-year admission. This may change over time as rules and regulations are added by the Immigration and Naturalization Service. Of course, accompanying family members (spouse or children) may be admitted under the same terms and conditions of the principal. There is an annual numerical limitation of 5500 TN visas for Mexican citizens. Accompanying dependents of Mexican TN professionals are also counted against this annual limitation.

CANADIAN AND
MEXICAN
TRADERS AND
INVESTORS

NAFTA extends the benefits of the E Treaty Trader provisions to citizens Canada and Mexico. A Canadian or Mexican citizen seeking admission under this section must apply for a visa from a U.S. Consular Officer abroad in order to enter in E status. Regulations as to the issuance of these visas will be published shortly by the Department of State. Please also note that services have now been added to the above definition of "Trade."

INTRA-COMPANY
TRANSFEREE

The only substantial change in the application of the L-1 visa provisions to Canadian citizens is that the citizen may have the option of presenting all supporting documents, etc. at the designated border points, thus circumventing the need for previously approved petitions by the Immigration and Naturalization Service. I believe this will be difficult to implement as the volume of documentation required for these visas can sometimes be quite onerous and unless one arrives at the border point early (three hours is recommended), it is doubtful that the border official will be able to properly analyze the documents. Unless the INS border inspector has sufficient time to review the alien's documents, the foreign person will be admitted under parole and an appointment will be scheduled at the Immigration and Naturalization office nearest the Canadian citizen's intended place of work in order to have the supporting documents thoroughly reviewed.

Mexican citizens will still have to apply for the L-1 visa at the Northern Regional Service Center of the INS.

CANADIAN AND MEXICAN CITIZENS SEEKING CLASSIFICATION IN ACTIVITIES AT A PROFESSIONAL LEVEL

Under the provisions of the NAFTA, Canadian and Mexican citizens can enter the United States temporarily to "engage in business activities at a professional level." In order to qualify under this category, individuals must provide proof of Canadian or Mexican citizenship and documentation showing that they are engaged in one of the professions listed in Schedule Two to Annex 1502.1. "Schedule Two" follows this subsection. An important advantage of this provision is that the Canadian citizen will be able to enter the United States without first having a petition filed by an employer requesting the alien's admission. The implementing legislation of the FTA amends the Immigration and Naturalization Act and includes as professionals: disaster relief and insurance claims adjusters, computer systems analysts, and management consultants. NAFTA provides that individuals who lack a baccalaureate or licenciatura degree must demonstrate at least four years of experience, or the equivalent of the time normally spent acquiring a baccalaureate degree in the United States.

A Canadian or Mexican citizen who otherwise qualifies, will be provided with an I-94 Form under the classification symbol TN with an initial entry period not to exceed one year. Extensions of stay may be granted in increments of one year.

Although NAFTA does not require that a petition be filed on behalf of a Canadian business professional, the implementing regulation specifies that the level of documentation "be on a par with that required for non-immigrant classifications for which petitions are required. Mexican citizens will have to file a formal visa petition (Form I-129) at the Northern Regional Service Center." Canadian citizens do not need to file a visa petition and may present their credentials and documentation of job offers directly to the INS inspector at the border. For either Mexicans or Canadians the following documentation must be presented:

☞ the professional activity to be engaged in.

☞ the purpose of entry.

☞ the anticipated length of stay.

☞ the educational qualifications or appropriate credentials which demonstrate that the Canadian or Mexican citizen has professional level status.

☞ proof that the Canadian or Mexican citizen complies with all applicable state laws and/or licensing requirements for the occupation to be engaged in.

☞ the arrangements for remuneration for services to be rendered.

☞ extensions of stay may be granted in increments of one year. The application for an extension of stay is to be accompanied by a letter from the employer confirming the continuing need for the alien's temporary services and specifying the additional time needed.

In addition to the above, NAFTA provides for the admission of Canadian and Mexican citizens who are coming to engage in certain professional activities. A list of those specific professions which have been identified by the act and enabling legislation is reproduced below:

(For purposes of brevity, the term baccalaureate degree includes the licenciatura degree issued in Mexico.)

☞ Accountant—baccalaureate degree

☞ Architect—baccalaureate degree or provincial license

☞ Computer Systems Analyst—baccalaureate degree

☞ Disaster Relief Claims Adjuster—baccalaureate degree or three years experience in the field of claims adjustment

☞ Economist—baccalaureate degree

☞ Engineer—baccalaureate degree or provincial license

☞ Forester—baccalaureate degree or provincial license

☞ Graphic Designer—baccalaureate degree, or post-secondary diploma and three year's experience

☞ Hotel Manager—baccalaureate degree and three year's experience

☞ Land Surveyor—baccalaureate degree or provincial/Federal license

☞ Lawyer—member of bar in province, L.L.B.; J.D.; L.L.L., or B.C.L

☞ Librarian—M.L.S. or B.L.S

☞ Management Consultant—baccalaureate degree or five years experience in consulting or related field

☞ Mathematician—baccalaureate degree

☞ Medical/Allied Professionals:

Clinical Lab Technologist—baccalaureate degree

Dentist—D.D.S., D.M.D., or provincial license

Dietitian—baccalaureate degree or provincial license

Medical Technologist—baccalaureate degree

Nutritionist—baccalaureate degree

Occupational Therapist—baccalaureate degree or provincial license

Pharmacist—baccalaureate degree or provincial license

Physician—(teaching and/or research only) M.D., or provincial license

Physio/Physical Therapist—baccalaureate degree or provincial license

Psychologist—provincial license

Recreational Therapist—baccalaureate degree

Registered Nurse—provincial license

Veterinarian—D.V.M.; D.M.V., or provincial license

☞ Range Manager (Range Conservationist)—baccalaureate degree

☞ Research Assistant (Working in a Post-Secondary Educational Institution)—baccalaureate degree

☞ Scientific technician/technologist—must work in **direct support** of professionals in the following disciplines: Chemistry, geology, geophysics, meteorology, physics, astronomy, agricultural sciences, biology, or forestry; must possess theoretical knowledge of the discipline; must solve practical problems in the discipline; must apply principles of the discipline to basic or applied research

☞ Scientist

Agriculturist (Agronomist)—baccalaureate degree

Animal Breeder—baccalaureate degree

Animal Scientist—baccalaureate degree

Apiculturist—baccalaureate degree

Astronomer—baccalaureate degree

Biochemist—baccalaureate degree

Biologist—baccalaureate degree

Chemist—baccalaureate degree

Dairy Scientist—baccalaureate degree

Entomologist—baccalaureate degree

Epidemiologist—baccalaureate degree

Geneticist—baccalaureate degree

Geologist—baccalaureate degree

Geophysicist—baccalaureate degree

Horticulturist—baccalaureate degree

Meteorologist—baccalaureate degree

Pharmacologist—baccalaureate degree

Physicist—baccalaureate degree

Plant Breeder—baccalaureate degree

Poultry Scientist—baccalaureate degree

Soil Scientist—baccalaureate degree

Silviculturist (forestry specialist)—baccalaureate degree

☞ Teacher for any of the following institutions:

College—baccalaureate degree

Seminary—baccalaureate degree

University—baccalaureate degree

☞ Technical Publications Writer—baccalaureate degree, or post-secondary diploma and three year's experience.

☞ Urban Planner—baccalaureate degree

☞ Vocational Counselor—baccalaureate degree

The Canadian and Mexican citizen must present to the Immigration and Naturalization inspector at the port of entry a verification of citizenship, a letter and any other required documents which demonstrate that the individual possesses the requisite educational background and experience for the profession claimed. Canadian citizens must also establish that they are qualified to engage in the employment indicated. Of course, a dependent spouse and children may also be admitted under the same visa category so long as these are also NAFTA nationals. If the dependents are not NAFTA citizens, they may be admitted as a B-2 visitors.

Canadian citizens in this classification may be re-admitted to the United States for the remainder of the period authorized on the original Form I-94 which they received at the border at the time of the initial entry, without presentation of the original letter or documentation. A Canadian admitted under this section may apply for an extension of stay on Form I-539, which is standard for requests of extensions of stay. The application for extension shall be accompanied by a letter(s) from the United States employer(s) confirming the continued need for the

NAFTA citizen's services and stating the length of additional time needed.

A Mexican citizen seeking the TN visa must file a formal petition on Form I-129 and will be adjudicated as if the petition were a normal H-1B visa petition. The petition must be filed at the Northern Service Center of the Immigration and Naturalization Service. The Notice of Approval must then be presented to the appropriate U.S. consulate in Mexico which will issue the visa.

A request to change U.S. employers is also made on the Form I-539, which must then be accompanied by a letter from the new employer describing the services to be performed, the time needed to render such services and the terms of remuneration for services. Employment with a different or with an additional employer is not authorized prior to approval by the INS of the request for extension of stay.

In addition, NAFTA provides for a procedure that allows for certain Canadian business persons to enter the United States temporarily. This would enable these persons to enter the United States for the purpose of extending performance of after-sales, service and training throughout the life of a warranty or service agreement.

A Canadian is permitted to present a Form I-129 petition together with supporting documentation at a U.S. port of entry rather than having to file the petition in advance at a regional Immigration and Naturalization office. Since these visa petitions generally require much documentation, it is recommended that individuals appear at the border at least three hours in advance of their scheduled departure.

The Intra-Company Transferee (L-1 Visa)

The L-1 visa is one of the most flexible and sought-after temporary visas which provide for employment.

Section 101(a)(15)(L) of the Immigration and Nationality Act establishes the requirements for the L-1 visa, one of the most useful non-immigrant visas available to employees of foreign companies. The purpose of the L-1 visa is to facilitate the transfer of key employees to the United States from companies that are affiliated with or related to United States corporations. This visa is very useful because it is not limited to specific countries with which the United States may have entered a treaty. Nationals of all countries are eligible, provided the specific qualifications for the visa are satisfied.

Duration of stay. The L-1 visa has a duration of seven years for "Managers" and "Executives" and five years for persons of "specialized knowledge." The duration of stay is issued for an initial period of three years and may be extended for additional period of two years. In the case of a new office, the visa is issued for one year and may be extended for two periods of three years.

REQUIREMENTS

Duration of employment. The employee who is to be transferred must have been continuously employed by the overseas (extra-United States) company for a period of at least one year out of the last three years prior to entry into the United States. Short business or pleasure trips to the United States during the one year period will not disqualify the employee from the visa; however, extended trips or visits to the United States may be considered by the INS as an interruption of the one-year foreign employment requirement.

Intra-company relationship. The prior employer/foreign company must be related to the U.S. company, either as a subsidiary, affiliate or division. This unity of identity is satisfied by any of the above legal relationships, and must in most cases, be documented to the INS. The documentation of the U.S.-foreign corporation relationship may not need to be documented in the case of large, well-known multi-national corporations such as Ford Motor Company, Monsanto, Dupont, etc.

In order to establish that the foreign-domestic entities are one and the same for immigration purposes, it is necessary that the corporations be controlled by the same person(s) (affiliate) or that one corporation controls the other (subsidiary). In order to document the above, one must show that the U.S. corporation owns at least fifty-one percent of the shares of the foreign corporation, (or vice-versa), or in the alternative that the same stockholders own fifty-one percent of each of the corporations. Another alternative, is to show that the foreign corporation is a branch or division of the U.S. corporation or vice-versa. The requirement of common control can be satisfied in certain instances even where the controlling entity does not own fifty-one percent of the stock. Thus, where persons own less than fifty-one percent of the foreign corporation, they must demonstrate effective control of that corporation through legal documents, contracts, or some other documented arrangement.

The INS has taken the position that the degree and nature of ownership of the foreign and U.S. companies must be identical. That is, indirect ownership of either the foreign or domestic company by way of another company or business entity would, in the opinion of the INS disqualify either the U.S. or foreign company from filing a petition for an L-1 visa. This overly technical interpretation of the law has been rejected by at least one federal court in the United States and it seems that the INS is backing away from this position. This is important because for many foreign persons it is preferable that they not own real estate directly in their own name or perhaps even in a company once removed from ultimate beneficial ownership of the U.S. company. Nonetheless, where otherwise possible it is beneficial to avoid tiers of ownership between a U.S. affiliate and foreign parent.

Here is an example. A Taiwanese family owns seventy-five percent interest in a Taiwanese manufacturing concern. The same family acquires a U.S. company, but instead of owning it in the same fashion as they own the Taiwanese parent, the family forms two foreign holding corporations (organized in the country of Barbados) which in turn own all the stock in the U.S. affiliate company. Even though the family indirectly owns the U.S. affiliate company in the same proportion as they own the Taiwanese company, the INS may make a technical objection on the basis that the forms of ownership of the companies differ. This scholarly attitude on the part of the INS may change on this subject, but as of the writing of this book, it represents the current posture of the INS. The reason why a foreign person may decide to hold U.S. business and real property interests using a multi-tiered corporate structure may be due to sound tax and other reporting requirement concerns, but there is no automatic understanding or acceptance by the INS of these otherwise very valid motivations.

In addition, the petitioning company must continue to be a "qualifying organization." Thus, the foreign company must continue to function as a viable business entity throughout the employment period of the L-1 visa holder. If the foreign entity ceases to exist or ceases to function as a viable business entity, then the L-visa status of the employee is jeopardized. This is an extremely important point for a small company to bear in mind.

Other qualifying companies. The immigration regulations permit entities other than a corporation to serve as a qualifying company. Partnerships and even sole proprietorships can serve as qualifying companies for L-1 visa purposes. In a non-corporate setting it is important to establish that the employing company is a separate entity from the employee being transferred. This fact is easier to establish with a corporation since a corporation is recognized as a separate legal entity from its owners. In the case of a larger, well-established company which operates in a legal form other than a corporation (or its equivalent), the L-1 visa may still be available but there will be a heavier burden of proof to establish the separate business and economic identity of the company.

In the case of a company that is contemplating the creation of a U.S. subsidiary or affiliate office, I recommend that either the company incorporate or that it create a separate corporation which will then act as the qualifying company for the L-1 visa. It must be remembered that mere creation of a corporation is insufficient. It will be necessary to transfer active and viable business activities to the corporation in order to allow it to serve as a qualifying company. Advanced and careful planning is the key to success in these endeavors.

Employee's qualifications. The law defines "manager," "executive" and "person of specialized knowledge" as follows:

Manager:

☞ Primarily manages the organization, or a department, subdivision, function, or component of the organization. The addition of the concept "function" gives the definition more usefulness for smaller companies or companies in which a key function is primarily managed and run by the same person.

☞ Primarily supervises and controls the work of other supervisory, professional or managerial employees, or manages an essential function within the organization, or a department or subdivision of the organization. In order to qualify as a "manager" under these regulations, a first-line supervisor must supervise professional persons. Thus, a manager would not qualify as such if he is the first-line supervisor of actual production personnel.

☞ Has the authority to hire and fire or recommend those as well as other personnel actions if another employee or other employees are supervised; if no other employees are supervised, functions at a senior level within the organizational hierarchy or with respect to the function managed.

☞ Exercises discretion over the day-to-day operations of the activity or function for which the employee has authority.

Executive:

☞ Directs the management of the organization or a major component or function. Note that this is similar to the third point under "manager" as defined above.

☞ Establishes the goals and policies of the organization, component, or function.

☞ Exercises wide latitude in discretionary decision-making.

☞ Receives only general supervision or direction from higher level executives, the board of directors or stockholders of the organization.

Person of Specialized Knowledge:

☞ Must have special or unique knowledge of the petitioning organization's product, service, research, equipment, techniques, management or other interests and its application in international markets, or an advanced level of knowledge or expertise in the organization's processes and procedures.

☞ *Special knowledge* is knowledge which is different from or exceeds the ordinary or usual knowledge of an employee in a particular field.

☞ A specialized knowledge professional is a person who has specialized knowledge and is a member of the professions.

There is no requirement that the position to be filled by the employee be identical to that previously held abroad, or that it have all of the same responsibilities, but the position in the United States must be at least of the equivalent classification as the employee's position abroad.

NEWLY FORMED
COMPANIES

The original purpose of the law was to provide for the transfer to the United States of managers and key persons from and by multinational corporations. However, the letter of the law as written also permits small companies to benefit from the L-visa—even companies that are composed of no more than two or three individuals.

The INS regulations have the following additional requirements for newly formed companies; A "newly formed company" is a company that has been in business for less than one year. A newly formed U.S. company which is a subsidiary or an affiliate of a foreign company must establish that it has obtained a place for conducting business, that the beneficiary had been employed abroad as a manager or executive and will continue in that capacity in the United States.

If the L-1 visa employee is a major stockholder of the company, proof must be submitted that the employee will be transferred abroad at the completion of temporary duties in the U.S.

All of the above points must be minutely documented to the INS. Indeed, one should provide, among other things: copies of the lease for the premises, copies of any business contracts, a cash projection for the business, and copies of accounting and bank records to indicate that both the foreign company and the United States parent are viable entities. Proof of economic viability usually requires documentation which establishes that the United States entity has the financial ability to cover the transferee's salary for at least the first year of operation. I also recommend the inclusion of documentation regarding the qualifying company's economic strength as well. The petition, together with the supporting documentation, must then be filed with the appropriate district office of the INS for processing. I cannot overemphasize the importance of presenting a well-organized and probative set of corroborating documents together with the Form I-129. See the instruction sheet for the Form I-129 which is included in appendix C. The success or failure of the petition will be based for the most part on the strength of the documentary evidence submitted in support of the petition. After approval of the petition, the employee may bring the letter of approval to the nearest U.S. Consular Post in order to apply for the issuance of the visa.

The purpose of this regulation is to prevent relatively small companies from sponsoring visas for their sole or family owner/manager when the real intention is to immigrate permanently to the United States. The regulation however, ignores economics and business realities and often results in an overly mechanistic view of a business organization.

The regulations further state that in defining "executive or managerial" for L-visa purposes the INS will review the size of the company and the total number of employees employed by the company. The regulations seem to be creating an additional requirement of size and/or structure that is not contained in the original law and is subject to attack in the court systems. This new development requires close study and analysis by any foreign company seeking to expand operation into the United States.

Company must be "doing business." The law also requires that the petitioning company be in the business of providing regular, systematic and continuous goods and/or services. The regulations specifically exclude the mere presence of an agent or office of the qualifying organization in the U.S. and abroad as being acceptable. The law clearly favors entrepreneurial activities rather than passive investments. Indeed, if the person is not needed to actively manage or supervise a key function of the organization, that person probably does not need to be physically present in the United States—or at least that is the attitude of the government on this issue.

Alien's intent. An important consideration for this visa (as is the case with all of the others discussed in this book) is the question of intent. This applies both as to the employer and the employee. In both cases, it is required that the intention be one of a temporary nature. In the context of the L-1 visa, the problem of intent has been largely eliminated.

It is now permissible for an employee to have a "dual intent" with respect to intention as to the duration of stay. That is, the employer and employee may have the present intention of remaining in the United States on a temporary basis in compliance with the requirements of the L-1 visa, while at the same time, having an intention to file a petition for a permanent visa at some point in the future. The INS must be satisfied that both the employer and the employee agree that the employee will return abroad if the permanent visa is not approved during the valid period of the stay authorized by the L-1 visa. Putting the intention into words, it can be thought of as saying:

It is my intention to remain in the United States on a temporary basis during the period of time that my L-1 visa is valid. I may decide to remain in the United States as a permanent resident by filing an application for a permanent visa but I agree that I will depart the United States in the event that the L-1 visa expires before I obtain my permanent visa.

Usually, the mere statement of intention by the employer is sufficient to establish the petitioner's intention to comply with the law, unless the transferee is also a principal owner of the company and/or the U.S. corporate enterprise is a new venture. In these cases additional documentation is required to establish the circumstances under which the transferred employee will depart the United States.

This visa does not require that the foreign employee maintain a home abroad but if he does, it is obviously helpful on the issue of temporariness.

The reason for this high degree of attention to the question of intent by the INS is that the L-visa, at least with respect to executives and managers, lends itself to a relatively easy conversion to a permanent visa.

Normally, an alien must have received a job offer from a U.S. employer which has been certified by the Department of Labor as not displacing qualified local workers or negatively affecting the U.S. labor market. This process can take a long time. A manager or executive who holds an L-1 visa can qualify for a first preference employment-based permanent visa as a multinational manager or executive without the necessity of a labor certification. This is a highly coveted advantage.

As a result of the long time delays in obtaining a permanent visa, an employee may need to extend his L visa before the permanent visa is approved. A new policy determination by the INS states that the filing of a request for labor certification or of a petition for a permanent visa will not "per se" disqualify a person from obtaining an extension to the L-visa. In other words, the Immigration and Naturalization representative will look at other evidence to determine whether or not—at the time a person applies for an extension of his L-visa—that person has a true intention to return home in the event that the permanent visa is denied.

Even though the distinction between dual intent and a preconceived permanent intent may be somewhat unclear, the distinction must be thoroughly understood by the employee and the employer in order to avoid difficulties with INS. This is especially the case where the person is the employee of a small business or a business in which a substantial interest is held.

CHANGE OF
STATUS

If the alien is already in the United States and otherwise qualifies for the L-1 visa, he or she may elect to file for a "Change of Status," while he or she is in the United States so as to avoid the necessity of a trip abroad to a U.S. Consulate. When persons holding a B-1 visa file for a Change of Status for purposes of establishing the office and they have been in the United States for an extended period, there may be an interruption of the required one-year foreign employment.

As a result of the legal complexity concerning the requirements of the L-visa, the employer and/or employee should seek the advice and counsel of a qualified immigration attorney before any definite steps are taken.

TEMPORARY WORKERS

H-1B VISA

This is one of the most important non-immigrant visas available to qualified foreign persons wanting to come to the United States in order to work. The administrative regulations defining this visa state:

> An H-1B classification applies to an alien who is coming temporarily to the United States:
>
> (1) To perform services in a specialty occupation (except registered nurses, agricultural workers, and aliens of

129

extraordinary ability or achievement in the sciences, education, or business) described in section 214 (i)(1) of the Act,..., and for whom the Secretary of Labor has determined and certified to the Attorney General that he prospective employer has filed a labor condition application under section 212 (n)(1) of the Act;

(2) To perform services of an exceptional nature requiring exceptional merit and ability relating to a cooperative research and development project or a co-production project provided for under a Government-to-Government agreement administered by the Secretary of Defense;

(3) To perform services as a fashion model of distinguished merit and ability and for whom the Secretary of Labor has determined and certified to the Attorney General that the prospective employer has filed a labor condition application under section 212(n)(1) of the Act." 8 C.F.R. 214.2(h)(ii)(B).

This visa is highly sought because, unlike many other types of visas, the position that is being filled by the alien can be permanent; it is only the need for the alien that must be temporary. Furthermore, the foreign national is not required to have any prior employment experience with the same employer nor does the employer have to be international in character.

Specialty occupation. "...an occupation which requires theoretical and practical application of a body of highly specialized knowledge in such fields of human endeavor including, but not limited to, architecture, engineering, mathematics, physical sciences, medicine and health, education, business specialties, accounting, law, theology, and the arts, and which requires the attainment of a bachelor's degree or higher in a specific specialty, or its equivalent, as a minimum for entry into the occupation in the United States."

This definition describes a classic profession which requires the application of a theoretical body of knowledge to particular circumstances.

In the field of fashion modeling, prominence is defined as a high level of achievement evident by a degree of skill and recognition substantially above that ordinarily encountered to the extent that a person described as prominent is renowned, leading, or well known in the field of fashion modeling.

Employer's requirements. Before filing an H-1B petition, the prospective employer (petitioner) must file a labor condition application with the Department of Labor. The *labor condition application* is a representation that the petitioner has agreed to pay the H-1B beneficiary the prevailing wage for the job.

The labor condition application is not a document to be taken lightly. It presupposes that the employer has made a determination as to the prevailing wage for the job and then will pay the foreign employee accordingly. If it is determined by the government that an employer has violated the terms of the labor condition application, the employer can be fined. One of the conditions of the H-1B visa is that the employer is obligated to pay the cost of transporting the foreign employee abroad in the case of termination. The law does not provide for a sanction in the event of a violation of this provision and it is difficult to imagine how this provision could be enforced or who could enforce it.

Employee's (beneficiary) requirements for a specialty occupation. In order to qualify as a specialty occupation, the beneficiary-employee must meet one of the following criteria:

- ☞ hold a United States baccalaureate or higher degree as required by the specialty occupation from an accredited college or university.

- ☞ hold a foreign degree determined to be equivalent to a United States baccalaureate or higher degree required by the specialty occupation from an accredited college or university.

☞ hold an unrestricted state license, registration, or certification which authorizes full practice of the specialty occupation and be immediately engaged in that specialty in a state of intended employment.

- If a temporary license is available and the foreign person is allowed to perform the duties of the occupation without a permanent license and an analysis of the facts demonstrate that the alien under supervision is authorized to fully perform the duties of the occupation, H classification may be granted. This might be the case for certain health-related occupations such as physical therapists, for which occupations a state might provide a temporary license pending completion of all requirements for permanent licensure.

- In certain occupations which generally require licensure, a state may allow an individual to fully practice the occupation under the supervision of licensed supervisory personnel in that occupation. In such cases, if the facts demonstrate that the alien under supervision can fully perform the duties of the occupation, H classification will be granted. For example, this might be the case with architects who might be able to fully perform their functions as long as they work under the authorization of an employer-architect's state license.

☞ have education, specialized training, and/or progressively responsible experience that is equivalent to completion of a United States baccalaureate or higher degree in the specialty occupation and have recognition of expertise in the specialty through progressively responsible positions directly related to the specialty.

☞ proof of the filing of a labor condition application must accompany a petition for fashion modeling for H-1B classification.

☞ an evaluation from an official who has authority to grant college-level credit for training and/or experience in the specialty at an accredited college or university which has a program for granting such credit based on an individual's training and/or work experience.

☛ the results of recognized college-level equivalency examinations or special credit programs such as the College Level Examination Program (CLEP) or Program on Non-Collegiate Sponsored Instruction (PONSI).

☛ an evaluation of education by a reliable credentials evaluation service which specializes in evaluating foreign educational credentials.

☛ evidence of certification or registration from a nationally recognized professional association or society for the occupational specialty that is known to grant certification or registration to persons in the specialty who have achieved a certain level of competence.

☛ a determination by the INS that the equivalent of the degree required by the specialty occupation has been acquired through a combination of education, specialized training, and/or work experience in areas related to the specialty and that the alien has achieved recognition of expertise in the specialty occupation as a result of such training and experience. For purposes of determining equivalency to a baccalaureate degree in the specialty, three years of specialized training and/or work experience are required by the INS for each year of college-level training the alien lacks. In addition, the INS requires that the alien produce at least one type of documentation such as recognition of expertise in the specialty occupation by at least two recognized authorities in the same specialty occupation; membership in a recognized foreign or United States association or society for the specialty occupation; published material by or about the alien in professional publications, trade journals, books, or major newspapers; licensure or registration to practice a specialty occupation in a foreign country, or achievements which a recognized authority has determined to be significant contributions to the field of the specialty occupation.

The INS has issued a new I-129 Petition which is used for all of the above visas. The new form includes a relatively clear and useful set of instructions. The instruction sheet is included in appendix C. It is important to understand that the form requires complete and accurate documentation in order to comprise a completed petition.

Duration of stay. The H-1B visa is issued for three years and may be extended once. Foreign persons who are issued an H-1B visa in order to work on a Department of Defense project are issued a visa valid for five years.

Annual quota. There is a maximum of 65,000 visas to be issued annually for this visa. This is the only non-immigrant visa which has a numerical limitation quota.

Employers must always establish that they have the financial resources to pay the alien's salary and are otherwise a viable economic entity. If aliens are an owner or part owner of the business, they must convince the Immigration and Naturalization Service that their intention to remain in the United States is only of a temporary nature, regardless of their ownership interest in the company. If the company does not have other employees or does not have the other indicia of a going enterprise then the H visa petition may be denied. Even though the Form I-129 is deceptively simple, the employer and employee must accompany the petition with substantial documentation to establish their intent, qualifications, and financial ability. The instruction sheet for the form I-129 has been included in this book as an appendix and it is instructive to peruse the form in conjunction with the material presented in this section.

Once the visa is obtained, it may be extended for an additional three-year period. This provides for a maximum six-year duration of stay. In filing a request for the extension, the employer will have to justify the need to maintain the employee on a temporary basis for an additional three years, and the employee will have to prove an ongoing temporary intent that he/she will, in fact, leave the United States as soon as the duration of stay of the visa expires. The filing by the H-1B foreign national for a labor certification as the first step in a petition for a permanent visa, will not in and of itself disqualify the alien from obtaining the H-1.

Physicians. The law originally provided a "loophole" permitting foreign physicians to enter the United States to practice medicine (direct patient care); however, that loophole has been partially closed and foreign physicians may perform direct patient care if they; (1) have a license or other interim authorization otherwise required by the state of intended employment to practice medicine and; (2) have a full and unrestricted license to practice medicine in a foreign country or have graduated from a medical school in the United States or a foreign country.

If the physician is being admitted primarily to teach or conduct research for a public or nonprofit private educational or research institution, only condition (2) mentioned above requires compliance. As far as the petitioning employer is concerned, it must establish that the alien is coming to the United States primarily to teach or conduct research as described above or, if coming to provide patient care, has passed the Federation Licensing Examination (FLEX) or equivalent and is competent in English or is a graduate of an accredited medical school. In order to demonstrate competency in English the alien must pass the English proficiency test given by the Educational Commission for Foreign Medical Graduates (ECGMG).

Further details about the experience of implementing these new rules will determine the feasibility of utilizing this visa category for aliens who intend to practice medicine in the United States, albeit on a temporary basis. It is possible to enter the United States with this visa and then adjust status to that of permanent residency if conditions and circumstances warrant.

ALIENS OF
EXTRAORDINARY
ABILITY

O-1 Visa. This visa category benefits aliens of extraordinary ability in the sciences, arts, education, business, or athletics. For persons other than in the motion picture and television industry, extraordinary ability is shown by "sustained national or international acclaim." It appears that at least with respect to business, sciences, and education, the standard for eligibility could be quite high—perhaps the equivalent of a Noble Prize winner.

Foreign persons who are engaged in the motion picture and television industry, extraordinary ability is shown through a "demonstrated record of extraordinary achievement." The documentation required will include letters and print-media articles of acclaim, copies of awards as well as portfolios indicating the nature and extent of the performer's activities.

Consultation with local industry groups. The law also requires that the INS consult with union and management groups in the motion picture and television industry on an advisory basis prior to issuance or denial of the visa. The recent rule of the INS provides that petitioners for both O and P aliens must obtain an advisory opinion before submitting the petition. If the petition lacks the advisory opinion, then the INS will ask a peer group or labor union for an advisory opinion only if the INS agrees that the petition merits expeditious handling. If the INS does not feel that the case merits expeditious handling, it will deny the petition. Needless to say, the INS is generally not sympathetic to the custom in the entertainment industry of last-minute scheduling and promotion, and a petition should also provide proof as to the expeditious nature of the contracting arrangement. The attitude of many of the INS personnel is that the failure of the petitioner to plan properly does not mandate that the INS adopt a "crisis" approach to the adjudication of the petition. There is some logic to this position.

The INS rules provide that a labor union or peer group must act on an INS request for an advisory opinion within fifteen days after receiving a copy of the petition.

In the event there is no union or other "peer" group with which to consult, the INS may issue the visa regardless. The law is an improvement over the prior one practiced under the old H-1 regulations which did not provide for consultation with management as well as labor groups. The advisory opinions by unions or management groups which recommend denial must be in writing and the INS must attach such opinions to its final decision.

Duration. There is a three-year limitation on the initial duration of this visa. The duration of the visa shall be sufficient for the completion of the event(s) or activity but for no longer than three years. However, extensions of stay are granted only in order to complete the event(s) or activity.

Standards for "extraordinary ability." The administrative Code of Federal Regulations establishes the standards for determining extraordinary ability as follows:

☞ receipt of a major internationally recognized award such as the Nobel Prize.

☞ at least three of the following forms of documentation:

- Documentation of the alien's receipt of nationally or internationally recognized prizes or awards for excellence in the field of endeavor.

- Documentation of the alien's membership and association in the field for which classification is sought which requires outstanding achievement of their members as judged by recognized national or international experts in their disciplines or fields.

- Published material in professional or major trade publications or major media about the alien relating to the alien's work in the field for which classification is sought, which shall include the title, date and author of such published material and any necessary translation.

- Evidence of the alien's participation on a panel or individually, as a judge of the work of others, in the same or in an allied field of specialization as that for which classification is sought.

- Evidence of the alien's original scientific scholarly or business-related contributions of major significance in the field.

- Evidence of the alien's authorship of scholarly articles in the field in professional journals or other major media.

- Evidence that the alien has been employed in a critical or essential capacity for organizations and establishments that have a distinctive reputation.

- Evidence that the alien has commanded and/or commands a high salary or other remuneration for services evidenced by contracts or other reliable evidence.

The INS has promulgated the final rules establishing the standards for determining extraordinary achievement or extraordinary ability in the arts. They are reproduced from the Federal Register (Vol. 57, No. 69, April 9, 1992) as follows:

> (A) Evidence that the alien has been nominated for or has been the recipient of significant national or international awards or prizes in the particular field such as an Academy Award, an Emmy, a Grammy, or a Directors Guild Award; or (B) At least three of the following forms of documentation:
>
> (1) Evidence that the alien has performed and will perform services as a lead or starring participant in productions or events which have a distinguished reputation as evidenced by critical reviews, advertisements, publicity releases, publications, contracts, or endorsements;

(2) Evidence that the alien has achieved national or international recognition for achievements evidenced by critical reviews or other published materials by or about the individual in major newspapers, trade journals, magazines, or other publications;

(3) Evidence that the alien has performed in a lead, starring, or critical role for organizations and establishments that have a distinguished reputation evidenced by articles in newspapers or trade journals;

(4) Evidence that the alien has a record of major commercial or critically acclaimed successes as evidenced by such indicators as title, rating, standing in the field, box office receipts, credit for original research or product development, motion picture or television ratings, and other occupational achievements reported in trade journals, major newspapers, or other publications;

(5) Evidence that the alien has received significant recognition for achievements from organizations, critics, government agencies, or other recognized experts in the field in which the alien is engaged. Such testimonials must be in a form which clearly indicates the author's authority, expertise, and knowledge of the alien's achievements; or

(6) Evidence that the alien has commanded or now commands a high salary or other substantial remuneration for services in relation to others in the field, as evidenced by contracts or other reliable evidence; or

(C) If the above standards do not readily apply to the beneficiary's [alien] occupation, the petitioner may submit comparable evidence in order to establish the beneficiary's eligibility."

A recent opinion letter from the Acting INS Assistant Commissioner for Adjudications has stated that O-1 aliens can petition for themselves and thus, do not need to be hired by a U.S. employer.

O-2 Visa. This visa is used for those foreign persons who accompany and/or assist the O-1 alien in the athletic or artistic performance. The person must be an integral part of the performance of the O-1 visa person and must have critical skills and experience with the O-1 alien that are not of a general nature and cannot be readily replicated by other individuals.

O-2 visa applicants who assist persons in the movie and television industry must have a pre-existing and long-standing working relationship with the O-1 alien and in the event of filming, must be needed for purposes of maintaining continuity of filming both inside and outside of the United States.

Unlike O-1 aliens, O-2 visa applicants must show that they have a foreign residence which they have no intention of abandoning; consultation is also required for this group but only from labor organizations experienced in the skill involved. Depending on how the regulations are drafted, this requirement of consultation could result in delays and conflict since the opinion of a labor organization and the principal O-1 alien could differ on the question of O-2 alien's importance to the O-1 visa holder.

Dependent family members of O-1 and 2 aliens are issued O-3 visas, but they are not authorized to work.

P-1 Visa. This visa is for two types of internationally recognized individuals:

- ☞ athletes who compete individually or as part of a team at an "internationally recognized level of performance,"

- ☞ Entertainers who perform as part of a group that has received international recognition as "outstanding" for a "sustained and substantial period of time." The INS has recently promulgated rules and regulations establishing the standards for these terms. They are reproduced as follows from the Federal Register (Vol. 57, No. 69, April 9, 1992):

A P-1 athlete must have an internationally recognized reputation as an international athlete or he or she must be a member of a foreign team that is internationally recognized. The athlete or team must be coming to the United States to participate in an athletic competition which has a distinguished reputation and which requires participation of an athlete or athletic team that has an international reputation.

(A) Standards for an internationally recognized athlete or athletic team. The petition for an athletic team must be accompanied by evidence that the team as a unit has achieved international recognition in the sport. Each member of the team is accorded P-1 classification based on the international reputation of the team. A petition for an athlete who will compete individually or as a member of a United States team must be accompanied by evidence that the athlete has achieved international recognition in the sport based on his or her reputation. A petition for a P-1 athlete or athletic team shall include:

(1) a tendered contract with a major United States sports league or team, or a tendered contract in an individual sport commensurate with international recognition in that sport, and

(2) Documentation of at least two of the following:

(i) Evidence of having participated to a significant extent in a prior season with a major United States sports league;

(ii) Evidence of having participated in international competition with a national team;

(iii) Evidence of having participated to a significant extent in a prior season for a United States college or university in intercollegiate competition;

(iv) A written statement from an official of a major United States sports league or an official of the governing body of the sport which details how the alien or team is internationally recognized;

(v) A written statement from a member of the sports media or a recognized expert in the sport which details how the alien or team is internationally recognized;

(vi) Evidence that the individual or team is ranked if the sport has international rankings; or

(vii) Evidence that the alien or team has received a significant honor or award in the sport.

(viii) Criteria and documentary requirements for members of an international recognized entertainment group. A P-1 classification shall be accorded to an international group to perform as a unit based on the international reputation of the group. Individual entertainers shall not be accorded P-1 classification to perform separate and apart from a group. Except as provided in paragraph (p)(4)(iii)(C)(2) of this section, it must be established that the group has been internationally recognized as outstanding in the discipline for a sustained and substantial period of time. Seventy-five percent [75%] of the members of the group must have had a sustained and substantial relationship with the group for at least one year and must provide functions integral to the group's performance.

(B) Standards for members of internationally recognized entertainment groups. A petition for P-1 classification for the members of an entertainment group shall be accompanied by:

(1) Evidence that the group, under the name shown on the petition, has been established and performing regularly for a period of at least one year;

(2) A statement from the petitioner listing each member of the group and the exact dates for which each member has been employed on a regular basis by the group; and

(3) Evidence that the group has been internationally recognized in the discipline. This may be demonstrated by the submission of evidence of the group's nomination or receipt of significant international awards or prizes for outstanding achievement in its field or by three of the following different types of documentation:

(i) Evidence that the group has performed and will perform as a starring or leading entertainment group in productions or events which have a distinguished reputation as evidenced by critical reviews, advertisements, publicity releases, publications, contracts, or endorsement.

(ii) Evidence that the group has achieved international recognition and acclaim for outstanding achievement in its field as evidenced by reviews in major newspapers, trade journals, magazines, or other published materials;

(iii) Evidence that the group has performed and will perform services as a leading or starring group for organizations and establishments that have a distinguished reputation evidenced by articles in newspapers, trade journals, publications, or testimonials;

(iv) Evidence that the group has a record of major commercial or critically acclaimed successes, as evidenced by such indicators as ratings, standing in the field, box office receipts, record, cassette, or video sales, and other achievements in the field as reported in trade journals, major newspapers, or other publications;

(v) Evidence that the group has achieved significant recognition for achievements from organizations, critics, government agencies, or other recognized experts in the field. Such testimonials must be in a form that clearly indicates the author's authority, expertise, and knowledge of the alien's achievements; or

(vi) Evidence that the group has commanded or now commands a high salary or other substantial remuneration for services comparable to others similarly situated in the field as evidenced by contracts or other reliable evidence.

(C) Special provisions for certain entertainment groups— (1) Alien circus personnel. The one-year group membership requirement is not applicable to alien circus personnel who perform as part of a circus or circus group, or who constitute an integral and essential part of the performance of such circus or circus group, provided that the alien or aliens are coming to join a circus that has been recognized nationally as outstanding for a sustained and substantial period of time as part of such a circus. (2) Certain nationally known entertainment groups. The director may waive the international recognition requirement in the case of an entertainment group which has been recognized nationally as being outstanding in its discipline for a sustained and substantial period of time in consideration of special circumstances. An example of a special circumstances would be when an entertainment group may find it difficult to demonstrate recognition in more than one country due to such factors as limited access to news media or consequences of geography."

The one year membership requirement may be waived if the new member is replacing another member because of illness or other urgent circumstances or in the event the new member adds to the group by performing a critical role.

Note that entertainers who perform individually cannot be issued this visa.

In addition to the above, at least twenty-five percent of the P-1 entertainers must have had a "sustained and substantial" relationship with the group for a period of at least one year and all must provide integral functions to the group's performance.

The Attorney General of the United States acting through the District Director of the applicable Immigration and Naturalization District office may waive the "international" requirement or consider other types of evidence to sustain the substantial recognition factor for the entertainment group. This provision will benefit entertainment groups that may be quite talented and recognized in their country or region but who do not yet have an international acclaim or recognition.

P-2 Visa. The P-2 visa is issued to artists and entertainers participating in a reciprocal exchange program between foreign-based organizations and U.S.-based organizations that are engaged in the temporary exchange of artists and entertainers. This applies to both individuals and groups. Future administrative regulation will define the details for the eligibility and documentary requirements for these visas.

P-3 Visa. This visa is applicable to artists and entertainers who perform "under a program that is culturally unique."

Duration of stay for the P Visa. The duration of stay under both P-2 and P-3 visas is the time needed for the specific performance or event. P-1 athletes, however, may be allowed a duration of stay of up to ten years. This is a very sound provision since many professional athletes are required or encouraged to sign multi-year contracts with the team organizations for which they are playing.

Other eligibility requirements. P visa applicants must have a residence in a foreign country which they have no intention of abandoning (Remember this requirement does not apply to O visa applicants) and foreign persons must be entering to work in their respective fields of endeavor.

EDUCATIONAL/TRAINING VISAS

These sections will discuss each of three types of educational-training visas which are available to qualified foreign persons. They all share the common purpose of serving to upgrade the educational and/or vocational skills of foreign persons but differ markedly about the approaches that are taken to fulfill these goals.

H2-A AND
H2-B VISA

The H-2A visa applies to persons coming to the United States to perform agricultural work of a temporary or seasonal nature. This is a specialized visa process and the INS has published a handbook which provides details to prospective farm employers on the requirements of this visa.

The H-2B visa applies to persons whose job skills or occupation do not rise to the level of an H-1B applicant and who are coming to the United States to perform temporary work for a United States employer. The need for the employee must be temporary even though the job itself may not be of a temporary nature. Thus, if the employer needs a worker for a one-time occurrence or to meet seasonal or intermittent needs, then the employer may hire the foreign person after obtaining a labor certification from the Department of Labor to the effect that there are no U.S. persons available to perform the job requested and the employment of the alien will not adversely affect wages and working conditions of workers in the United States. In fact, because of the expense and inconvenience involved in obtaining the labor certification, I personally do not feel that this visa category is very useful, at least not in my experience. The visa is only issued for a one year period, so that only very unique positions and circumstances would justify the expense and trouble involved in obtaining this visa.

This visa is used by U.S. companies to employ both skilled and unskilled aliens on a temporary basis. There are two parts of the "temporariness" concept that must be noted. First, the position that the alien is filling must be of a temporary nature, and secondly, the company's need for the designated position must also be temporary. This visa is issued for a duration of one year at a time and may be extended, with some difficulty, up to a maximum period of three years. Another feature of the H-2 visa which differentiates it from the H-1B visa is that a Department of Labor "certification" must usually be issued as a precondition to the issuance of the visa. This is a marked difference from the H-1 visa which does not require a Department of Labor certification.

Eligibility requirements. Most of the eligibility requirements for this visa pertain to the employer rather than the employee even though, of course, the alien employee must be qualified for the position. As previously stated a United States employer is required to file a request for a labor certification from the Department of Labor as a prerequisite to the filing of an H-2B petition. It is incumbent upon the employer to prove to the Department of Labor that there are no U.S. workers available in the location of the job offering who are willing and able to perform the required work at current and prevailing wage rates. In addition, the employer will need to prove that the employment of the alien workers will not adversely affect the U.S. labor market.

The procedure above is identical to the procedure required for a Department of Labor certification for an immigrant visa, except that the Department of Labor is only interested in "Part A" of the Labor Certification request, which deals with the employer's needs and job offering. "Part B" of the ETA-750 lists the alien's qualifications, and does not have to be completed. If the Department of Labor denies the certification, it is still possible to obtain the H-1B visa if the employer can convince the INS of the unavailability of local labor to perform the job. This is not an easy task and, frankly, is probably not worth the effort.

Temporariness. Assuming that the Department of Labor issues a labor certification, the employer must still prove to the satisfaction of the Immigration and Naturalization Service that the need for the position is temporary and that the position itself is temporary. An example of these conditions is where a United States employer starts a new manufacturing operation and requires the assistance of a foreign expert who can train the employer's existing U.S. workers and give consulting advice to the management on the organization and administration of the new operation. In this example, the position is temporary in that it has a defined beginning and end; the need is temporary since the employer's need will terminate with the completion of the job.

It is important to note that the mere designation of a termination date is insufficient proof of "temporariness" to the Immigration and Naturalization Service. Rather, it is required that the employer give operational evidence as to the projected termination of the position as well as the employer's need for that position in order to support the visa.

Alien's qualifications. In order for alien to be the beneficiaries of an H-2 petition, they must establish their qualifications to perform the job requested. The job may be skilled or unskilled and can range from a high degree of technological expertise to that of a seasonal, unskilled laborer. In any event, aliens must prove that they are qualified by work experience or training or both to perform the job.

In addition, aliens must prove that their intention in entering the United States is temporary and that they maintain a home in a foreign country to which they intend to return as soon as their job tour is over.

Special problems. It is nearly impossible to adjust the H-2 Visa to that of a permanent resident alien. The Immigration and Naturalization Service has consistently maintained in a series of judicial and administrative rulings that the initial certification by an employer that the position as well as the employer's need were temporary preclude a later contention that the same position and need has now changed to that of permanent nature. In essence, the Immigration and Naturalization Service treats the initial petition as a warranty by the employer that the temporary character of the position will not change in the future to that of a permanent position to justify the employment of the alien.

It is possible for an employer to file a permanent visa petition or a petition to change the status on behalf of an employee's temporary visa so long as it is for a different employment position with different responsibilities than those which formed the basis for the issuance of the original H-2 visa.

Application requirements. The application for an H-2 visa, as indicated above, consists of essentially two steps. The first is the completion of the Department of Labor certification by the employer, and the second is the processing of the actual petition via Form I-129 by the employer with the Immigration and Naturalization Service. It is not necessary that the employer obtain the Department of Labor certification as a prerequisite to the issuance of the H-2 visa. That is, if the labor certification request is denied, the employee may offer rebuttal evidence to the Immigration and Naturalization Service, together with the letter of denial by the Department of Labor and attempt to persuade the Immigration and Naturalization Service to issue the visa, notwithstanding the Department of Labor denial. However, the Immigration and Naturalization Service normally gives much weight and credence to the finding of the Department of Labor in these matters.

Issuance of the H-2 visa. In the event the visa is granted, then the Immigration and Naturalization Service will issue its approval notice on a Form I-171C, which is sent to the employer. The employer will then forward this original form, together with its petition to the appropriate U.S. Consulate abroad. The U.S. Consulate will then make a file for the beneficiary (or beneficiaries) and issue the individual visas. The petition filed by the employer can be for multiple workers for the same position.

Duration of time and extension process. The H-2 visa is granted for a one-year period and may be extended for additional periods of one year to a maximum of three years. The extension request is accomplished by filing an additional Form I-129, which is now used as an extension application and requires both an additional Department of Labor certification and additional filing fee.

Obviously, the necessity of having to go through a second Department of Labor certification militates against extending the H-2 Visas beyond the original one-year period. It is very difficult to file successfully a change of non-immigrant status from a different non-immigrant classification to an H-2 classification. The likelihood that an alien who is in the United States in another non-immigrant status and coincidentally discovers a temporary job for which he is immediately qualified is rare. The reverse, however, is not as unlikely, in that it may be possible to change an H-2 visa to that of a different non-immigrant classification so long as the beneficiary is eligible for that visa, and the visa is for a totally different position from that which supported the H-2 petition.

H-3 VISA   This visa is offered to qualified foreign trainees who enter the United States with the purpose of participating in an established occupational training program. The visa anticipates that the alien will not be entering the United States for the purpose of engaging in productive employment, even though some degree of productive employment may be permissible so long as it is incidental to the training and is otherwise inconsequential in nature.

Eligibility. Most of the eligibility requirements pertain to the U.S. company or entity under whose auspices the alien will be entering the United States. In order to support an H-3 visa, the United States company must file a preliminary petition with the Immigration and Naturalization Service to participate in an established training and/or educational program. If the company does not have its own approved and fully structured in-house training program, then it will have to seek the assistance of one or more blanket agencies which have already been authorized by the United States Information Agency to sponsor the entry of qualified foreign persons as J-1 trainees. Training of the foreign persons cannot anticipate an eventual job offer by the U.S. employer.

The law assumes that the H-3 visa holder will undergo training which will be useful in the alien's home country. The documentary proof must show that the employer is not seeking to train the foreign person for eventual U.S. employment, but rather for employment abroad.

In addition to the above, the U.S. employer must prove that the type of training it offers the alien is unavailable in the alien's home country. This very often can be established by showing that the U.S. company's activities in the United States (or even on a worldwide basis) are unique.

Aliens must prove that their intention is to enter the United States only for a temporary period of time, and that they will return to a home or foreign domicile which they have no intention of abandoning.

Duration of the visa. This H-3 visa is valid for the documented length of the approved training program which usually means an outside limit of two years. It is technically possible to extend the visa beyond a two-year period of time, but such a request will generally be met with skepticism by the Immigration and Naturalization Service. Where a number of foreign trainees will be undergoing the same training, it is possible to include all of them in a single petition filed by the U.S. company or training agency. The U.S. employer must establish that the majority of time spent by the alien in the United States will be a bona fide training-instructional program, as opposed to on-the-job productive employment. If from a description of the position and its attentive duties, it seems as if the employer is gaining direct benefits from the alien's activities in the United States, then the H visa may be denied.

F-1 VISA

The F-1 visa is available to persons who seek to enter the United States for the purpose of engaging in a full time academic program. The visa extends to persons enrolled at the elementary school level through the postgraduate and doctoral level of university education. In theory, the requirements for obtaining a visa are simple and straightforward. However, it is often difficult for persons from certain countries where there is a high incidence of visa fraud to obtain this visa.

Duration of stay. The F visa is granted for a period of stay known as "duration of status" ("DS"). That is, the visa is valid for the entire period of the proposed academic program. If an individual enrolls in a four-year college program leading to an engineering degree, the visa will be valid for the entire four-year university program, so long as the individual otherwise maintains an educational status and does not violate the terms of the visa. Upon the completion of the academic program—the basis for the visa—the foreign students must then apply for an extension of that visa if they decide to pursue an additional course of study. If a student changes institutions before the completion of the academic program, an extension application is not required even though the Immigration and Naturalization Service must be notified of the change.

Conditions of eligibility. The foreign student must be coming to the United States to engage in a full-time course of study, all of which is defined by regulations. Generally, full time status requires a minimum of twelve semester hours (or credit hours) on the university level or an equivalent—assuming that the university considers this to be a full-time course of study and charges a full time tuition rate. For secondary or elementary grade school programs, the student must be enrolled in a course of study that the institution normally considers as minimum in order to obtain the diploma. Enrollment in associate degree institutions is also acceptable to support an F visa as long as the student is involved in a full-time course of study; usually, requiring a minimum of twelve hours.

Since the institution will be certifying on a Form 1-20A that the student is in fact enrolled in a full-time course of study, that institutional certification is almost always accepted by the Department of State as proof that the full-time course of study requirement will be met.

Visa processing. In order to obtain the F visa, the student must apply for and receive admission to an approved educational institution in the United States. In addition to any other required documentation, the student will also receive a completed Form I-20A-B which will be filled out by the school and will require little information from the student other than a signature in two places. Most of the information that is on the Form I-20A-B is provided by the school so the student should review the form to make sure that it is accurate. The existing Form I-20A-B is an eight-page document which is submitted to the Visa Office at the time the student applies for his visa. In addition, the student will prepare and execute a Form OF-156, which is a general non-immigrant visa application form. It is important that all questions are properly answered. In particular, those questions from pages 19 through 30 should accurately reflect the student's temporary intention.

There is an exception to the above procedure. Occasionally prospective students will not yet have chosen a particular institution at which they will study and may enter the United States on a B-2 visa and then make a change of non-immigrant visa when they have made their selection. In this case, students will appear before the visa officer and prove their student intention and financial ability and may then receive a B-2 visa which will be stamped "prospective student/school not chosen." This will be very helpful when the students later make an application to change their status after they have chosen their school. This notation is very important because without it, students may find it very difficult to change their status to that of an F visa from a tourist visa. That is because the Immigration and Naturalization Service very often considers these change requests as evidence that the prospective student entered the United States on a fraudulent basis (preconceived intent), bypassing the normal F visa application process. A notation will thus avoid that problem since it will establish that there has been no fraudulent intent.

Persons seeking to enter the United States under F visa status must present a valid passport with the F visa stamped therein, together with the Form I-20A-B. Students will then be examined at the border with respect to the school that they will be attending and the duration of the program. If the immigration officer is satisfied that the person is entitled to the F visa, then the student will be given the I-94 arrival/departure record with the notation "DS" stamped therein, (which means Duration of Status), as well as a portion of the I-20 form (i.d. copy): the alien must keep both documents. Certain types of on-campus employment are permissible if it is the type of employment that is normally done by students and does not displace U.S. labor. Thus, the position of library or laboratory assistant employment is permissible. A sample Form I-20A-B is included in appendix D and Form OF-156 is in appendix F.

Eligible institutions. In order to qualify for the F visa, the student must be enrolled in an institution which has been approved for that purpose by the attorney general. All public elementary, secondary, and post-secondary institutions are approved by the attorney general and most private institutions with established reputations and recognizable names are also approved. When applying for enrollment in an educational institution, unless it is public, the alien should inquire that the private institution is in fact approved by the attorney general. The student must be enrolled in an educational program that provides academic training as opposed to purely vocational-type training. A vocational or business school whose curriculum is basically non-academic would not support an F visa.

Financial requirements of the student. Prospective students must prove to the U.S. Consul abroad that they have sufficient funds to pay for the educational training as well as their maintenance for the duration of the program. This requirement very often causes great difficulty to applicants for this visa. The funds must be currently available and not be based upon some speculation of funding by the student. In this regard, the Department of State (the Visa Office) will want proof that the student—himself, herself or through family—has sufficient funds to pay for the expenses. Where a student has family or close friends that agree to provide room and board, an affidavit to this effect and supported by proof of their financial stability would be very helpful.

The law has created a pilot (temporary) program which permits prospective students to engage in part time employment during their course of study in positions which do not displace U.S. labor. This is an exception to the general rule which prohibits F-2 students from gainful employment. In general, the foreign student cannot project anticipated earnings from part-time or full-time employment as a means of support during the educational program. If the prospective student is married, the spouse can accompany the F-1 visa holder but is not permitted to work. The only exception to this rule occurs if the financial circumstances that were reasonably relied upon by the alien change unexpectedly. In this case the student would have to make an application in the United States for permission to work.

English language proficiency. The student must be proficient in the English language or must be enrolled in a course of study that will enable proficiency in English. These matters are all covered in Form I-20A-B which is filled out by the educational institution and serves as a prerequisite for the issuance of the visa.

"I SEE YOU'RE APPLYING FOR A STUDENT VISA!"

Proof of temporary intent. Perhaps the largest stumbling block for persons applying for the F visa is the requirement that the persons have a purely temporary intent, and that they have a domicile to which they shall return at the completion of the educational program. This require-ment can cause great difficulty for those persons who are of modest financial means, young, and are traveling to the United States alone or at least without immediate family. Under these circumstances the Department of State is concerned that the individuals may be entering the United States only for the purpose of employment and will disap-pear into the U.S. economy as soon as they leave the airport. It is highly recommended that when a student is interviewed by the visa officer of the U.S. consulate, in addition to the required documents, such as the Form I-20A-B and the other non-immigrant visa petition documents, the student also bring proof of ties to a home country to document this temporary intent. In this regard, family photographs and/or information as to membership in various civic and social organizations would be important. Perhaps proof that the student will be returning to a job at the completion of schooling or any other evidence of ties to the home country would be very helpful.

Practical training. A student may also apply for a period of practical training which cannot exceed a total of twelve months, including time spent in such practical training during the normal course of the stu-dent's academic training: summer vacations, mid-semester breaks, etc. The requirements are essentially that the practical training is related to the course of study of the alien's educational training in the United States and that the student be unable to receive his practical training in his home country. In both instances, this is a matter of documentary proof and the Immigration and Naturalization Service will have to rule on the application. In general, the fact that a school official will certify that the practical training sought by the student will benefit academic training is normally sufficient. In this regard, a Form I-538 is filled out, together with documentary information as to the unavailability of that type of training in the student's home country.

J-1 VISA   The J-1 visa assumes that the foreign employee will be actively engaged in on-the-job training under employment circumstances equivalent to that of a U.S. employee in the same position. In other words, it is expected that the employer will be gaining some productive benefits from the foreign employee's activities even though the main purpose of the employee's presence in the United States is to gain on-the-job, practical training.

Duration of stay. The duration of stay under the J-1 visa is limited to the time required to complete the particular program for which the foreign person was admitted.

Eligibility. Again, most of the eligibility requirements focus on the U.S. employer determining whether or not the sponsor has been designated by the United States Information Agency as an exchange-visitor program sponsor. Thus, a company having its own established program may seek to bring foreign employees to the United States in accordance with its already-approved program. In the event it does not have such a program, it may seek to bring the foreign employee under one of various umbrella programs which have already been designated by the United States government. These umbrella programs are sponsored by other organizations who, at the request of the U.S. employer, will place a foreign exchange visitor with the sponsor in a United States company. Under some circumstances, the United States company may decide to establish their own exchange-visitor program by filing an application directly with the United States Information Agency. Obviously, this is a time-consuming and expensive step and it would only be feasible under the rarest of circumstances. A small to medium-sized company which did not have experience with foreign exchange visitors in the past might find it difficult to obtain such approval from the United States Information Agency.

This visa is very often used for the purposes of bringing "au pairs" to the United States.

This visa is useful for advanced courses of training such as for medical school graduates who must have at least passed Parts I and II of the National Board of Medical Examiners Examination or the Foreign Medical Graduate Examination in Medical Sciences (FMGEMS).

The visa is obtained at the U.S. Consulate abroad. The alien must obtain and complete a Form IAP-66, a Form OF 156, Application for Nonimmigrant Visa, must show evidence of means of support while in the United States, proof of an intention to depart the United States upon completion of the program and provide the appropriate fee. The alien must also prove proficiency in the English language.

The J visa holder's dependent family members will also receive J-2 visas which will enable them to accompany the J-1 visa holder to the U.S. There is no prohibition against the J-2 visa holder engaging in employment so long as the employment is not for the purpose of providing financial support for the J-1 visa holder.

Requirements. The foreign business trainee must be employed on a full work week basis and must receive compensation equal to at least the prevailing minimum wage and under the prevailing working conditions for the particular industry involved. The purpose of the training must be to improve the visitor's skills for use in the visitor's home country. Consequently, the alien must maintain a foreign residence which he or she has no intention of abandoning. Any indication by foreign exchange visitors that they may be harboring an intention to remain in the United States on a permanent basis may cause the visa to be denied to them.

Two-year foreign residency period. One of the most unusual characteristics of this visa category is that the foreign exchange visitor will be barred from filing a permanent visa petition or for applying for a change of status to a foreign H or L visa for a period of two calendar years from the date of U.S. training completion. This rule is applicable to those exchange visitors whose programs have been financed in whole or in part by: the United States government; their own governments, or by persons who are nationals of countries that the United States Information Agency has determined require the skills and services of people with the alien's special training.

Since the nature and purpose of the J visa is to encourage sponsorship entry of third world persons to the United States, neither the United

States nor the home country would want the foreign exchange visitor to remain in the United States at the completion of the training program. This would be self-defeating with respect to the program and probably makes poor politics between the United States and the alien's home country. Nonetheless, there are procedures to waive the two-year foreign residency requirement but they are not liberally granted.

While the nature of the waiver application process is beyond the scope of this book, it is possible to highlight the general four conditions which provide for the waiver. They are as follows:

☞ A waiver may be requested by a United States governmental agency on behalf of the exchange alien. This is usually couched in terms of being beneficial to the United States security interest or to that of the public good. Obviously, these situations are somewhat rare.

☞ A waiver may be obtained when the foreign residence requirement would result in exceptional hardship to the U.S. citizen or permanent resident spouse or child. What constitutes "exceptional hardship" is very often difficult to establish in advance, and generally requires intervention of legal counsel. Thus, when a United States citizen marries a foreign exchange visitor while that person is in the United States, it would be very difficult to justify extreme hardship since the U.S. citizen voluntarily embraced the situation. In any event, legal assistance is generally required to properly present an extreme hardship.

☞ Another ground for obtaining a waiver of the two-year foreign residency requirement is on the basis of a "no-objection" letter issued by the alien's government to the United States Information Agency stating that the foreign government has "no objection" to the alien remaining in the United States. The United States government is not bound by this no-objection letter and if the United States government will be paying all or a substantial portion of the foreign exchange visitor's costs, then such a letter would have little influence. In any event, these no-objection letters are unavailable to foreign medical graduates.

☞ If the alien can prove that he or she would be subject to persecution in the home country on the basis of race, religion, political opinion, nationality or membership in a particular social group, then the two-year waiting period may be waived. Proof as to the exception should be conducted along the same line as a request for political asylum.

The application process. The most practical method of bringing an exchange alien into the United States is under an established umbrella program. The sponsoring agency who has already been designated by the United States Information Agency will issue a certificate of eligibility for the exchange visitor status (Form IAP-66) directly to the foreign national and will help arrange the transfer of the alien to the United States for practical training. The J visa holder must present a passport with a valid J visa stamped in it together with a Form IAP-66 upon arrival at the border.

Q VISA   The Q visa is a new visa category that permits entry of a person into the United States for purposes of participating in a program designed to provide practical training or employment and the sharing of the history, culture and traditions of the alien's home country. This exchange program will be administered by the Immigration and Naturalization Service instead of the United States Information Agency. The visa is valid for a period of fifteen months and may be applied for either at the U.S. Consulate in the alien's home country or in the United States by way of an application for a Change of Status. Final administrative regulations will establish the detailed requirements for the petition.

K VISA   This visa is issued by the U.S. Consulate abroad to the fiancé of a United States citizen. It is a temporary visa that requires that the foreign person contract marriage within ninety days of entry into the United States. The visa presumes that upon the celebration of the marriage, the foreign person will then apply for a permanent visa to the United States and will adjust his/her status in the United States.

The essential requirements are that the parties must establish that they have physically met within the last two years and are intent on getting married. In the case of those persons whose religious principals prohibit their meeting before the wedding, the Department of State has relaxed the requirement of a physical meeting but requires proof of the parties' membership in the religion which in fact prohibits the physical meeting prior to the marriage. The proofs required in order to substantiate the physical meeting have no limitation and in cases that I have handled, I have offered photographs taken of the parties together in myriads of circumstances including: birthday celebrations, other weddings involving other parties and even a ribald photograph or two taken while the parties were celebrating in a nightclub. The United States Consular officers are not squeamish in this regard and will accept documentation which establishes the statutory and regulatory requirements. Remember, a picture is worth a thousand words.

The United States citizen is the petitioner and must establish that he or she is a United States citizen. Both parties must establish that they are otherwise free to contract marriage. Thus, if he or she has been married before, proof of the termination of the previous marriage must be submitted.

If the foreign person marries a person other than the original Petitioner, he or she will be precluded from adjusting status to permanent residency in the United States. Rather, upon approval of a Form I-130 from the United States citizen or permanent resident spouse, the beneficiary will have to travel abroad to have the visa issued by the United States consulate abroad.

In any event, the beneficiary is still subject to the two-year conditional visa provision as explained in the section concerning permanent residency based upon marriage to a United States citizen (Spouse of a U.S. citizen) on page 67 of this book.

**"ER -- EXCUSE ME, BUT I HAVE JUST A FEW MORE QUESTIONS
ON YOUR 'K' VISA FORM..."**

R VISA   This non-immigrant visa category closely follows the immigrant visa category for special immigrant religious workers. The immigrant religious worker category expires on October 1, 2000 but the R visa category will continue to apply indefinitely.

The principal difference between the immigrant religious worker visa and the R non-immigrant visa is that the R visa category has a five-year limitation.

The State Department has recently issued a cable to all diplomatic and consular posts which establish the guidelines for adjudication of this visa. The cable itself was reproduced in 69 Interpreter Releases 412 (April 6, 1992 edition) and the relevant section is as follows:

> ...There is no requirement in the INA that applicants for R status establish that they have a residence in a foreign country which they have no intention of abandoning. The (IMMACT90) limits R non-immigrants to a total period of stay not to exceed five years. The alien's stated intention to depart the United States when his or her status ends is normally sufficient to satisfy (IMMACT90),

absent specific indications or evidence that the alien's intent is to the contrary.

Consular officer is responsible for adjudicating R non-immigrant visas. By not mandating a preliminary petition process for R non-immigrants, Congress placed responsibility and authority with consular officers to determine whether the requirements of (IMMACT90) are met for aliens seeking that classification and requiring visas. Consular officers shall process R visa applications in light of these regulations and notes, requesting advisory opinions from the department when deemed necessary or required per (this cable).

The criteria for classification of an R religious worker are:

- ☛ The alien is a member of a religious denomination having a bona fide nonprofit, religious organization in the United States.

- ☛ The religious denomination and its affiliate, if applicable, are exempt from taxation, or the religious denomination qualifies for tax-exempt status.

- ☛ The alien has been a member of the organization for two years immediately preceding admission.

- ☛ The alien is entering the United States solely to carry on the vocation of a minister of that denomination, or

- ☛ At the request of the organization, the alien is entering the United States to work in a religious vocation or occupation for that denomination or for an organization affiliated with the denomination, whether in a professional capacity or not, or

- ☛ The alien is the spouse or child of an R-1 non-immigrant who is accompanying or following to join him or her, and

- ☛ The alien has resided and been physically present outside the United States for the immediate prior year, except for brief visits for business or pleasure, if he or she has previously spent five years in this classification.

Characteristics of a religious denomination. A religious denomination will generally have the following elements or comparable indications of its bona fides:

- ☞ some form of ecclesiastical government.

- ☞ a recognized creed and form of worship.

- ☞ a formal code of doctrine and discipline.

- ☞ religious services and ceremonies.

- ☞ established places of religious worship.

- ☞ religious congregations.

Requirements for a nonprofit organization. A bona fide nonprofit organization, as described in the Internal Revenue Code of 1986, must meet the following criteria:

- ☞ No part of the net earnings of the organization may benefit any private shareholder or individual;

- ☞ No substantial part of the organization's activities may involve propagandizing or otherwise attempting to influence legislation.

- ☞ The organization may not participate or intervene in any political campaign, including publishing or distributing statements on behalf of (or in opposition to) any candidate for public office.

Membership. Aliens must establish that they have been a member of the qualifying organization for at least two years immediately preceding application for a visa or for admission. Unlike an applicant for a special immigrant visa as a religious worker, an applicant for R non-immigrant classification needs only to have been a member of the organization for the required two-year period and needs not to have been engaging in qualifying ministerial, vocational, or occupational activities in addition to membership.

Ministers of religion. Only individuals authorized by a recognized religious denomination to conduct religious worship and to perform other duties usually performed by authorized members of the clergy of that religion may be classified as ministers of religion. The term does not include lay preachers or other persons not authorized to perform such duties. In all cases, there must be reasonable connection between the activities performed and the religious calling of a minister. Evidence that a person qualifies as a minister of religion is normally available in the form of official ecclesiastical recognition such as certificates or ordination, licenses, formal letters of conferral, etc.

Ordination of ministers. Ordination of ministers chiefly involves the investment of the individual with ministerial or sacerdotal functions, or the conferral of holy orders upon the individual. If the religious denomination does not have formal ordination procedures, other evidence must be presented to show that the individual has authorization to conduct religious worship and perform other services usually performed by members of the clergy.

A deacon of any recognized religious denomination may be considered to be a minister of religion. Practitioners and nurses of the Christian Science Church and commissioned officers of the Salvation Army are considered to be ministers of religion.

Buddhist monks. The ceremony conferring monkhood status in the Buddhist religion is generally recognized as the equivalent of ordination. Whether or not a Buddhist monk qualifies as a minister of religion depends upon the activities he is seeking to pursue in the United States. However, in order to qualify for R status, a Buddhist monk must both establish his own qualifications as a minister of religion, and must demonstrate that he is seeking to enter the United States for the sole purpose of conducting religious worship and providing other traditional religious services.

Evidence forming the basis for R classification. An alien seeking classification as a religious worker makes application directly to a consular officer, or if visa exempt, to an immigration officer at a U.S. port of entry. No petition, labor certification or prior approval is required. The alien shall present evidence which establishes to the satisfaction of the consular or immigration officer that he or she will be providing services to a bona fide nonprofit, religious organization or its affiliate, and that he or she meets the criteria to perform such services. The alien shall present evidence that the religious denomination, or its affiliate, qualifies as a nonprofit religious organization in the form of:

1. A certificate of tax-exempt status issued by the Internal Revenue Service.

2. In the case of a religious denomination which has never sought tax-exempt status, documentation demonstrating that the organization would qualify for tax exemption, if such status were sought. In all cases involving claimed eligibility for tax exemption, the consular officer must forward all pertinent documentation along with an evaluation of the evidence presented to the Department for an advisory opinion.

Certification from employing religious organization. An authorized official of the specific organizational unit of the religious denomination or affiliate which will be employing or engaging the alien in the United States must prepare a letter certifying the following:

☛ if the alien's religious membership was maintained (in whole or in part) outside the United States, the foreign and United States religious organizations belong to the same religious denomination.

☛ immediately prior to the application for the non-immigrant visa or application for admission to the United States, the alien has been a member of the religious organization for the required two-year period.

☛ that (as appropriate):

• if the alien is a minister, he or she is authorized to conduct religious worship for that denomination and to perform other duties usually performed by authorized members of the clergy of that denomination. The duties to be performed should be described in detail.

- if the alien is a religious professional, he or she has at least a United States baccalaureate degree or its foreign equivalent; such a degree is required for entry into the religious profession.

- if the alien is to work in a nonprofessional religious vocation or occupation, he or she is qualified in that vocation or occupation. Evidence of such qualifications may include, but need not be limited to, evidence establishing that the alien is a monk, nun, or religious brother or sister, or that the type of work to be done relates to a traditional religious function.

☛ the arrangements made for payment for services to be rendered by the alien, if any, including the amount and source of any salary, a description of any other types of compensation to be received (including housing, food, clothing, and any other benefits to which a monetary value may be affixed) and a statement whether such payment shall be in exchange for services rendered.

☛ the name and location of the specific organizational unit of the religious denomination or affiliate for which the alien will be providing services within the United States.

☛ if the alien is to work for a bona fide organization that is affiliated with a religious denomination, a description of the nature of the relationship between the affiliate and the religious denomination.

A consular officer may request any appropriate additional evidence which is necessary to verify the qualifications of the religious denomination, the alien, or the affiliated organization.

Aliens in R-2 status (spouses and dependents of the R alien) are not authorized to accept employment. The consular officer shall take this into account in evaluating whether family members have furnished adequate evidence of their self-support while in the United States. R-2 non-immigrants are permitted to study during their stay in the United States.

R visa recipients should have all qualifying documentation available when applying for admission in the event that it is requested by an INS officer at the port of entry.

Length of stay. The initial period of admission for an R non-immigrant may not exceed three years. To extend a religious worker's stay, the organizational unit of the religious denomination or affiliate must file Form I-129, petition for the non-immigrant worker at the INS Service Center having jurisdiction over the place of employment, and provide a letter from an authorized official of the organizational unit confirming the worker's continuing eligibility for R classification. An extension may be authorized for a period of up to two years. The religious worker's total period of stay may not exceed five years.

Maintaining Visa Status 5

Now that you have obtained your visa to the United States, at great expense and after much preparation and hard work, it is important that you understand how to maintain your visa so that you do not inadvertently lose it. There are traps for the careless that can jeopardize either a non-immigrant or an immigrant (permanent residency) visa. This chapter will give some examples.

Problems for Non-Immigrants

Overstay of I-94

The first and most important danger in maintaining visa status is for a non-immigrant to inadvertently overstay the duration of stay permitted by the Form I-94. This form on the following page is the small white card which is inserted in the alien's passport upon inspection and admission to the United States by the INS inspecting officer.

Just for a moment let us review the situation. Foreign persons obtain visa status in one of two ways:

☞   by obtaining their visas from a U.S. Consulate abroad, in which case the visa is affixed in their passports; or

☞ by receiving the desired visa status through a Change of Status approved by the Immigration and Naturalization Service while they are already in the United States.

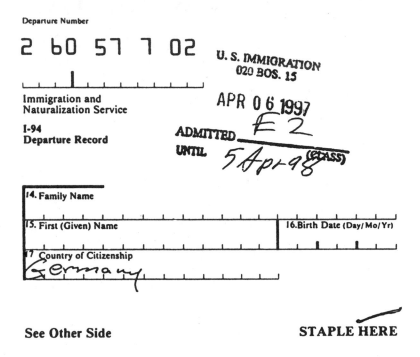

With respect to the visa stamped into the passport, the time period of visa validity measures the time within which an alien may seek to enter the United States in that particular visa category. In other words, the visa in the passport establishes the time period in which a person may seek to cross the border into the United States. The duration of time the foreign person is allowed to remain in the U.S.A., after entry is not determined by the validity period of the visa. This time period is known as *Duration of Stay* and is determined by the date designated on the Form I-94 (Arrival-Departure Record). For example, when a person enters the U.S. with a B-1/B-2 visa which normally has a duration of ten years, the immigration officer at the border will normally allow the arriving alien to remain in the U.S. for a period of six months. The date of required departure will be designated on the Form I-94. If a person enters with a different type of visa, say an H-1 or an L-1, the lawful period of stay may be one or two years.

If the foreign person remains in the United States beyond the date stated in the Form I-94 by even one day, without first having filed an application for an Extension of Stay, the underlying visa is automatically and immediately terminated—the visa becomes void. This means that if the person attempts to use that visa again to reenter the United States, he or she is subject to (removal) exclusion from the United States on the basis of not holding a valid visa. Understand further that if a person is formally *removed*, that is to say, is turned away at the border, he or she will not be able to reenter the United States for a period of five years. The only exception to this penalty occurs if the immigration inspector allows the foreign person to withdraw his application for entry.

If a foreign person is removed from the United States at the border, the person will need to return to the country of nationality and reapply for another visa as a condition of re-entry. The risk, of course, is that the U.S. Consulate may not issue the visa again if the foreign person has already violated the terms of the original visa. Obviously if the overstay is only for a slight period of time (one or two days) and is only a technicality, there is a better chance that the U.S. Consulate will reissue the visa. However, if there has been a substantial overstay, then there is a good chance that the U.S. Consulate will not reissue the visa. There is no appeal from a denial by the U.S. Consulate.

DEPENDENTS   All of the above applies to the principal visa holder's dependents as well. Let us create a hypothetical case as an example of a problem that often occurs with dependents and visa maintenance. Assume that a foreign person, Mr. Schiller, holds an L-1A visa as the executive of a large subsidiary of a foreign owned company. He is married to Olga and has two children, ages eight and eleven. Olga does not work outside the home and takes care of all household duties and especially the education and upbringing of the children. The Schillers are a typical busy young family and Olga is very active in the school parents/teachers association and also directs the children's various outside activities. This includes driving both children around to soccer and hockey practice and games as well as gymnastics and music education.

In the jargon of visa law, Mr. Schiller is known as the *principal* visa holder, while Olga and the children are known as *derivative* visa holders. Mr. Schiller is required by the conditions of his job to travel often in and out of the United States. Olga and the children do not accompany Mr. Schiller on any of these trips. Inadvertently, the duration of stay as noted on the Form I-94 expires as to Olga and the children and they remain beyond the period of authorized stay for seven and a half months. This is only discovered at a holiday party when one of Olga's friends casually remarks to her that she has heard that the wife and children of executives must also file for an Extension of Stay. This family now faces a life changing crisis that cannot be easily remedied. This is because Olga cannot now "extend her stay" of visa status and must return to her country of origin in order to reapply for a visa. More important, she is subject to the three-year bar against reentry. How did this happen?

Upon entry to the United States the principal visa holder, as well as the derivative visa holders, received Forms I-94 which allowed each of them to remain in the U.S. for an entire year. Every time a visa holder departs and then re-enters the United States, he or she will receive permission to remain in the U.S. for another year or perhaps two years and this will be noted on a new Form I-94. This is how Mr. Schiller continued to receive new Forms I-94 each of which extended his duration of stay for a period of one year from entry. He has always remained in status. However, if the derivative visa holders have not departed and reentered the United States, they will need to file a form known as an Application to Extend/Change Non-immigrant Status (Form I-539) in order to remain longer than the year which they originally received. Olga and the children never departed the United States after their initial entry. They never paid attention to their own visa affairs, expecting that if Mr. Schiller were in status so would they be. Neither Mr. Schiller nor his employer considered the duration of status of Olga and the children as separate from Mr. Schiller's status. Since Olga and the children, the derivative visa holders, did not file an application to extend their status (Form I-539) with the INS they overstayed their Duration of Stay and thus their visas became void. What is more important, since Olga overstayed the Form I-94 by 180 days or more, when she travels to her home country to apply for a new visa, she will then automatically trigger the three-year ban to the United States. There are no waivers or exceptions to these bureaucratic consequences. The Schillers must either return to their country of origin in order to remain together as a family unit or Mr. Schiller must remain alone in the United States while Olga lives out her three-year ban from the United States. This is not fiction nor is it farfetched. It is a real problem based upon real events.

THE THREE AND TEN YEAR BARS AGAINST RE-ENTRY

The law now states that if a foreign person is illegally present in the United States for 180 days but less than one year, upon that person's departure from the United States he or she will be prohibited from reentering the U.S. for a period of three years from the date of the departure. *Illegal presence* is a period of time which accrues after the expiration of the duration of stay as noted on the Form I-94, or after the government has declared in some formal manner that the foreign person has either violated the terms of the non-immigrant visa or that the person's visa status has been terminated. In our example, these are the consequences to the principal visa holder's wife, who is here with her husband on an L-1 (she has an L-2), who does not extend her I-94 at the expiration of the year and then remains illegally present in the United States for 180 days.

- ☛ Her L-2 visa is void from the day after the expiration of the Form I-94, thus

- ☛ She cannot extend her visa status from within the U.S., thus

- ☛ She will be required to apply for a new L-2 visa in her country of last residence, thus

- ☛ Upon her departure from the United States, she will then be barred from reentering the United States for a period of either three or ten years.

There are no waivers to these consequences available to non-immigrants.

All this even though the wife's overstay was inadvertent and otherwise innocent and absolutely unimportant in any real sense to the INS. The same consequences befall the children who may be over the age of eighteen years. Furthermore, if a person overstays the expiration date noted on Form I-94 by more than one year, he or she is then prohibited from reentering the United States for a period of ten years!

There are some very limited waivers available for persons who can prove that the application of either of these bars to reentry would cause an extreme hardship to a U.S. citizen or permanent resident, spouse, child, or parent. Needless to say even if a foreign person were eligible to apply for these limited waivers, it is very difficult to obtain these waivers, and for non-immigrant persons they are unavailable.

INCONSISTENCY WITH NON-IMMIGRANT VISA STATUS:

A non-immigrant can also lose his or her non-immigrant visa status by engaging in activities which are inconsistent with the visa that the person holds or for causing the INS border inspector to believe that to be the case.

E-2 VISAS

In addition to the requirement of not violating the terms of the duration of stay a treaty investor also has a substantive problem with which to contend for purposes of visa maintenance. Remember that one of the requirements for obtaining an E-2 investor visa is to ensure that the investment is not "marginal." The regulations state in the negative that a marginal enterprise is "…one that does not have the present or future capacity to generate more than a minimal living for the treaty investor and his or her family."

On a positive note the regulations also state as follows:

☛ *Marginal enterprise*. A *marginal enterprise* is an enterprise that does not have the present or future capacity to generate more than enough income to provide a minimal living for the treaty investor and his or her family. An enterprise that does not have the capacity to generate such income, but that has a present or future capacity to make a significant economic contribution, is not a marginal enterprise. The projected future capacity should generally be obtainable within five years from the date the alien commences normal business activity of the enterprise.

Most prudent business persons are advised to reinvest their profits back into their enterprises in order to expand their businesses, capture market share, etc., rather than to borrow expansion capital from outside sources. In addition many foreign business persons and entrepreneurs are not accustomed to borrowing from third party sources when they have the capital at hand. However, in the context of visa law they should seriously consider preserving and showing their enterprise's financial surplus as a net profit, and thus net income, and then expand the enterprise' growth with borrowed funds. The reason for this is the arcane notion of profit and income that the government bureaucracy utilizes in adjudicating reissuance of visas.

If the company has been relatively successful, the investor/owner has a choice as to whether to fund the company's expansion with its own profit or to borrow from an outside source. Most conservative economists would encourage most businesses to fund their own growth and not borrow from outside sources. This, however, is not always a good idea in the E-2 visa context because a government examiner who may know very little about business may deny the reissuance of the visa if the company's financial books do not reflect a net profit. Indeed, in certain hostile Consulates the treaty officers seem to be looking for excuses to deny treaty visas, not withstanding that the investor has in good faith already relocated his person, family, assets and life's energy to the U.S. Thus under most circumstances it would be advisable to borrow from a third party, perhaps using the profit as collateral by the creation of some sort of sinking fund or other special account, to fund the growth and expansion.

A complex financial statement which attempts to demonstrate that the enterprise utilized its financial surplus to fund its acquisition of personnel, equipment, or inventory creates a problem for the investor. Most government examiners are not financial analysts. They are looking for conceptually clear and simple evidentiary guideposts. A financial statement or income tax return that clearly demonstrates a healthy net income is good. A similar report which documents the hiring of many employees is also good.

I recommend that a treaty investor/entrepreneur hire a competent financial professional that can advise him on the best method of demonstrating income and profitability and funding the continuing growth of the business.

Additionally, the comprehensive business plan that served as the basis for original visa issuance should be carefully prepared so that it does not become the basis for the denial of the E-2 visa reissuance. The business plan should be realistic and also express the conditions which support the financial projections. So, if some of these conditions change and the company is not as profitable as anticipated, the investor will at least have a basis for explaining any income differential from the original projections and modifying the business plan accordingly. Indeed, the original comprehensive business plan should be a "living" document and the company's performance should be charted against it throughout the life of the investment.

L-1A VISA

For new companies, the L-1A visa is issued somewhat liberally for the first year. Thereafter in order to extend the term of the L-1A visa as well as the duration of stay beyond the first year, the business must demonstrate that it is making legitimate progress in its development and is engaged in the actual provision of goods and services. Therefore, a new company should commence operations as soon as possible after visa issuance. Additionally the company must demonstrate that its executive or manager is not merely acting in the capacity of the actual provider of the company's service. The government examiner will search for defined levels of employment and function. It thrives on organization and flow charts. It is not a good argument that the young company may be better off with fewer levels of employees and departments.

I recommend that as much as is reasonably possible, new businesses should put into place the most dramatic increases in capital and personnel growth before the end of its first year. I advise that the company concentrates on meeting a three, four, or five year plan rather than try to justify its costs on its single and first year basis and that it organizes itself accordingly. The government examiner who is adjudicating the petition has, in all probability, not had to contend with meeting a payroll or satisfying a contract at all costs and does not sympathize with the plight of the manager who must do anything and everything to get the job done. Also, as with the E-2 visa, the comprehensive business plan should be considered as a living, dynamic document against which the company's performance should be documented.

THE POWER OF EXPEDITED REMOVAL

The law now gives the immigration inspector at the border the power to turn a person away from the United States, without a hearing and without review of any kind, if the inspector determines that the person is either entering the United States with fraudulent documents or entering for a purpose other than that which is authorized by the visa. This power was clearly meant to apply to aliens who attempt to enter the U.S. with no documents or with fraudulent documents. But the law as written also applies to a person who has a valid visa but who is determined by the INS inspecting officer to be entering the U.S. for a purpose other than that permitted under the particular visa.

Thus, a person who is entering the United States with a B-1/B-2 visa may be turned away at the border if the inspector feels that this person is entering the United States in order to reside permanently (perhaps to join with a U.S. citizen or permanent resident of the opposite sex in a long term relationship) or to engage in unauthorized employment. The above activities are inconsistent with that of a B-1 or B-2 visa. So, if an immigration inspection officer makes a determination at the border that the foreign person is not entitled to enter the U.S. on the basis of the visa which the foreign person holds, then the officer has the right and the authority to turn the alien away (*removal*) without offering the opportunity to make a phone call or provide any other evidence to support the foreign person's case. Furthermore, removal by the officer prohibits that person from reentering the United States for a period of five years. There is no appeal to this decision by the inspecting officer. Indeed, there is not even a method under the law for the government itself to undo the action of an inspecting officer that may clearly have been wrong. Obviously this is a very dangerous provision. It poses a special problem for foreign persons who own real estate in the United States, who may have close relatives in the United States, and who may not have a standard type job outside the United States.

Let us create another hypothetical example. Harold Smith is a single, young-looking man in his mid-forties from England who earned a lot of money as a commodities trader. He has always been a freelance or independent consultant to established commodities and stock brokerage houses in Europe. He does not actually maintain an office but is always "on-call" as to his clients. He has purchased an expensive and nice condominium apartment on the beach on the west coast of Florida and uses it at least two times a year. His trips to the United States are usually for periods of one month or so at a time. This year, however, he has already been in the U.S. for a total of three months. He decides to come once again to his U.S. beach apartment to experience and enjoy the traditional Thanksgiving holiday in order to relax a bit and to work on a proposal which he intends to make to a large international commodities brokerage house. He brings all of his research documents with him as well as the telephone numbers of his most important clients so that he can "stay in touch." He receives a bargain price for round trip airfare on an airline which flies through Memphis, Tennessee, a newly developing U.S. international destination.

Upon inspection at the INS immigration counter, the INS inspector questions why this relatively young person is traveling for a third time to the U.S. The inspector also finds out that Harold owns real estate in the U.S. while only renting a flat in his home country. The inspector also finds various documents in Harold's luggage which relate to his work including a list of work items which he must complete in the U.S. These include a number of clients to telephone and some research to be done on the financial status of a U.S. mining company. Harold did not bring any documentation as to the nature of his job, other than that he is an independent consultant. Finally, the INS inspector finds a Florida driver license as well as a Florida issued credit card, all in Harold's name. Harold explains that the driver license is a matter of convenience for writing checks and for otherwise providing personal identification in Florida and the credit card was issued as a courtesy by his Florida bank for starting a checking account. The INS inspector speaks rudely to Harold, addressing him disparagingly by his first name and suggests that Harold is really coming to the U.S. to work illegally. Harold becomes irate and says things to the INS inspector that he later regrets. Harold is placed back on the next airplane and is removed from the U.S. He cannot come back for at least five years, not even to arrange the sale of his apartment and its contents.

How could Harold have avoided his disastrous encounter with the INS border inspector? What might anyone who is similarly situated do or not do in order to avoid bureaucratic difficulties at the border? The following is a list of suggestions and recommendations applicable to most non-immigrants though it is clearly not complete and may not be applicable to all persons in all circumstances:

First, do not travel to the U.S. with a U.S. state issued driver license or U.S. issued credit cards or bank check books. Leave these here in the U.S. Their presence on your person will only cause questions and suspicions. Also, the law of the state of your final destination may be different from the law of the state in which you are attempting to clear U.S. immigration and the INS examiner may be unfamiliar with the law of any state other than his or her own. It may be difficult, for instance, to convince the inspecting officer that the state of your destination requires all residents who reside therein for sixty consecutive days to obtain a state issued driver license. The same advice applies to U.S. issued credit cards and check books.

Do carry travelers' checks as well as travel and resort brochures. In the case of business travelers who hold employment authorized visas, do carry documents which identify your employment in the United States.

Second, foreign persons should purchase a round trip ticket from a point outside the United States. The money saved by buying and using "back to back" round trip airline tickets is not worth the frustration and difficulty at the border with a suspicious INS inspector.

Third, if a foreign person owns a U.S. home or apartment, that person should carry in his luggage proof of ownership or lease of a residence outside the U.S. as well as evidence of his/her foreign income or financial means. If one has purchased a holiday home in the U.S., preserve all the marketing materials, brochures, etc., which were used to market the property as these will often confirm that the property is suitable as a holiday home. This is important if a foreign person seeks admission at a port of entry other than the state of final destination. In the example above, the INS inspector will not necessarily know (or care) that the west coast of Florida is a popular destination for Europeans and that there is a large vacation or holiday home industry there.

Fourth, avoid entering the U.S. at new or developing U.S. international destinations. Always try to enter in the state of final destination.

Fifth, foreign persons should not carry work related documents with them upon entry to the U.S. Often these documents create confusion and suspicion in the minds of INS inspectors and may require explanations which a foreign person may be unable to make in the limited and intimidating environment of an immigration border inspection. These suggestions also apply to letters from and to persons of the opposite sex with whom a foreign person may be involved, since the INS inspector may determine that the purpose of entry is to reside permanently in the U.S. with the love interest.

Sixth, a foreign person should carefully examine the Form I-94 before leaving the inspection counter to make sure the date of required departure is clear. Also the foreign person should carefully document the date of expiration of the Form I-94 and arrange to either file an extension or depart the U.S. on a timely basis.

Seventh, during the inspection interview always be honest and forthright and remain courteous and respectful of the INS examiners regardless of their attitude or demeanor. Most INS inspectors are courteous persons who are merely enforcing the law and regulations which others in the government have enacted. Outbursts of angry words or return sarcasm directed at the occasionally rude border inspector by a foreign person will not be helpful. The immigration inspector has tremendous authority and will probably not be in a mood to be counseled as to good manners by a foreign person. When patience is about to fail, the foreign person should retain the attitude that he or she is dealing with a ruthless and strong bully who is guarding the entrance to a place which the foreign person wishes to visit.

Of course, the foreign person should not engage in gainful employment or in any business activity which is unauthorized by the visa in the passport.

Finally, illegal conduct that results in a conviction in a U.S. court can be a permanent bar from entering the United States. Do not believe what is depicted in the movies or is otherwise bandied about in pubs and train stations. The United States' immigration laws *are* enforced.

It is important to understand the difference in cultures between the bureaucracy which is administering these visa regulations and that of a typical foreign person entering the United States. A non-immigrant visa for a person entering the United States on a temporary basis is usually not an end in itself. Rather, it is a means to an end. A person is either coming to be a student, to run a business, to get married, or any number of things, and the visa is the way to accomplish them. Normally after a person has entered the United States, the visa status is relegated to a secondary importance. However, for the U.S. visa immigration authorities, the visa is of the utmost importance—it is their life. Consequently, what may be an inadvertent oversight to a foreign person, is a grievous violation to the bureaucrat, who is charged with the responsibility of administering the laws.

Understand also that the United States legal regimen charges a person with the knowledge of the law, no matter how complex. Thus, even if a person seeks in good faith to extend his or her visa and then inadvertently mails it to the wrong immigration office he may lose his visa. This is because by the time the application is filed at the correct office the original authorized time period may have expired and the foreign person may be out of status. It is ineffective to claim that the late filing was caused by an honest mistake by the alien or that the application had been mistakenly sent to a wrong INS office, even by the mistake of an INS employee. This author has seen letters from the Immigration Service rejecting requests to extend visa status when a foreign person inadvertently mailed the extension request on a timely basis but to the wrong immigration office and by the time the application was filed at the correct INS office the filing was late.

PROBLEMS FOR IMMIGRANTS

When a foreign person who is already a permanent resident remains outside of the United States for more than six months but less than one year, upon reentry that person is subject to the same type of inspection as would be given to any other foreign person. The fact that he or she has a permanent residency visa does not avoid the necessity of having to prove all over again to the satisfaction of the INS inspector at the border that he or she is entitled to reenter as a permanent resident. The burden of proof is on the foreign person to prove that he or she is still a permanent resident and not on the INS to prove that the person has abandoned the permanent residence. The foreign person must prove that he or she has not abandoned by intention or action his or her permanent residence. Only in visadom is it standard to require a person to prove a negative.

One of the easiest ways of abandoning permanent residence of the United States, other than by remaining outside of the U.S. for at least one year without first having obtained a Re-entry Permit, is by failing to pay taxes within the United States or by failing to maintain a United States domicile.

If the permanent resident remains outside the United States for a period of one year without having first received or obtained a reentry permit, the government will assume that person has abandoned residency unless the person can prove by documents and otherwise that he or she has not abandoned residency.

One can also lose his permanent residence by a series of actions which when taken in their totality, indicate to the government an abandonment of permanent residency. A person who maintains a residence as well as a job outside the United States and only lives a short period of time each year in the United States, say two months, can be considered to have abandoned his residency, this is because the inspector believes that the foreign person is domiciled outside the United States and is just visiting the United States for the purpose of maintaining the visa. In these cases if the person must travel abroad, then I strongly recommend that if he is going to be outside the United States for a period of six months or more, that he obtain in advance of his departure, a document called a *Reentry Permit*. This document is valid for a period of two years and will allow a person to reenter with much less stress. Here are some suggestions:

First, if the trip outside the U.S. is for longer than six months, apply for a reentry permit before departing the United States.

Second, if business or personal commitments require extensive time and travel outside the United States always arrange to file a U.S. federal income tax return and carry it with you upon reentry. Always try to return the United States within six months of departure. Try to maintain a U.S. home or residence and carry the documentation on your person upon your return to the United States

The above examples have been prepared from actual situations with the hope of causing the foreign person to be scrupulous in understanding the requirements of the visa law even after entry to the U.S.

TAXES, PROFESSIONAL SERVICES, AND PRE-ENTRY PLANNING

6

It is important that an investor or other business visitor to the United States (for brevity, we will designate all such persons "investors" in this chapter) understand some pertinent business customs and practices in the United States. This section will provide some ideas and examples which may be helpful to a business person who is contemplating an initial business visit to the United States for the purpose of completing a transaction that will have certain visa consequences.

If I had to characterize a society with a single concept, I would characterize the United States as the information society. We are a nation driven by the need to record statistics and data on almost any notable economic activity. While it is sometimes difficult for the lay person to discover needed information, it is almost always possible to find someone who can provide a service for the discovery, compilation, and analysis of that information. This wealth of access to information is one of the primary advantages of investing in the United States. Information is almost always available to analyze, and investments or transactions can be accomplished in a proper and professional manner. Nonetheless, many foreign persons in the United States do not take advantage of these facilities and very often encounter unnecessary problems in the development and execution of their plans.

If a person wishes to develop an enterprise or a business in a particular location in the United States, one merely has to ask for the critical information and it is usually obtainable. If it is not obtainable, then that in and of itself is a relevant finding. Here are some examples:

In the United States almost every state has an economic development agency or industrial promotion board or some other similar bureaucracy whose function it is to stimulate investment and economic growth in that state. These agencies will gladly provide a wealth of information and statistics, free of charge. It is wise to spend some time corresponding and obtaining information from these sources about the demographic and economic trends within the state, the state's employment policies and existing labor market. These agencies may also provide information about the individuals and professionals who may be of assistance in a particular field of endeavor.

In addition to state governmental programs, there are also local and regional chambers of commerce and related organizations, all of whom may be very helpful to a prospective entrepreneur. The best way to approach the chambers of commerce is to already have a particular plan or scheme in mind and then discuss this with the key person of that body. The local chamber of commerce can be very helpful in pointing out local trends and in making recommendations as to banks and other professional services and providers who can be of assistance. The local chamber of commerce also will have much statistical and economic data which can be helpful in further analyzing one's plans. It is often good to compare any data or other demographic information obtained from the state with the local chamber of commerce and to explore any discrepancies between the two of them.

One should also not overlook other sources of information which may be obtained from local or regional trade or industrial associations which are easily identifiable through industrial and/or trade journals. These organizations will also have statistical and economic data which will be much more specific to an industry and which will enable one to do a comparison between conditions as portrayed on a general basis by the local chambers of commerce and the information otherwise obtained from the trade or industrial association.

THE LEGAL SYSTEM

The system of law in the United States is probably very different from legal systems with which most foreign persons are familiar. Our system of law evolved from the Common Law of England with its emphasis on the rule of precedent and the lack of a rigid (and predictable) code of law. Parties in a business environment are basically free to establish for themselves the benefits and responsibilities of their transaction or their business relationship. Subsequently, the law as it applies to any specific situation may be difficult to discover; thus, the proliferation of lawyers, both general practitioners and specialists. While it is clearly beyond the scope of this book to engage in a general discussion of all the attributes of the legal system as they would affect the affairs of a foreign person, one point needs to be made very clearly: Most states in the United States have laws, judicial precedents, and customs that give preference to the words of a contract as opposed to the oral understanding of the parties. This is especially true with respect to the acquisition of real estate, business ventures, and other types of commercial investments. Thus, the written instrument is given considerable weight in any dispute by two legally capable parties. Foreign persons must be careful that they clearly know and understand the consequences of any documents that they sign because they will be bound to that document.

LAWYERS

Much has been written and discussed about the proliferation of lawyers in the United States. While it is true that the United States does have a larger number of attorneys than other countries, it is important to remember that the attorney handles many of the functions which, in other countries, are dealt with by notaries and other judicial and quasi-judicial officers. In addition, U.S. law is based on the Common Law of England which is a jurisprudence molded by judicial precedent rather than by a detailed code. Additionally, one should bear in mind that the United States, whether as a result or a cause of the preceding, is a very complex society and has a profusion of business and legal rules which cannot be mastered by a single individual. It must also be remembered that the laws of each state may vary and may also differ from the laws of the federal government: it is also possible that both federal and state laws may deal with the same subject matter.

It is money well spent to consult with any competent attorney who is experienced or sensitive in dealing with foreign buyers before any purchase transaction is consummated. Such consultation can be very illuminating and can ensure that the transaction is structured in the most favorable terms for the foreign person. The American Immigration Lawyers Association (AILA) is an organization of lawyers who strive to achieve some degree of expertise in the field of U.S. immigration law. A foreign person who is interested in obtaining a visa to the United States should consider utilizing the services of a member of this organization. There are members of this organization in many foreign countries. Also, each state has a bar association which can identify lawyers who hold themselves out as experts in a particular field, including immigration law. Referral advice can also be obtained from other professional associations, such as accountants and other types of business and professional consultants.

The foreign investor should, at some point in negotiations, and certainly before any documents are signed, seek professional assistance. The list of possible consultants includes qualified accountants and an expert who is knowledgeable in the particular field or business of interest to the investor.

One of the most helpful benefits gained by this practice is learning the terms applicable to that particular business. There are many business and legal terms that are in use in various jurisdictions of the United

States which have no counterpart in a foreign culture. Many terms and customs vary from state to state or town to town in the United States. In the real estate field, for example, the use of the terms "escrow agent," "title insurance," and "trustee," are all terms that must be clearly understood by a prospective investor or entrepreneur.

In the United States, the parties are presumed to have read and understood a document that bears their signatures. It is too late after a signature has been applied to a document to state that one had a misconception as to what the document meant or what the meaning was of a particular paragraph. The United States is not a multi-lingual society and very little sympathy is extended for those who cannot understand the language.

REAL ESTATE BROKERS, BUSINESS BROKERS, AGENTS IN GENERAL

One of the benefits of seeking to invest in the United States is that there is virtually no field or endeavor for which one cannot find a person or entity willing to provide a consulting service. This is the case with respect to the acquisition of land, buildings, shopping centers, and business opportunities. Real estate brokers are trained and licensed in each state, and are presumably expert in the selling and purchasing of real estate of all types. This includes residential and commercial properties ranging anywhere from the most humble of acquisitions to major urban income-producing properties costing hundreds of millions of dollars. The same can also be said with respect to acquisition of a United States business enterprise. Real estate brokers can render valuable services in that they can identify suitable acquisitions within the structural and financial parameters that the foreign investor establishes.

While it is advisable to use the services of a real estate professional, it is important to understand that in many states a real estate broker, unless special arrangements are made at the beginning of the transaction, represents and works for the seller of property. This is the case even though the real estate broker may never have met the owner of the property that is being sold. In the United States, property listing services are often utilized by real estate professionals. In this system a broker who obtains authorization to sell a property (*listing*) for a person will record that property in a central listing index called a multiple listing file or multiple property list file, or some other such designation. This list will then be circulated to other real estate professionals who can read a description of the property being sold together with the price and terms, etc. When these other real estate brokers find a prospective buyer who may be interested in purchasing property with those characteristics, they will present the compatible properties from their multiple listing sources to the prospect.

The industry custom, however, is that the seller will pay a commission to whoever sells this property and the "selling" broker is usually a sub-agent of the "listing" broker. The commission is usually divided by the listing broker, that is the broker who listed the property, and the selling broker, the broker that procures the buyer. Thus, even though the selling broker may have a personal relationship with the buyer, the broker represents the seller, who, as indicated previously, may be a stranger. The broker's legal and ethical duty is to protect the interest of the seller and obtain for that seller the highest price under the most favorable terms possible.

Obviously, this typical system is not the ideal way for the foreign buyer to approach the purchase of a real estate acquisition in the United States. Since foreign persons do not normally understand the dynamics or the customs of the local market they are usually at a great disadvantage compared to local persons and may not be in a position to derive the best bargain possible. For these reasons, it is strongly recommended that a foreign person acquiring real property and/or business enterprises in the United States utilize a real estate agent who is committed to representing the buyer only, i.e., a buyer's broker. In this manner, the foreign buyer will derive the most benefit from the experience and skill of the real estate professional. Normally, the foreign person will agree to pay the buyer's broker an agreed upon fee or commission but this in no way involves a price disadvantage as the broker should be able to reduce the price to the seller by the amount of the commission the buyer is paying. Again, knowing how this system works enables one to gain an advantage.

If real estate brokers state that even though they are being paid by and contracted to the seller, they will protect the interest of the buyer/investor, the buyer should be forewarned of a potential conflict of interest and should proceed with caution. However, if the seller acknowledges and accepts this arrangement, it is usually permissible although not recommended. The laws of most states do not permit a professional to represent both sides of a transaction. This situation is now in a state of change and many states are considering a modification of the customary rules of agency so as to allow a real estate professional to represent both parties to a real estate transaction, or in some cases, to represent neither side to a real estate transaction. This is a matter of local law and custom that must be determined on a state-by-state basis and it is the responsibility of the alien to do so. As stated in the Introduction, the United States is a dynamic society and constantly revises many of its legal norms and customs.

The concept of *real property* includes raw vacant land, apartment buildings, shopping centers, warehouses, and even hotels and motels. Closely related to real estate brokerage (and licensed in the same manner in many states) are business brokers. These are people who specialize in the acquisition and sale of commercial business enterprises which may or may not have any real estate as part of their assets.

Additionally, there is an international association of real estate brokers who specialize in international real estate transactions. This organization is known by its initials, FIABCI, which stands for International Real Estate Federation. The organization is composed of real estate professionals from many countries who specialize in representing foreign purchasers (and sellers) and who are experienced in dealing with the needs of foreign persons. There probably are FIABCI members in your home country who can serve as a good referral source to a local U.S. FIABCI member for the foreign buyer. This organization is headquartered in Paris, France and has members throughout the world.

In the United States there is a national professional real estate association known as the *National Association of Realtors* (*NAR*). This organization has state and local boards throughout the country and has an international sub-group named the *International Section of the NAR*. The members of this section manifest a special interest in the needs and desires of prospective foreign real estate investors.

If you are interested in acquiring or developing a hotel or motel in the United States, you can also contact an organization known as the Hotel and Motel Brokers of America, which is headquartered in Kansas City, Missouri (telephone number 816/891-7070) and whose members are specialists in the acquisition and sale of hotel and motel properties in the United States. The acquisition of a hotel or a large motel, especially one that has other enterprises within it such as a restaurant and/or sports facilities, etc., is generally a good investment for a foreign buyer. This business combines the security of United States real estate with the growth potential of an entrepreneurial enterprise and can qualify an individual to obtain an E visa.

There are many other well qualified real estate professionals in other organizations who may also be of service to a foreign buyer, but it is important to remember the key consideration: to insure that the real estate professional is working as a buyer's agent.

ACQUIRING AND DEVELOPING A U.S. BUSINESS ENTERPRISE

An existing U.S. business enterprise is the best option. I agree with the school of consultants who generally favor the acquisition of an existing U.S. business enterprise, including a franchised business, as a means of establishing the basis of an L, E or H-1B visa. For purposes of this discussion I will refer to all of these as "business visas."

The Small Business Administration publishes statistics on the dynamics of developing business enterprises in the United States. Perhaps in no other country in the world does the entrepreneurial zeal thrive more than in the U.S. Yet, the other side of the fabled stories of successful enterprises which are developed from the bottom up is the reality of the high percentage of business failures—especially among newly formed enterprises. While the statistics may vary slightly, the consensus is that approximately seventy-five percent of all new businesses fail within the first two years.

It is for this reason that it is generally advantageous to purchase an existing U.S. business enterprise—one that has preferably been an existence for at least five years. One of the greatest advantages of this process is that the purchaser buys an existing administrative and marketing apparatus. The existing business has at least survived the critical beginning period and has established the basis for its future growth. This is true even in the case of some troubled businesses. In fact, the troubled business also usually presents the opportunity to identify the source of the business' difficulties. Thus, the new owner can concentrate on correcting the problem areas and avoiding the mistakes of the past.

The foreign purchaser must be aware of a few key points in the business acquisition process:

First, the foreign prospective buyer should do a thorough due diligence analysis. The term, *due diligence* is defined as a critical analysis of the key characteristics of a business that will predict its future success or failure. The due diligence inquiry includes the study of the enterprise's financial books and records, a review of the company's past and present marketing techniques, inspection of the key items of equipment and fixtures and consideration of the competitiveness of the company's product or services.

The prospective foreign buyer should negotiate for a due diligence period of at least twenty-one days as well as for a visa contingency clause. The latter would enable the foreign person to nullify the purchase agreement in the event their visa petition is denied.

Second, the prospective buyer should take advantage of the due diligence period and conduct a thorough analysis of all the key components of the enterprise. Very often, this will involve the hiring of one or more technical or financial experts. I cannot overemphasize the importance of hiring and utilizing the best consultants that can be afforded. Foreign buyers must remember that even though they may be familiar with the nature of the business enterprise they are investigating, they are unfamiliar with the local business, administration, and legal environment of the enterprise. Assume nothing—heed everything.

Third, the prospective buyer should remember that in business dealings in the U.S., personal relationships may be important but the formal written agreement is paramount.

Fourth, during the negotiation period the prospective buyer should remember that even though the status as a foreign purchaser may generate inconvenience to the seller, foreign status also presents an advantage to the seller. The advantage results from the fact that the buyer must invest a greater percentage of capital in the purchase transaction than the typical U.S. buyer. This fact alone should give the prospective buyer a stronger negotiating position.

Fifth, a good business broker can be invaluable in the selection of a business acquisition and in the negotiation process. The business broker (or Merger and Acquisition Specialist) is a person who specializes in the sale and purchase of existing business enterprises. The foreign entrepreneur must remember that traditionally a business broker is paid by and owes allegiance to the seller. In that capacity the broker will always attempt to place the business in the best possible light. Additionally, the broker will try to assess whether or not the buyer is financially qualified to complete the acquisition and whether or not the buyer is qualified to manage the business. Therefore, while buyers should be candid with their broker, they should not offer information that could prejudice their bargaining position. Very often reputable business brokers will also work as an agent for the buyer or, in some cases, will agree to honor the confidences of both seller and buyer. The nature of the relationship should be established at the commencement of the transaction process, not at the end. Depending upon the particular State, the occupation of a business broker or merger and acquisition specialist is often regulated by law.

Finally, the prospective foreign buyer should not attempt to acquire and manage a U.S. business enterprise without a substantial capital reserve. At the very least, the buyer should reserve sufficient capital to cover personal living expenses for at least one year as well as a sufficient cash reserve to cover the enterprise's operating costs for approximately six months. Planning conservatively for capital needs is essential not just for success but also for peace of mind. The foreign entrepreneur will be immersed in the many details of adjusting to life in this fast-paced society and it would be inappropriate to burden oneself with unnecessary stress caused by the normal ebb and flow of the business cycle.

FRANCHISED
BUSINESSES

For a variety of reasons the foreign entrepreneur may prefer to establish a new business enterprise in the community in which he has selected. Perhaps there are no suitable existing business enterprises that suit or interest the buyer. Or perhaps the buyer just desires to pursue a particular type of business enterprise. Perhaps one's dream requires the creation of something new, something in which the buyer can claim credit for developing. If this is the case, then there is another exciting option that, if not unique to the U.S., is nonetheless a product of the American business dynamism—a franchised business opportunity.

There are more than 500,000 franchised businesses in the United States and franchising is one of this country's fastest growing methods of doing business. A franchised business is a method of operation in which the originator or developer of a successful product or service authorizes another business operator to utilize the originator's trademark, business methods, products or services. The originator is called the *franchiser* and the *franchisee* is the one who purchases the right to use the trademark and system of business. A franchisee usually receives assistance with the site selection for the business, personnel training, business organization, marketing, and product supply. The franchisee usually pays an initial fee as well as on-going royalties. These fees enable the franchiser to provide training, research, development and support for the entire business. In essence, the franchisee acquires the franchiser's experience, expertise, and operational system.

Franchising has a much greater percentage of success than businesses started without the benefits of a franchise system. One of the reasons for this success is the requirement by U.S. federal law that a franchiser provide the prospective franchisee with extensive documentation as to the considered business. This documentation is contained in the Uniform Franchise Offering Circular (UFOC). This document provides detailed information on the initial investment required, the amount of working capital, current and past litigation and monetary claims, identity and experience of the principal executives, advertising reserves, degree of managerial experience required and much more. The UFOC provides the prospective franchisee with the tools with which to conduct an effective due diligence inquiry. Additionally, the prospective franchisee should contact other franchisees in the system and obtain as much information and comment as possible from these business owners.

Nonetheless, it is good sense to hire an experienced franchise consultant or attorney to assist in the analysis of the UFOC. Unlike traditional enterprises, the franchise alternative offers a lower risk of failure to the entrepreneur.

Franchising is especially relevant for foreign executives and managers because most franchisers do not want an overly individualistic person as a franchisee. Experience has demonstrated to franchisers that the ability to follow a proven business plan coupled with executive and managerial ability provides the best combination for franchise success. These characteristics are also generally beneficial for foreign buyers since it is prudent for foreign persons to allow themselves to be taught the local U.S. business customs and business practices. So there seem to be a combination of advantages which favor the franchised business for foreign entrepreneurs.

Some franchises, however, are so controlled that there is very little room for executive or managerial discretion. In that case, the franchised business might not sustain an L-1 or E-2 visa. That type of tightly controlled franchise is easy to identify and can be avoided. In any event, utilizing a visa contingency clause in the franchise agreement will provide the foreign entrepreneur with the ability to apply for the franchise without risking the loss of a deposit in the event the visa is denied. In fact, most franchised businesses still require a high level of executive and managerial ability (as well as time and energy) in order to succeed and there is an administrative precedent for the suitability of a franchised business for visa purposes.

Perhaps foreign persons can franchise their successful business methods from their home countries into the United States and thus provide others with the opportunity to share in their success.

Anyone interested in the option of franchising may contact the International Franchise Association, 1350 New York Avenue, N.W., Suite 900, Washington, D.C. (U.S.A.), telephone (202) 628-8000, facsimile (202) 628-0812 for more information. Additionally, there is a permanent franchise exhibition at The Merchandise Mart, 200 World Trade Center, Chicago, Illinois 60654.

Tax Planning and Other Economic Considerations

This section will briefly discuss the various U.S. federal income tax and estate tax consequences as they may affect a foreign person seeking entry into the United States. It is not meant to be a profound or complete analysis of all of the subjects and issues which are pertinent to such an individual, but is merely designed to acquaint a person with important topics. Any foreign person who contemplates an investment into the United States should consult a qualified international tax attorney or accountant for advice regarding the income and or estate tax consequences of the investment. Very often it will be necessary for the U.S. tax professional to consult with the client's tax and business advisors in order to ensure complete coverage of all the pertinent issues.

GENERAL PRINCIPLES: RESIDENCY VS. NON-RESIDENCY

The United States federal government collects taxes from its residents on the basis of a federal income tax as well as by gift and estate taxes. The agency in charge of taxes is the Internal Revenue Service. Additionally, every State as well as its various local subdivisions and municipalities may also collect taxes. The United States is one of the few countries in the world whose central government taxes its citizens and residents on their worldwide income. This very often is a substantial factor to be considered in the overall strategic financial planning by an inbound foreign person. For income tax purposes, there is a profound difference between a citizen, a resident and a non-resident. These designations may, in fact, have nothing to do with the immigration definition of these same terms.

A United States resident, for tax purposes, is any person who is either a U.S. citizen or a person deemed to be a resident of the United States in accordance with the Rules and Regulations of the Internal Revenue Code. A person deemed to be a resident of the United States, for tax purposes, is anyone who is the holder of a permanent visa to the United States (green card). This is sometimes called the *green card* test. This is an absolute test and if a person is a permanent U.S. resident alien, the person is automatically and absolutely a resident for income tax purposes under current U.S. law.

In addition to the so-called green card test there is also the *substantial presence* test. This test imposes U.S. tax residency on foreign persons who spend a designated time in the United States. These so-called substantial presence tests are as follows:

Any person who is present in the United States for thirty-one or more days in the present year is treated as a United States resident if the person has also spent 183 more days in the current year or 183 days over a three year period using the following formula.

- ☞ In the current year, one day of actual presence equals one day for the legal formula (1=1).

- ☞ In the previous year, one day of actual presence equals one-third of a day (1=$^1/_3$).

- ☞ For the next previous year, one day of actual presence equals one-sixth of a day (1=$^1/_6$).

For example, if a person were to reside in the United States for ninety days in 1998, ninety days in 1997, and ninety days in 1996, that person would not be considered a U.S. resident for tax purposes since the total of the above formula does not equal 183 days.

- ☞ 1998: 90 actual days = 90 equivalent days

- ☞ 1997: 90 actual days = 30 equivalent days

- ☞ 1996: 90 actual days = 15 equivalent days

Total = 135 days of equivalent presence in the United States under the substantial presence test and thus, not a U.S. resident for income tax purposes. In applying the above formula, any actual travel days in the United States must also be counted in the equation. For instance, if one enters the United States at 11:30 p.m. on a given day, that entire day is counted as one actual day of presence in the United States. Similarly, if one departs the United States at 12:30 a.m., that entire day also is counted in the equation.

There are some specific exemptions that apply to this formula; for instance, a person who remains in the United States for an extended period because of a medical emergency or who is posted in the United States as a diplomat. There are other exemptions applying to teachers, job trainees, and students. In addition to the above formula, if persons meet the substantial presence test under the mathematical computation but can prove that they maintain a home abroad and have closer connections with another jurisdiction, (i.e., they pay taxes in the other jurisdiction), then they may preserve their status as a non-U.S. resident for income tax purposes. This possible exception, however, applies only to an individual who has been present in the United States for less than 183 days in the current year.

U.S. INCOME TAXATION FOR NON-RESIDENCY

As to non-residents, the United States taxes four categories of income, as follows:

- ☛ Income that is effectively connected with a U.S. trade or business. This type of income is taxed on a net taxable income basis, using the normal progressive tax rates otherwise applicable to U.S. taxpayers. Business losses and expenses are allowed to be deducted from gross income in the calculation of net income which is subject to taxation.

- ☛ Income which is known as "fixed or determinable, annual or periodic income" which is not connected with a U.S. trade or business. This category does not include interest income generated by deposits in qualified U.S. financial institutions such as banks or insurance companies. This latter form of investment interest is not taxable at all.

- ☛ Capital gains income of a foreign person who is physically present in the U.S. for more than 183 days in the calendar year. Obviously, a person physically present in the United States for more than 183 days in the calendar year will almost always be deemed to be a U.S. taxpayer in any event.

☞ Gain on the sale or other disposition of U.S. real property interests ("USRPI").

Fixed or determinable annual or periodical income is taxed at a flat rate of thirty percent on the gross amount unless that amount has been reduced by treaty. In addition to the burden of taxation, the tax amount must be withheld at the source of payment by the "withholding agent." This person is usually the last person who has control of the income before it is transferred or conveyed to the foreign person. This type of income is normally considered passive income, such as dividends, interest, or royalties, etc.

Thus, it may be in one's financial interest to be considered engaged in a U.S. trade or business if one is receiving rents from real estate investments. Also, there may be a tax treaty in effect between the United States and the foreign person's home country, which may reduce the rate for fixed or determinable annual income or periodical income. Additionally, capital gains—that is, the amount of gain realized when a capital asset is sold, associated with United States property and other than real property—is not taxable so long as the person receiving that income has not been physically present in the United States for 183 or more days. Capital gains on the sale of real property, however, is taxable regardless of the length of time a person has been in the United States.

If the income is from a source outside the United States, then it would not be taxable unless that income is effectively connected with a U.S. trade or business. There are a number of complex rules that determine the source of income, and the application and effect of these rules usually requires professional assistance.

WITHHOLDING REQUIREMENTS

A primary concern of a foreign person who owns real estate or other income producing assets in the U.S. is the requirement of withholding a certain percent of the income to cover tax liability. In order for the withholding rules to apply, the following requirements must exist:

☞ There must be a withholding agent. The Internal Revenue Service rules are very broad in defining which persons are required to withhold funds otherwise payable to a foreign person. This definition includes real estate brokers, attorneys, other trustees, lessees or mortgagees of real or personal property.

☞ Only U.S. sources of income are subject to withholding.

☞ The items which are subject to withholding are fixed, determinable, and annual or periodic income such as interest, dividends, rent, salaries, and other fixed or determinable annual or periodical gains and profit income. Income from the sale of property, real or personal, is not considered fixed, determinable, annual, or periodic. So capital gains are not subject to withholding unless they involve real estate.

☞ The income must not be effectively connected with a U.S. trade or business.

☞ The recipient of the income or money must be either a nonresident or alien, foreign partnership or foreign corporation.

☞ If there is a treaty or other special rule or exception, then the withholding requirement may be avoided.

☞ As to partnerships, it should be noted that a domestic partnership is required to withhold and remit to the IRS all fixed determinable annual and periodic income (which is not effectively connected with a U.S. trade or business), which is included in the distributive share of a foreign partner, even if the income is not actually distributed. If the partnership distributive income is effectively connected, then withholding is not required. However, IRS rules and regulations now require a U.S. partnership to withhold and make quarterly estimated tax payments on a foreign partner's share of partnership income which is effectively connected with U.S. trader business regardless of whether distributions of income are made to the partners.

☞ Trusts, U.S. source, income which is fixed or determinable, annual or periodic, and which is distributed through a trust's foreign beneficiary, is subject to withholding.

☞ It is extremely important that a foreign person understand that the tax characterization of a business entity by the IRS may determine whether distribution is a dividend and thus taxable by thirty percent as opposed to any other type of distribution. For example, if a foreign entity is called or designated as a trust or partnership but is defined by the IRS as a corporation, then a distribution may be determined to be a dividend. The United States has signed a network of treaties dealing with income tax and withholding requirements with other countries. The primary purpose of the U.S. income tax treaties is the prevention of double taxation. However, some treaties may provide some insular and legitimate tax avoidance opportunities. The advantages offered by U.S. tax treaties have been utilized by corporations formed or otherwise resident within the treaty jurisdiction, controlled by well-advised foreign taxpayers whose personal residences are countries not having a treaty with the U.S., or whose treaty may not be suitable for a particular transaction or investment.

NON-RESIDENT ENGAGED IN TRADE OR BUSINESS IN THE UNITED STATES

If a non-resident alien is engaged in a trade or business in the United States, then all the income effectively connected with that trade or business is taxable at the same rates and according to the same rules as for a United States citizen or resident. There is no clear cut definition as to what constitutes a United States trade or business. The determination usually involves a review of the activities of the person and the frequency and nature of those activities. Any business activity that involves significant contacts in the United States or that operates from, or in connection with, a fixed or permanent office may well cause the taxpayer to be treated as engaged in a trade or business in the United States.

Various countries have treaties with the United States that provide that the host country will only tax the profits of an enterprise if the alien maintains a "permanent establishment" in that country. There are various definitions as to what denotes a "permanent establishment" but it normally includes the maintenance of a business, an office or factory which is in place or is expected to remain in place for a period of twelve months or more. Normally, the use of an independent contractor or agent for the representation of a foreign enterprise in the United States will not result in a finding of a permanent establishment unless that independent contractor has wide and general authority to act on behalf of the principal and normally does so.

UNITED STATES
REAL PROPERTY

A recent amendment to the United States Federal Tax Code known as the Foreign Investment Real Property Tax Act (known as "FIRPTA") essentially places non-resident aliens on an equal footing with United States residents with respect to the tax on the net gains from the sale of United States real property interests. The gain is taxed as if the gain were effectively connected with a United States trade or business. A person is taxable only on the net gain realized in the business and can offset the gross amount realized with expenses, depreciation, etc.

The definition of what is a real property interest is quite broad and covers most interests in real property; i.e., land and buildings, except an interest which is purely that of a lender or creditor. Ownership by foreign persons of a hotel or motel, for example, is considered ownership of a United States real property interest.

In addition, if a United States corporation owns the United States real property interest, and that interest amounts to at least fifty percent of the sum of all property owned by that corporation, then it will be considered a United States real property holding corporation and the corporate sale of stock will also result in taxation. Payment of the tax is secured by way of a mandatory withholding of ten percent of the amount realized on disposition of that United States real property interest. The tax may not equal the ten percent, but the withholding agent is required to secure that amount and submit it to the Internal Revenue

Service. This is to ensure there will be a fund of money to pay the tax when it is annually determined. The following are exceptions to this withholding requirement:

☞ The property is purchased by a person for use as a residence and the value is $300,000.00 or less.

☞ The property being sold was not considered an interest in U.S. real property; however, according to the law, a U.S. real property interest includes not only real property owned directly by an individual, but also real property owned by a U.S. corporation which, is itself, principally owned by a foreign person. If the property is held by a foreign corporation, and only the shares of stock are sold, then FIRPTA does not apply since the purchaser is only buying shares of stock in a foreign corporation.

☞ The transferred property's corporate stock is transferred under an established U.S. securities market, or the transferor has executed and furnished a "non-foreign affidavit" certifying that the transferor is not a foreign person.

Any non-resident alien who was engaged in a trade or business in the United States during the taxable year or had his income subject to tax by the United States is required to file an IRS Form 1040NR. There are certain exceptions to this which can be discussed with a tax expert.

Thus, if United States real property taxation considerations are important to a foreign investor, the above information needs to be addressed in the pre-immigration planning stages.

U.S. ESTATE AND GIFT TAXES

The tax computation for a gross estate in the case of a nonresident alien involves calculations very similar to that for a U.S. person. The following special rules should be kept in mind by any foreign person when making an investment in the United States for acquisition of income-producing assets:

☞ The situs (that is, the legal residence) of real property is determined by its physical location. Thus, real property situated in the

United States is considered as having a U.S. situs. Mortgages and liens on real property as a result of loans are not considered as real property for this purpose. These are considered intangible assets, but if the debt obligation is of a U.S. person, then it is U.S. situs property.

☞ As to corporate stock, stock of a U.S. corporation is U.S. situs, whereas stock of a foreign corporation is considered foreign situs regardless of the place of management or location of the stock certificates. As to foreign partnerships, the rule is somewhat unclear. The situs of the partnership is where the partnership business is carried on or managed, not necessarily where the assets are located. What is unclear is whether or not a foreign partnership, which is engaged in a U.S. business, subjects its entire partnership interest as U.S. situs rather than just its U.S.-based situs assets.

☞ The situs of currency is its physical location and it is treated just as other tangible personal property.

☞ Debt obligation of a U.S. person is considered a U.S. situs property except where the obligation of a U.S. corporation for more than eighty percent of the gross income of the organization comes from an active foreign source for a three-year prior period.

☞ The physical location of the assets of sole proprietorship determines its situs.

☞ Property held through a reputable or grantor trust, of which the decedent is the grantor, can be U.S. situs property.

☞ Intangible personal property is considered as U.S. situs if it was issued by or enforceable against a resident of the U.S., a domestic corporation or a governmental unit.

☞ The formula and method for the computation of the tax is identical to that of a U.S. tax payer with one exception: the marital deduction is not allowed the foreign person unless it was granted by treaty, or unless the surviving spouse is a U.S. citizen, or unless the property is conveyed through a qualified domestic trust. Furthermore, after making the required computations, the rates now range from eighteen to fifty-five percent of the adjusted estate.

The United States imposes estate taxes upon the estate of a non-resident alien if that alien has assets situated in the United States at the time of death. A *non-resident* for purposes of the estate and gift tax laws refers to a person who is not "domiciled" in the United States. *Domicile* is normally defined to be that place where a person intends to live permanently, a place that a person has selected as the permanent home. The question of domicile can sometimes be difficult to define precisely. In general, it has been held by the courts that a person can only have one domicile even though there may be many residences. It does not necessarily follow, however, that a person who is domiciled in the United States must be a "resident" for estate tax purposes. Though this result would generally follow, it is technically possible for persons to have a foreign residence (and passport) even though they might be domiciliaries of the United States based upon other considerations and circumstances.

The determination of "residence" for estate tax purposes is of paramount importance to a foreign person in the United States because if the person is deemed to be a resident, that is, domiciled in the United States, then the United States government may impose an estate tax on the worldwide property held by that person. If the foreign person is considered to be a non-resident alien, then the United States can only impose a federal estate tax on the assets located in the United States at the time of death. The tax rate applicable to a non-resident alien is the same as would apply to a citizen except that certain normal tax-credit devices (the marital deduction) are inapplicable. This fact could make a devastating impact on the total tax liability of a foreign person and requires careful study.

In this situation, the source rules are very important as to what constitutes U.S.-located (situs) property. Currency and other tangible personal property are considered to have a situs based upon physical location. Corporate stock of a U.S. corporation has a U.S. situs while corporate stock of a foreign corporation has a foreign situs, regardless of where the stock certificates are actually located.

Thus, in most situations when aliens do not intend to reside in the United States for extended periods of time, it is not advisable to hold even residential property or what I consider as "casual property" (condominium, apartment, raw land, etc.) in the United States in their own name.

It is better to have U.S. real property owned by a foreign corporation or a U.S. subsidiary corporation owned by a foreign corporation, since under these circumstances the property will not be deemed as situated in the United States. Of course, this suggestion must be balanced with the foreign person's other tax interests to ensure that there are no other income tax or other problems created by this device. In general, though, the above is a preferred way of holding property in the United States by a non-resident person. However, before a commitment is made, it is advisable to discuss the tax and other economic consequences of these purchases with a trained professional. This is one of those instances where an hour or two of consultation before taking what may be irrevocable steps can be worth much money and much peace of mind.

GENERAL PLANNING REQUIREMENTS

There are many planning considerations which should be addressed by a foreign person seeking to make investment in the U.S. prior to that direct investment. Some of them can be characterized as follows:

☛ Initially, the foreign person must establish priorities with respect to the transfer of assets to the United States. There is always the objective to minimize U.S. and other taxation earnings in this position (gains) at the various levels of operation and in avoidance of U.S. state tax. In addition, there may be some other very valid immigration objectives which may conflict with some of the above tax concerns and the foreign person will need to determine which objective shall be paramount.

☛ Where will the investor maintain residence?

☛ Are there plans in the immediate future or in the near future to relocate?

☛ Compare the U.S. tax regimen with the individual and corporate income tax rates and state tax rates in the country of residence or in the country where assets generating income are located.

☛ The availability of tax treaties which may change the withholding rules or other U.S. tax requirements otherwise applicable to a non-resident or resident alien.

☛ Is the investor making a unique trans-national acquisition in the United States, or is the investor making a long term plan to transfer assets to the U.S.

☛ Is the investor already engaged in a business outside of his/her home country? Where? What are the tax ramifications?

☛ If there are other existing U.S. investments, are they producing income or loss?

☛ Is there need for anonymity on the part of the foreign investor?

☛ How will the investment be financed, and by whom?

☛ What are the home country laws concerning the repatriation of foreign income earnings for individual residents?

☛ What is the anticipated time that the investment will be held? Short term or long term?

☛ What are other relevant business considerations?

The tax rates for income which is effectively connected with a U.S. trade or business is the same as for residents and is based on a progressive schedule. In addition, the tax is imposed on the net gain of the enterprise. In certain cases a foreign person may elect to be taxed as if engaged in a U.S. trade or business. It may be beneficial to be taxed as a U.S. trade or business so as to avoid the imposition of a tax on the gross income derived from investments in the United States. The rules for this type of election are beyond the scope of this book but the election option is mentioned here only to make the reader aware of the availability of this procedure.

INVESTMENT REPORTING REQUIREMENTS

The federal government maintains various investment disclosure laws which provide for the filing of certain reports by a foreign person who owns either agricultural land or other types of business enterprises. The financial threshold for the reporting requirements of commercial business is generally $1,000,000 of cost, or the actual value of the business assets whenever less than 200 acres of real estate involved.

The U.S. Department of Commerce regulations require the reporting of a transaction when a foreign person acquires ten percent or more interest in a U.S. business (including real estate). A foreign BE-13 is filed by a U.S. business within forty-five days after the investment. If the foreign person or entity directly acquires United States real property interest, the form is filed in the name of that foreign person entity and describes the real property acquired. Form BE-13 identifies each foreign person owning a United States business enterprise and discloses the ultimate beneficial foreign owner, that is, the person or entity in the chain of ownership that is not more than fifty percent owned by another person. Additionally, Form BE-13 requests the name, ownership percentage and country of location of each foreign owner. If the ultimate beneficial owner is an individual, however, only the country of residence must be disclosed. Exemptions from filing this form include the acquisition of real estate for personal residence; acquisition of a United States business by a U.S. affiliate of a foreign person that merges the U.S. business into its business if the cost is less than 1 million and less than 200 acres of U.S. land is acquired, and an acquisition for establishment of a United States business if its total assets are less than or equal to $1 million and it does not own 200 or more acres of United States land. Bearing in mind, then, the recent provisions for a United States investor visa as defined in this book, it is clear that upon investment of $1 million for the acquisition of a U.S. business, reporting to the Department of Commerce may be required if the business and its assets includes 200 or more acres of United States land.

Department of Commerce reports are to be used solely for analytical or statistical purposes and are confidential. However, anonymity can never be fully guaranteed. If anonymity is needed, a request for confidentiality can be made in writing to the Department of Commerce. Failure to file the above forms or to provide the information required under these forms may result in civil penalty not exceeding $10,000 or criminal penalty of a fine not exceeding $10,000, or imprisonment up to one year, or both. The reporting requirements should be taken seriously.

The U.S. Department of Agriculture has a series of reporting requirements for the purpose of monitoring the disposition of agricultural land. *Agricultural land* is defined as land currently used or used within the past five years for agricultural, forestry, or timber production purposes unless the land is ten acres or less and the income from the products on the land amounts to less than $1,000.00 on an annual basis, or the land is for personal use. In addition, some states have their own reporting requirements, while other states may have some restrictions on the type of real estate that can be purchased by a non-U.S. resident. These factors should be examined carefully beforehand by a foreign person to ensure that the purchase of certain U.S. assets will be compatible with the investor's overall business plan.

The tax regimen of the United States obviously provides for a considerable amount of disclosure of the foreign person's interest in the

United States. In addition to the tax reporting requirements for acquisitions, there are also the non-tax reporting requirements under the Department of Agriculture and Department of Commerce rules and regulations mentioned in the previous paragraphs.

In addition, there is now a regimen of reporting requirements known as EXON-FLORIO regulations. The regimen authorizes the President of the United States to block or suspend an acquisition by a foreign entity of a United States business if it negatively affects national security. Administration of this law has been delegated to the Committee of Foreign Investment in the United States (SFIUS). Consequently, it is recommended that a foreign person making a transaction that could possibly result in the acquisition of control of a U.S. business, and possibly affect U.S. security, give notice to the SFIUS. The reason for doing so is to eliminate within a designated time period any potential (future) action by the United States to require the foreign investor to divest itself of the transaction investment. The law gives the United States up to three years to issue a divestiture order. Therefore, it is certainly worthwhile to give a written notice in advance of the investment and force the government to reveal any interest that it may have in the transaction.

A Final Word

The immigration law of the United States is not only broad and complex; it is also subject to constant modification. In addition, the economic environment of the United States is dynamic and fast-paced. The prospective foreign entrepreneur or business executive must successfully maneuver within the systems of both of these critical areas at the same time. These circumstances make it difficult for the small sized foreign business entrepreneur to attempt to manage all these issues by him or herself. A friend of mine used the analogy of attempting to learn simultaneously how to juggle crystal goblets and bounce on a trampoline to describe this endeavor.

The necessity of pre-entry planning cannot be over-emphasized, especially since the transfer of a successful enterprise will result in certain U.S. state and federal income tax consequences. The strategy of pre-entry planning is also beneficial to those individuals who seek a long-term visa to the United States based upon employment, education, or other personal interests. As an example, U.S. persons who desire to obtain a K visa for a "significant other" should carefully read the section in this book concerning the requirements for that visa as well as the Introduction and Preface to this book. In this manner, persons will understand the documentation requirements and the reasoning behind these requirements. Thus, the key to success for obtaining any visa entry into the United States is planning—particularly long term.

I enjoy hearing from my readers and you may contact me at my business office which is located at:

28100 U.S. 19 N., Suite 502
Clearwater (Tampa), Florida, 33761
United States of America
Internet address: http://ilw.com/carrion/
E-mail address: 73344,267@compuserve.com

Appendix A
INS Offices

Following are the addresses of the INS District Offices and Sub-offices where papers may be filed. When more than one district is located in a state, you will need to check with one of the offices to determine the correct jurisdiction for filing your papers. Correspondence should be addressed to "Immigration and Naturalization Service, U.S. Department of Justice."

Note: Addresses are subject to change.

INS HEADQUARTERS
425 Eye Street NW
Washington, DC 30536

INS REGIONAL OFFICES

Eastern Operations
70 Kimball Ave.
S. Burlington, VT 05403-6813

Central Operations Regional Office
7701 N. Stemmons Freeway
Dallas, TX 75247

Western Operations Regional Office
24000 Avila Road
P.O. Box 30080
Laguna Niguel, CA 92607-0080

INS SERVICE CENTERS

California
P.O. Box 10589
Laguna Niguel, CA 92607-0589

Nebraska
850 "S" Street
Lincoln, NE 68501

Texas
P.O. Box 851488
Mesquite, TX 75185-1488

Vermont
P.O. Box 9589
St. Albans, VT 05479-9589

EASTERN REGION DISTRICT OFFICES

Albany Sub-Office
James T. Foley Federal Courthouse
445 Broad, Rm. 227
Albany, NY 12207

Atlanta District Office
77 Forsyth Street SW
Atlanta, GA 30303-0253

Baltimore District Office
Nations Bank Center
100 S. Charles, 11th Fl.
Baltimore, MD 21201

Boston District Office
JFK Federal Building
Government Center
Room 1700
Boston, MA 02203

Brooklyn Sub-Office
(Citizenship only for Queens, Kings, Nassau, Suffolk, and Richmond)
505 Fulton Street
Brooklyn, NY 11201

Buffalo District Office
130 Delaware Avenue
Buffalo, NY 14202

Charlotte Amalie, St. Thomas, VI Sub-Office
Federal District Court Bldg.
P.O. Box 610
Charlotte Amalie
St. Thomas, VI 00801

Charlotte Sub-Office
6 Woodlawn Green
Room 138
Charlotte, NC 28217

Cleveland District Office
Anthony J. Celebreeze Federal Bldg.
1240 E. 9th St., Rm. 1917
Cleveland, OH 44199

Detroit District Office
Federal Bldg.
333 Mt. Elliott Street
Detroit, MI 48207-4381

Ft. Lauderdale/Port Everglades Sub-Office
1800 Eller Drive, Ste. 401
P.O. Box 13054
Port Everglades Station
Ft. Lauderdale, FL 33316

Hartford Sub-Office
Ribicoff Federal Bldg.
450 Main Street
Hartford, CT 06103-3060

Jacksonville Sub-Office
400 W. Bay St., Rm. G-18
P.O. Box 35029
Jacksonville, FL 32202

Key West Sub-Office
301 Simonton St., Rm. 224
P.O. Box 86
Key West, FL 33040

Louisville Sub-Office
Gene Snyder U.S. Custom House, Rm. 604
601 W. Broadway
Louisville, KY 40202

Memphis Sub-Office
1341 Sycamore View
Suite 100
Memphis, TN 38134

Miami District Office
7880 Biscayne Blvd.
Miami, FL 33138

Nassau, Bahamas Sub-Office
U.S. Immigration/Nassau
7415 N.W. 19th St., Ste. H
Miami, FL 33126

New Orleans District Office
Postal Services Building
701 Loyola Ave., Rm. T-8011
New Orleans, LA 70113

Newark District Office
Federal Building
970 Broad Street
Newark, NJ 07102

New York District Office
26 Federal Plaza
New York, NY 10278

Norfolk Sub-Office
Norfolk Commerce Park
5280 Henneman Drive
Norfolk, VA 23513

Orlando Intl. Airport
P.O. Box 620848
Orlando, FL 32863

Philadelphia District Office
1600 Callowhill St.
Philadelphia, PA 19130

Pittsburgh Sub-Office
2130 Federal Building
1000 Liberty Avenue
Pittsburgh, PA 15222

Portland District Office
176 Gannett Drive
Portland ME 04106

Providence Sub-Office
200 Dyre Street
Providence, RI 02903

San Juan District Office
P.O. Box 365068
San Juan, PR 00936

St. Albans Sub-Office
P.O. Box 328
St. Albans, VT 05478

Tampa Sub-Office
5509 W. Gray St., Ste. 207
Tampa, FL 33609

Washington District Office
4422 N. Fairfax Drive
Arlington, VA 22203

West Palm Beach Sub-Office
4360 N. Lake Blvd.
Ste. 107
Palm Beach Gardens, FL
33419-6254

**CENTRAL REGION—
DISTRICT OFFICES**

Albuquerque Sub-Office
517 Gold Ave., Rm. 1010
P.O. Box 567
Albuquerque, NM 87103

Austin Sub-Office
3708 S. Second Street
P.O. Box 6496
Austin, TX 78704

Brownsville Sub-Office
1500 E. Elisabeth Street
Brownsville, TX 78520

Chicago District Office
10 W. Jackson Blvd., #600
Chicago, IL 60604

Dallas District Office
8101 N. Stemmons Freeway
Dallas, TX 75247

Denver District Office
4730 Paris Street
Denver, CO 80239

El Paso District Office
1545 Hawkins Blvd., Ste. 167
El Paso, TX 79925

Harlingen District Office
2102 Tegge Ave.
Harlingen, TX 78550

Helena District Office
2800 Skyway Drive
Helena, MT 59601

Houston District Office
126 North Point
Houston, TX 77060

Kansas City District Office
9747 N. Conant Avenue
Kansas City, MO 64153

Oklahoma Sub-Office
4149 Highline Blvd., Ste. 300
Oklahoma City, OK 73108

Omaha District Office
3736 S. 132nd Street
Omaha, NE 68144

San Antonio District Office
U.S. Federal Building
8940 Four Winds Drive
San Antonio, TX 78239

St. Paul District Office
2901 Metro Drive
Suite 100
Bloomington, MN 55425

**WESTERN REGION
DISTRICT OFFICES**

Agana Sub-Office
Pacific News Bldg.
Room 801
235 Archbishop Flores
Agana, GU 96910

Anchorage District Office
620 E. 10th Ave, #102
Anchorage AK 99501-3701

Fresno Sub-Office
865 Fulton Mall
Fresno, CA 93721

Honolulu District Office
595 Ala Moana Blvd.
Honolulu, HI 96813

Las Vegas Sub-Office
3373 Pepper Lane
Las Vegas, NV 89120

Los Angeles District Office
300 N. Los Angeles St.
Los Angeles, CA 90012

Phoenix District Office
2035 N. Central Avenue
Phoenix, AZ 85004

Portland District Office
511 NW Broadway
Portland, OR 97209

Reno Sub-Office
1351 Corporate Blvd.
Reno, NV 89502-7102

Sacramento Sub-Office
711 "J" Street
Sacramento, CA 95814

San Diego District Office
880 Front St., Ste. 1234
San Diego, CA 92101

San Francisco District Office
630 Sansome Street
San Francisco, CA 94111-
2280

San Jose Sub-Office
280 S. First St., #1150
San Jose, CA 95113

Seattle District Office
815 Airport Way So.
Seattle, WA 98134

Tucson Sub-Office
300 West Congress
Room 1T
Tucson, AZ 85701-1386

The following states have no INS office. The states come under the jurisdiction of the district listed with the state. You must check with that district to see whether the state is serviced by a sub-office within the district.

Alabama (Atlanta)

Arkansas (New Orleans)

Delaware (Philadelphia)

Iowa (Omaha)

Kansas (Kansas City)

Mississippi (New Orleans)

New Hampshire (Boston)

North Dakota (St. Paul)

South Dakota (St. Paul)

West Virginia (Philadelphia)

Wyoming (Denver)

Note: In addition to the regional and district offices, the INS maintains Regional Service Centers in each region, where many of the routine petitions and applications are sent for adjudication. The addresses are listed in the above list under the heading "INS SERVICE CENTERS."

APPENDIX B
FORM I-765

INSTRUCTIONS FOR
APPLICATION FOR EMPLOYMENT AUTHORIZATION
Form I-765

The Immigration and Naturalization Service (INS) recommends that you retain a copy of your completed application for your records.

INDEX

PART 1. GENERAL.

Purpose of the Application. Certain aliens who are temporarily in the United States may file a Form I-765, Application for Employment Authorization, to request an Employment Authorization Document (EAD). Other aliens who are authorized to work in the United States without restrictions should also use this form to apply to the INS for a document evidencing such authorization. Please review Part 2 ELIGIBILITY CATEGORIES to determine whether you should use this form.

If you are a Lawful Permanent Resident, a Conditional Resident, or a nonimmigrant authorized to be employed with a specific employer under 8 CFR 274a.12(b), please do **NOT** use this form.

DEFINITIONS.

Employment Authorization Document (EAD): Form I-688; Form I-688A; Form I-688B; or any successor document issued by the INS as evidence that the holder is authorized to work in the United States.

Renewal EAD: an EAD issued to an eligible applicant at or after the expiration of a previous EAD issued under the same category.

Replacement EAD: an EAD issued to an eligible applicant when the previously issued EAD has been lost, stolen, mutilated, or the previously issued card contains erroneous information, such as a misspelled name.

Interim EAD: an EAD issued to an eligible applicant when the INS has failed to adjudicate an application within 90 days of receipt of a properly filed EAD application or within 30 days of a properly filed initial EAD application based on an asylum application filed on or after January 4, 1995. The interim EAD will be granted for a period not to exceed 240 days and is subject to the conditions noted on the document.

PART 2. ELIGIBILITY CATEGORIES.

The INS adjudicates a request for employment authorization by determining whether an applicant has submitted the required information and documentation, and whether the applicant is eligible. In order to determine your eligibility, you must identify the category in which you are eligible and fill in that category in question 16 on the Form I-765. Enter only **one** of the following category numbers on the application form.

NOTE: **Category (c)(13) is no longer available.** You may <u>not</u> renew or replace your EAD based on (c)(13). If you have an EAD based on that category, please review the categories below to determine if you are eligible under another category.

APPLICATIONS TO BE FILED AT SERVICE CENTERS.

Asylee, (granted asylum)--(a)(5). File your EAD application with a copy of the INS letter granting you asylum. It is not necessary to apply for an EAD as an asylee until 90 days before the expiration of your current EAD.

Refugee--(a)(3). File your EAD application with either a copy of your Form I-590, Registration for Classification as Refugee, approval letter or a copy of a Form I-730, Refugee/Asylee Relative Petition, approval notice.

Paroled as a Refugee--(a)(4). File your EAD application with a copy of your Form I-94, Departure Record.

Asylum Applicant (with a pending asylum application) who Filed for Asylum on or after January 4, 1995--(c)(8). If you filed a Form I-589, Request for Asylum and for Withholding of Deportation, <u>on or after January 4, 1995, you must wait at least 150 days</u> before you are eligible to apply for an EAD. If you file your EAD application early, it will be denied and you will have to file a new application. File your EAD application with:

- A copy of the INS acknowledgement mailer which was mailed to you; or

- Other evidence that your Form I-589 was filed with the INS; or

- Evidence that your Form I-589 was filed with an Immigration Judge at the Executive Office for Immigration Review (EOIR); or

- Evidence that your asylum application remains under administrative or judicial review.

Asylum Applicant (with a pending asylum application) who Filed for Asylum and Withholding of Deportation Prior to January 4, 1995 and is *NOT* in Exclusion or Deportation Proceedings--(c)(8). You may file your EAD application at any time; however, it will only be granted if the INS finds that your asylum application is not frivolous. File your EAD application with:

- A complete copy of your previously filed Form I-589; and

- A copy of your INS receipt notice; or

- A copy of the INS acknowledgement mailer; or

- Evidence that your Form I-589 was filed with EOIR; or

- Evidence that your asylum application remains under administrative or judicial review; or

- Other evidence that you filed an asylum application.

Asylum Applicant (with a pending asylum application) who Filed an Initial Request for Asylum Prior to January 4, 1995, and *IS IN* Exclusion or Deportation Proceedings--(c)(8). If you filed your Request for Asylum and Withholding of Deportation (Form I-589) prior to January 4, 1995 and you ARE IN exclusion or deportation proceedings, file your EAD application with:

- A date-stamped copy of your previously filed Form I-589; or

- A copy of Form I-221, Order to Show Cause and Notice of Hearing, or Form I-122, Notice to Applicant for Admission Detained for Hearing Before Immigration Judge; or

- A copy of EOIR-26, Notice of Appeal, date stamped by the Office of the Immigration Judge; or

- A date-stamped copy of a petition for judicial review or for *habeas corpus* issued to the asylum applicant; or

- Other evidence that you filed an asylum application with EOIR.

Asylum Applicant under the ABC Settlement Agreement--(c)(8). If you are an El Salvadoran or Guatemalan national eligible for benefits under the ABC settlement agreement, American Baptist Churches v. Thornburgh, 760 F. Supp. 796 (N.D. Cal. 1991), there are special instructions applicable to filing your Form I-765 which supplement these instructions. These instructions and the application can be obtained by asking for an "ABC packet" at your local INS office or by calling 1-800-755-0777.

Deferred Enforced Departure (DED)/Extended Voluntary Departure--(a)(11). File your EAD application with evidence of your identity and nationality.

F-1 Student Seeking Optional Practical Training in an Occupation Directly Related to Studies--(c)(3)(i). File your EAD application with a Certificate of Eligibility of Nonimmigrant (F-1) Student Status (Form I-20 A-B/I-20 ID) endorsed by a designated school official within the past 30 days.

F-1 Student Offered Off-Campus Employment under the Sponsorship of a Qualifying International Organization--(c)(3)(ii). File your EAD application with the international organization's letter of certification that the proposed employment is within the scope of its sponsorship and a Certificate of Eligibility of Nonimmigrant (F-1) Student Status--For Academic and Language Students (Form I-20 A-B/I-20 ID) endorsed by the designated school official within the past 30 days.

F-1 Student Seeking Off-Campus Employment Due to Severe Economic Hardship--(c)(3)(iii). File your EAD application with Form I-20 A-B/I-20 ID, Certificate of Eligibility of Nonimmigrant (F-1) Student Status--For Academic and Language Students; Form I-538, Certification by Designated School Official, and any evidence you wish to submit, such as affidavits, which detail the unforeseen economic circumstances that cause your request, and evidence you have tried to find off-campus employment with an employer who has filed a labor and wage attestation.

J-2 Spouse or Minor Child of an Exchange Visitor--(c)(5). File your EAD application with a copy of your J-1's (principal alien's) Certificate of Eligibility for Exchange Visitor (J-1) Status (Form IAP-66). You must submit a written statement, with any supporting evidence showing, that your employment is not necessary to support the J-1 but is for other purposes.

M-1 Student Seeking Practical Training after Completing Studies--(c)(6). File your EAD application with a completed Form I-538, Application by Nonimmigrant Student for Extension of Stay, School Transfer, or Permission to Accept or Continue Employment, Form I-20 M-N, Certificate of Eligibility for Nonimmigrant (M-1) Student Status--For Vocational Students endorsed by the designated school official within the past 30 days.

Dependent of CCNAA E-1 Nonimmigrant--(c)(2). File your EAD application with the required certification from the American Institute in Taiwan if you are the spouse, or unmarried child, of an E-1 employee of the Coordination Council for North American Affairs.

Dependent of NATO Personnel--(c)(7). File your EAD application with a letter from the Department of Defense or NATO/SACLANT verifying your principal alien's status, your status, and your relationship to your principal alien.

N-8 or N-9 Nonimmigrant--(a)(7). File your EAD application with the required evidence listed in Part 3.

Family Unity Program--(a)(13). File your EAD application with a copy of the approval notice, if you have been granted status under this program. You may choose to file your EAD application concurrently with your Form I-817, Application for Voluntary Departure under the Family Unity Program. The INS may take up to 90 days from the date upon which you are granted status under the Family Unity Program to adjudicate your EAD application. If you were denied Family Unity status solely because your legalized spouse or parent first applied under the Legalization/SAW programs after May 5, 1988, file your EAD application with a new Form I-817 application and a copy of the original denial. However, if your EAD application is based on continuing eligibility under **(c)(12)**, please refer to **Deportable Alien Granted Voluntary Departure.**

K-1 Nonimmigrant Fiance(e) of U.S. Citizen or K-2 Dependent--(a)(6). File your EAD application if you are filing within 90 days from the date of entry. This EAD cannot be renewed. Any EAD application other than for a replacement must be based on your pending application for adjustment under (c)(9).

Citizen of Micronesia or the Marshall Islands or Palau--(a)(8). File your EAD application if you were admitted to the United States as a citizen of the Federated States of Micronesia (CFA/FSM) or of the Marshall Islands (CFA/MIS) pursuant to agreements between the United States and the former trust territories.

B-1 Nonimmigrant who is the personal or domestic servant of a nonimmigrant employer--(c)(17)(i). File your EAD application with:

- Evidence from your employer that he or she is a B, E, F, H, I, J, L, M, O, P, R or TN nonimmigrant and you were employed for at least one year by the employer before the employer entered the United States or your employer regularly employs personal and domestic servants and has done so for a period of years before coming to the United States; **and**

- Evidence that you have either worked for this employer as a personal or domestic servant for at least one year or, evidence that you have at least one year's experience as a personal or domestic servant; **and**

- Evidence establishing that you have a residence abroad which you have no intention of abandoning.

B-1 Nonimmigrant Domestic Servant of a U.S. Citizen--(c)(17)(ii). File your EAD application with:

- Evidence from your employer that he or she is a U.S. Citizen; **and**

- Evidence that your employer has a permanent home abroad or is stationed outside the United States and is temporarily visiting the United States or the citizen's current assignment in the United States will not be longer than four (4) years; **and**

- Evidence that he or she has employed you as a domestic servant abroad for at least six (6) months prior to your admission to the United States.

B-1 Nonimmigrant Employed by a Foreign Airline--(c)(17)(iii). File your EAD application with a letter, from the airline, fully describing your duties and indicating that your position would entitle you to E nonimmigrant status except for the fact that you are not a national of the same country as the airline or because there is no treaty of commerce and navigation in effect between the United States and that country.

APPLICATIONS TO BE FILED AT LOCAL INS OFFICES.

Temporary Protected Status (TPS)--(a)(12). File your EAD application with Form I-821, Application for Temporary Protected Status.

- Initial TPS-based application only, include evidence of identity and nationality as required by the Form I-821 instructions.

- Extension of TPS status, include a copy (front and back) of your last available TPS document: EAD, Form I-94 or approval notice.

- Registration for TPS only without employment authorization, file the Form I-765, Form I-821, and a letter indicating that this form is for registration purposes only. No fee is required for the Form I-765 filed as part of TPS registration. (Form I-821 has separate fee requirements.)

Applying for Temporary Protected Status (TPS)/Temporary Treatment Benefits--(c)(19). *File your EAD application with your TPS application, Form I-821.* If you are using this application to register for TPS and do not want to work in the United States, you must submit a letter indicating this application is for registration purposes only. No fee is required to register.

Granted Withholding of Deportation--(a)(10). File your EAD application with a copy of the Immigration Judge's order. It is not necessary to apply for a new EAD until 90 days before the expiration of your current EAD.

Dependent of A-1 or A-2 Foreign Government Officials--(c)(1). File your EAD application with a Form I-566, Application for Employment by Spouse or Unmarried Dependent Son or Daughter of A-1 or A-2 Official or Employee of Diplomatic or Consular Establishment or G-4 Officer or Employee of International Organization, with the Department of State endorsement.

Dependent of G-1, G-3 or G-4 Nonimmigrant--(c)(4). File your EAD application with a Form I-566, Application for Employment by Spouse or Unmarried Dependent Son or Daughter of A-1 or A-2 Official or Employee of Diplomatic or Consular Establishment or G-4 Officer or Employee of International Organization, with the Department of State endorsement if you are the dependent of a qualifying G-1, G-3 or G-4 officer of, representative to, or employee of an international organization and you hold a valid nonimmigrant status.

Adjustment Applicant--(c)(9). File your EAD application with a copy of the receipt notice or other evidence that your Form I-485, Application for Permanent Residence, is pending. You may file Form I-765 together with your Form I-485.

Applicant for Suspension of Deportation--(c)(10). File your EAD application with evidence that your Form I-256A, Application for Suspension of Deportation, is pending.

Paroled in the Public Interest--(c)(11). File your EAD application if you were paroled into the United States for emergent reasons or reasons strictly in the public interest.

Deportable Alien Granted Voluntary Departure--(c)(12). File your EAD application with a copy of the order or notice granting voluntary departure, and evidence establishing your economic need to work.

Deferred Action--(c)(14). File your EAD application with a copy of the order, notice or document placing you in deferred action and evidence establishing economic necessity for an EAD.

Adjustment Applicant Based on Continuous Residence Since January 1, 1972--(c)(16). File your EAD application with your Form I-485, Application for Permanent Residence; a copy of your receipt notice; or other evidence that the Form I-485 is pending.

Final Order of Deportation--(c)(18). File your EAD application with a copy of the order of supervision and a request for employment authorization which may be based on, but not limited to the following:

- Existence of economic necessity to be employed;

- Existence of a dependent spouse and/or children in the United States who rely on you for support; and

- Anticipated length of time before you can be removed from the United States.

PART 3. REQUIRED DOCUMENTATION WITH EACH APPLICATION.

All applications must be filed with the documents required below, in addition to the evidence required for the category listed in Part 2 ELIGIBILITY CATEGORIES, with fee, if required.

If you are required to show economic necessity for your category (See Part 2), submit a list of your assets, income and expenses.

Please assemble the documents in the following order:

Your application with the filing fee. See Part 4 FEE for details.

If you are mailing your application to the INS, you must also submit:

- Form I-765 Signature Card. If one is not enclosed with your application, ask your local INS office for one. Sign the card in the blue box marked "signature". Your signature must fit within the blue box. DO NOT fold this card when you mail your application.

- A copy of Form I-94 Departure Record (front and back), if available.

- A copy of your last EAD (front and back).

- 2 photos with a white background taken no earlier than 30 days before submission to the INS. They should be unmounted; printed on thin paper; glossy; and unretouched. The photos should show a three-quarter front profile of the right side of your face, with your right ear visible. Your head should be bare unless you are wearing a headdress as required by a religious order to which you belong. The photo should not be larger than $1\frac{1}{2} \times 1\frac{1}{2}$ inches, with the distance from the top of the head to just below the chin about $1\frac{1}{4}$ inches. Lightly print your name and your A#, if known, on the back of each photo with a pencil.

PART 4. FEE.

Applicants must pay a fee of $70 to file this form unless noted below. If a fee is required, it will not be refunded. Pay in the exact amount. Checks and money orders must be payable in U.S. currency. Make check or money order payable to "Immigration and Naturalization Service." If you live in Guam make your check or money order payable to "Treasurer, Guam." If you live in the U.S. Virgin Islands make your check or money order payable to "Commissioner of Finance of the Virgin Islands." There will be an additional charge if your check is not honored.

Please do **not** send cash in the mail.

Initial EAD: If this is your initial application and you are applying under one of the following categories, a filing fee is not required:

- (a)(3) Refugee;
- (a)(4) Paroled as Refugee;
- (a)(5) Asylee;
- (a)(7) N-8 or N-9 nonimmigrant;
- (a)(8) Citizen of Micronesia, Marshall Islands or Palau.
- (a)(10) Granted Withholding of Deportation;
- (a)(11) Deferred Enforced Departure;
- (c)(1) or (c)(4) Dependent of certain foreign government or international organization personnel; or
- (c)(8) Applicant for asylum [an applicant filing under the special ABC procedures must pay the fee].

Renewal EAD: If this is a renewal application and you are applying under one of the following categories, a filing fee is not required:

- (a)(8) Citizen of Micronesia, Marshall Islands, or Palau.
- (a)(10) Granted Withholding of Deportation;
- (a)(11) Deferred Enforced Departure; or
- (c)(1) or (c)(4) Dependent of certain foreign government or international organization personnel.

<u>Replacement EAD</u>: If this is your replacement application and you are applying under one of the following categories, a filing fee is not required:

- (c)(1) or (c)(4) Dependent of certain foreign government or international organization personnel.

You may be eligible for a fee waiver under 8 CFR 103.7(c).

The INS will use The Community Service Administration Income Poverty Guidelines ("Poverty Guidelines") found at 45 CFR 1060.2 as the basic criteria in determining the applicant's eligibility when economic necessity is identified as a factor.

The Poverty Guidelines will be used as a guide, but not as a conclusive standard, in adjudicating fee waiver requests for employment authorization applications requiring a fee.

PART 5. WHERE TO FILE.

If your response to question 16 is:

(a)(3), (a)(4), (a)(5), (a)(7), or (a)(8)

mail your application to:

INS Service Center
P.O. Box 87765
Lincoln, NE 68501-7765

If your response to question 16 is:

(a)(6), (a)(11), (a)(13),
(c)(2), (c)(3)(i), (c)(3)(ii), (c)(3)(iii), (c)(5), (c)(6), (c)(7), (c)(8),
(c)(17)(i), (c)(17)(ii), or (c)(17)(iii)

mail your application based on your address to the appropriate Service Center:

If you live in: Connecticut, Delaware, the District of Columbia, Maine, Maryland, Massachusetts, New Hampshire, New Jersey, New York, Pennsylvania, Puerto Rico, Rhode Island, Vermont, Virginia, West Virginia or the U.S. Virgin Islands, mail your application to:

INS Service Center
P.O. Box 9765
St. Albans, VT 05479-9765

If you live in: Arizona, California, Guam, Hawaii or Nevada, mail your application to:

INS Service Center
P.O. Box 10765
Laguna Niguel, CA 92607-0765

If you live in: Alabama, Arkansas, Florida, Georgia, Kentucky, Louisiana, Mississippi, New Mexico, N. Carolina, Oklahoma, S. Carolina, Tennessee or Texas, mail your application to:

INS Service Center
P.O. Box 152122, Department A
Irving, TX 75015-2122

If you live elsewhere in the U.S., mail your application to:

INS Service Center
P.O. Box 87765
Lincoln, NE 68501-7765

If your response to question 16 is:

(a)(10), (a)(12),
(c)(1), (c)(4), (c)(10), (c)(11), (c)(12), (c)(14), (c)(16), (c)(18), or (c)(19)

apply at the local INS office having jurisdiction over your place of residence.

If your response to question 16 is (c)(9), file your application at the same local INS office or Service Center where you submitted your adjustment application.

If your response to question 16 is (c)(8) under the special ABC filing instructions and you are filing your asylum and EAD applications together, mail your application to the office where you are filing your asylum application.

PART 6. PROCESSING INFORMATION.

Acceptance. An application filed without the required fee, evidence, signature or photographs (if required) will be returned to you as incomplete. You may correct the deficiency and resubmit the application; however, an application is not considered properly filed until the INS accepts it. If your application is complete and filed at an INS Service Center, you will be mailed a Form I-797 receipt notice.

Decision on your application.

- **Approval.** If approved, your EAD will either be mailed to you or you may be required to appear at your local INS office to pick it up.

- **Request for evidence.** If additional information or documentation is required, a written request will be sent to you specifying the information or advising you of an interview.

- **Denial.** If your application cannot be granted, you will receive a written notice explaining the basis of your denial.

No decision

- **Interim EAD.** If you have not received a decision within 90 days of receipt by the INS of a properly filed EAD application or within 30 days of a properly filed initial EAD application based on an asylum application filed on or after January 4, 1995, you may obtain interim work authorization by appearing in person at your local INS district office. You must bring proof of identity and any notices that you have received from the INS in connection with your application for employment authorization.

PART 7. OTHER INFORMATION.

Penalties for Perjury. All statements contained in response to questions in this application are declared to be true and correct under penalty of perjury. Title 18, United States Code, Section 1546, provides in part:

> . . . Whoever knowingly makes under oath, or as permitted under penalty of perjury under 1746 of Title 28, United States Code, knowingly subscribes as true, any false statement with respect to a material fact in any application, affidavit, or other document required by the immigration laws or regulations prescribed thereunder, or knowingly presents any such application, affidavit, or other document containing any such false statement - shall be fined in accordance with this title or imprisoned not more than five years, or both.

The knowing placement of false information on this application may subject you and/or the preparer of this application to criminal penalties under Title 18 of the United States Code. The knowing placement of false information on this application may also subject you and/or the preparer to civil penalties under Section 274C of the Immigration and Nationality Act (INA), 8 U.S.C. 1324c. Under 8 U.S.C. 1324c, a person subject to a final order for civil document fraud is deportable from the United States and may be subject to fines.

Authority for Collecting this Information. The authority to require you to file Form I-765, Application for Employment Authorization, when applying for employment authorization is found at 8 U.S.C. 274A(b)(1)(C)(iii). Information you provide on your Form I-765 is used to determine whether you are eligible for employment authorization and for the preparation of your Employment Authorization Document if you are found eligible. Failure to provide all information as requested may result in the denial or rejection of this application. The information you provide may also be disclosed to other federal, state, local and foreign law enforcement and regulatory agencies during the course of the INS investigations.

Paperwork Reduction Act. The Immigration and Naturalization Service (INS) tries to create forms and instructions which are accurate and easily understood. Often this is difficult because immigration law can be very complex. The public reporting burden for this form is estimated to average three (3) hours and twenty-five (25) minutes per response, including the time for reviewing instructions, gathering and maintaining the data needed, and completing and reviewing the collection of information. The INS welcomes your comments regarding this burden estimate or any other aspect of this form, including suggestions for reducing this burden, to: U.S. Department of Justice, Immigration and Naturalization Service, 425 Eye Street, Room 5307, Washington, D.C. 20536; and to the Office of Management and Budget, Paperwork Reduction Project: OMB No. 1115-0163, Washington, D.C. 20503.

U. S. Department of Justice
Immigration and Naturalization Service

OMB # 1115-0163

Application for Employment Authorization

Do Not Write In This Block

Remarks	Action Stamp	Fee Stamp
A#		

Applicant is filing under 274a.12 _____

☐ Application Approved. Employment Authorized / Extended (Circle One) _____ (Date).

                until _____ (Date).

Subject to the following conditions: _____

☐ Application Denied.

    ☐ Failed to establish eligibility under 8 CFR 274a.12 (a) or (c).

    ☐ Failed to establish economic necessity as required in 8 CFR 274a.12(c) (14), (18) and 8 CFR 214.2(f)

I am applying for:
  ☐ Permission to accept employment
  ☐ Replacement (of lost employment authorization document).
  ☐ Renewal of my permission to accept employment (attach previous employment authorization document).

1. Name (Family Name in CAPS)   (First)   (Middle)

2. Other Names Used (Include Maiden Name)

3. Address in the United States (Number and Street) (Apt. Number)

(Town or City) (State/Country) (ZIP Code)

4. Country of Citizenship/Nationality

5. Place of Birth (Town or City) (State/Province) (Country)

6. Date of Birth (Month/Day/Year) 7. Sex ☐ Male ☐ Female

8. Marital Status ☐ Married ☐ Single ☐ Widowed ☐ Divorced

9. Social Security Number (Include all Numbers you have ever used)

10. Alien Registration Number (A-Number) or I-94 Number (if any)

11. Have you ever before applied for employment authorization from INS?
  ☐ Yes (If yes, complete below) ☐ No

Which INS Office? Date(s)

Results (Granted or Denied - attach all documentation)

12. Date of Last Entry into the U.S. (Month/Day/Year)

13. Place of Last Entry into the U.S.

14. Manner of Last Entry (Visitor, Student, etc.)

15. Current Immigration Status (Visitor, Student, etc.)

16. Go to Part 2 of the instructions, Eligibility Categories. In the space below, place the letter and number of the category you selected from the instructions (For example, (a)(8), (c)(17)(iii), etc.).

Eligibility under 8 CFR 274a.12

(   ) (   ) (   )

Certification

Your Certification: I certify, under penalty of perjury under the laws of the United States of America, that the foregoing is true and correct. Furthermore, I authorize the release of any information which the Immigration and Naturalization Service needs to determine eligibility for the benefit I am seeking. I have read the Instructions in Part 2 and have identified the appropriate eligibility category in Block 16.

Signature   Telephone Number   Date

Signature of Person Preparing Form if Other Than Above: I declare that this document was prepared by me at the request of the applicant and is based on all information of which I have any knowledge.

Print Name   Address   Signature   Date

Initial Receipt	Resubmitted	Relocated		Completed		
		Rec'd	Sent	Approved	Denied	Returned

Form I-765 (Rev. 04-25-95) N Page 7

226

Appendix C
Form I-129

General Filing Instructions.

Complete the basic form and relating supplement. Indicate the specific classification you are requesting. Please answer all questions by typing or clearly printing in black ink. Indicate that an item is not applicable with "N/A". If the answer is "none," write "none". If you need extra space to answer any item, attach a sheet of paper with your name and your alien registration number (A#), if any, and indicate the number of the item to which the answer refers. You must file your petition with the required Initial Evidence. The petition must be properly signed and filed with the proper fee. Submit the petition in duplicate if you check block "a" or "b" in question 4 of Part 2 on the form.

Classification; Initial Evidence.

These instructions are divided into two parts. The first looks at classifications which require a petition for an initial visa or entry and for any extension or change of status. The second looks at those classifications which only require a petition for a change of status or extension of stay.

▶ **Petition always required:** The following classifications always require a petition. A petition for new or concurrent employment or for extension where there is a change in previously approved employment must be filed with the initial evidence listed below, and with the initial evidence required by the separate instructions for a change of status or extension of stay. However, a petition for an extension based on unchanged, previously approved employment need only be filed with the initial evidence required in the separate extension of stay instructions.

H-1A. An H-1A is an alien coming to perform services as a registered professional nurse. The petition must be filed by a U.S. employer that provides health care services (including nursing contractors), and must be filed with:
- evidence the alien has a full and unrestricted license to practice professional nursing in the country where he or she obtained nursing education, or that the nursing education was received in the U.S. or Canada;
- evidence the alien has either;
  - passed the test given by the Commission on Graduate of Foreign Nursing Schools (CGFNS),

- a permanent license to practice professional nursing in the state of intended employment, or
- a permanent license to practice professional nursing in any state or territory of the U.S. and has temporary authorization to practice professional nursing in the state of intended employment;
- evidence the alien is fully qualified and eligible under the laws of the state or territory of intended employment to work as a professional nurse immediately after entry;
- a statement indicating you intend to employ the alien solely as a registered professional nurse; and
- a copy of the Department of Labor's current notice of acceptance of the filing of your attestation on Form ETA 9029.

H-1B. An H-1B is an alien coming temporarily to perform services in a specialty occupation. A specialty occupation is one which requires the theoretical and practical application of a body of highly specialized knowledge to fully perform the occupation and requires completion of a specific course of education culminating in a baccalaureate degree in a specific occupational specialty. Write H-1B1 in the classification requested block. The petition must be filed by the U.S. employer, and must be filed with:
- an approved labor condition application from the Department of Labor;
- evidence the proposed employment qualifies as within a specialty occupation;
- evidence the alien has the required degree by submitting either:
  - a copy of the person's U.S. baccalaureate or higher degree which is required by the specialty occupation,
  - a copy of a foreign degree and evidence it is equivalent to the U.S. degree, or
  - evidence of education and experience which is equivalent to the required U.S. degree;
- a copy of any required license or other official permission to practice the occupation in the state of intended employment; and
- a copy of any written contract between you and the alien or a summary of the terms of the oral agreement under which the alien will be employed.

H1-B. An H-1B is also an alien coming to perform services of an exceptional nature relating to a cooperative research and development project administered by the Department of Defense. A U.S. employer may file the petition. Write **H-1B2** in the classification requested block. It must be filed with:

- a description of the proposed employment and evidence the services and project meet the above conditions; and
- a statement listing the names of all aliens who are not permanent residents who are have been employed on the project within the past year, along with their dates of employment.

H-1B. An H-1B is also an artist, entertainer or fashion model who has national or international acclaim and recognition for achievements, individually or, in the case of entertainers, as part of a group, to be employed in a capacity requiring someone of distinguished merit and ability. (See the separate instructions for accompanying personnel.) A U.S. employer or foreign employer may file the petition. Write **H-1B3** in the classification requested block. It must be filed with:

- copies of evidence the alien or group is nationally or internationally recognized in the discipline by submitting at least 3 different types of documentation showing that the group:
  - has performed and will perform as a starring or leading entertainment group in productions or events which have a distinguished reputation as evidenced by critical reviews, advertisements, publicity releases, publications, or contracts,
  - has achieved national or international recognition and acclaim for outstanding achievement in their field as evidenced by reviews in major newspapers, trade journals, magazines, or other published material,
  - has received significant national or international awards or prizes for outstanding achievement in their field,
  - has performed and will perform services as a leading or starring group for organizations and establishments that have a distinguished reputation,

- has a record of major commercial or critically acclaimed successes, as evidenced by such indicators as ratings, or standing in the field, box office receipts, record, cassette, or video sales, and other achievements in the field as reported in trade journals, major newspapers, or other publications,
- has received significant recognition for achievements from organizations, critics, government agencies or other recognized experts in the field,
- has received significant recognition for achievements from organizations, critics, government agencies or other recognized experts in the field,
- commands a high salary or other substantial remuneration for services, evidenced by contracts or other reliable evidence;
- copies of evidence the services to be performed require a person of distinguished merit and ability and either:
  - involve an event, production or activity which has a distinguished reputation; or
  - the services are as a lead or starring participant in a distinguished activity for an organization or establishment that has a distinguished reputation or record of employing persons of distinguished merit and ability.

H-1B. An H-1B is also an alien coming temporarily to perform as an artist or entertainer, individually or as part of a group, in a unique or traditional art form. (See the separate instructions for accompanying personnel.) A U.S. employer or foreign employer may file the petiion. Write **H-1B4** in the classification requested block. It must be filed with:

- a description of the proposed activities and evidence they constitute a unique or traditional art form;
- affidavits, testimonials or letters from recognized experts attesting to the authenticity and excellence of the skills of the alien or group in presenting the unique or traditional art form and explaining the level of recognition accorded the alien or group in the native country and the U.S.;

- copies of evidence most of the performances or presentations will be culturally unique events sponsored by educational, cultural, or governmental agencies; and
- either:
  - an affidavit or testimonial from the ministry of culture, USIA Cultural Affairs Officer, the academy for the artistic discipline, a leading scholar, a cultural institution, or a major university in the alien's own country or from a third country,
  - a letter from a U.S. expert who has knowledge in the particular field, such as scholar, arts, administrator, critic, or representative of a cultural organization or government agency, or
  - a letter or certification from a U.S. government cultural or arts agency such as the Smithsonian Institution, the National Endowment for the Arts, the National Endowment for the Humanities, or the Library of Congress.

H-1B. An H-1B is also an alien coming temporarily to perform at a specific athletic competition as an athlete, individually or as part of a group or team, at a nationally or internationally recognized level of performance. (See the separate instructions for accompanying personnel.) A U.S. employer or foreign employer may file the petition. Write H-1B5 in the classification requested block. The petition must be filed with:
- a copy of the contract with a major U.S. sports league or team or contract in an individual sport commensurate with national or international recognition in that sport.
- copies of evidence of at least 2 of the following:
  - participation to a substantial extent in a prior season with a major U.S. sports league,
  - participation in international competition with a national team,
  - participation to a substantial extent in a prior season for a U.S. college or university in intercollegiate competition,
  - a written statement from an official of a major U.S. sports league or an official of the governing body of the sport detailing how the alien or team is nationally or internationally recognized,

- a written statement from a member of the sports media or a recognized expert in the sport detailing how the alien or team is nationally or internationally recognized,
- the individual or team is ranked if the sport has national or international rankings, or
- the alien or team has received a significant honor or award in the sport.

H-1B Accompanying Support Personnel. Accompanying support personnel are highly skilled aliens coming temporarily as an essential and integral part of the competition or performance of a H-1B artist, entertainer or athlete because they perform support services which cannot be readily performed by a U.S. worker and which are essential to the successful performance or services by the H-1B. The aliens must each also have significant prior work experience with the H-1B alien. Write *H-1BS* in the classification requested block on the petition. The petition must be filed in conjunction with the employment of a H-1B alien. The petition must be filed with:
- a statement describing the alien's prior and current essentiality, critical skills and experience with the H-1B;
- statements or affidavits from persons with first hand knowledge that the alien has had substantial experience performing the critical skills and essential support services for the H-1B; and
- a copy of any written contract between you and the alien or a summary of the terms of the oral agreement under which the alien will be employed.

H-2A. An H-2A is an alien coming temporarily to engage in temporary or seasonal agricultural employment. The petition must be filed by a U.S. employer or an association of U.S. agricultural producers named as a joint employer on the certification. The petition must be filed with:
- a single valid temporary agricultural labor certification, or, if U.S. workers do not appear at the worksite, a copy of the Department of Labor's denial of a certification and appeal, and evidence that qualified domestic labor is unavailable; and
- copies of evidence that each named alien met the minimum job requirements stated in the certification when it was applied for.

H-2B. An H-2B is an alien coming temporarily to engage in non-agricultural employment which is seasonal, intermittent, to meet a peak load need, or for a one-time occurrence. The petition must be filed by a U.S. employer with:
- either:
  - a temporary labor certification from the Department of Labor, or the Governor of Guam if the proposed employment is solely in Guam, indicating that qualified U.S. workers are not available and that employment of the alien will not adversely affect the wages and working conditions of similarly employed U.S. workers, or
  - a notice from such authority that such certification cannot be made, along with evidence of the unavailability of U.S. workers and of the prevailing wage rate for the occupation in the U.S., and evidence overcoming each reason why the certification was not granted; and
- copies of evidence, such as employment letters and training certificates, that each named alien met the minimum job requirements stated in the certification when it was applied for.

H-3. An H-3 is an alien coming temporarily to participate in a special education training program in the education of children with physical, mental, or emotional disabilities. Custodial care of children must be incidental to the training program. The petition must be filed by the U.S. employer with:
- a description of the training, staff and facilities, evidence the program meets the above conditions, and details of the alien's participation in the program; and
- evidence the alien is nearing completion of a baccalaureate degree in special education, or already holds such a degree, or has extensive prior training and experience in teaching children with physical, mental, or emotional disabilities.

H-3. An H-3 is also an alien coming temporarily to receive other training from an employer in any field other than graduate education or training. The petition must be filed by the U.S. employer with:

- a detailed description of the structured training program, including the number of classroom hours per week and the number of hours of on-the-job training per week;
- a summary of the prior training and experience of each alien in the petition; and
- an explanation of why the training is required, whether similar training is available in the alien's country, how the training will benefit the alien in pursuing a career abroad, and why you will incur the cost of providing the training without significant productive labor.

L-1. An L-1 is an alien coming temporarily to perform services in a managerial or executive capacity, for the same corporation or firm, or for the branch, subsidiary or affiliate of the employer which employed him or her abroad for one continuous year within the three-year period immediately preceding the filing of the petition, in an executive, managerial or specialized knowledge capacity. Write **L-1A** in the classification requested block on the petition.

L-1. An L-1 is also an alien coming temporarily to perform services which entail specialized knowledge, for the same corporation or firm, or for the branch, subsidiary or affiliate of the employer which employed him or her abroad for one continuous year within the three year period immediately preceding the filing of the petition, in an executive, managerial or specialized knowledge capacity. Specialized knowledge is special knowledge of the employer's product or its application in international markets or an advanced level of the knowledge of the employer's processes and procedures. Write **L-1B** in the classification requested block on the petition.

L Petition Requirements. A U.S. employer or foreign employer may file the petition, but a foreign employer must have a legal business entity in the U.S. The petition must be filed with:
- evidence of the qualifying relationship between the U.S. and foreign employer based on ownership and control, such as an annual report, articles of incorporation, financial statements or copies of stock certificates;

- a letter from the alien's foreign qualifying employer detailing his/her dates of employment, job duties, qualifications and salary, demonstrating that the alien worked for the employer for at least one continuous year in the three-year period preceding the filing of the petition in an executive, managerial or specialized knowledge capacity; and
- a description of the proposed job duties and qualifications and evidence the proposed employment is in an executive, managerial or specialized knowledge capacity.

If the alien is coming to the U.S. to open a new office, also file the petition with copies of evidence the business entity in the U.S.:
- already has sufficient premises to house the new office;
- has or upon establishment will have the qualifying relationship to the foreign employer;
- has the financial ability to remunerate the alien and to begin doing business in the U.S., including evidence about the size of the U.S. investment, the organizational structure of both firms, the financial size and condition of the foreign employer, and, if the alien is coming as an L-1 manager or executive to open a new office, such evidence must establish that the intended U.S. operation will support the executive or managerial position within one year.

Blanket L petition. An L blanket petition simplifies the process of later filing for individual L-1A workers and L-1B workers who are specialized knowledge professionals, which are persons who possess specialized knowledge employed in positions which require the theoretical and practical application of a body of highly specialized knowledge to fully perform the occupation and require completion of a specific course of education culminating in a baccalaureate degree in a specific occupational specialty.

A blanket L petition must be filed by a U.S. employer who will be the single representative between INS and the qualifying organizations. Write **LZ** in the classification requested block. Do not name an individual employee. File the petition with copies of evidence that:

- you and your branches, subsidiaries and affiliates are engaged in commercial trade or services;
- you have an office in the U.S. that has been doing business for one year or more;
- you have 3 or more domestic and foreign branches, subsidiaries, or affiliates;
- you and your qualifying organizations have obtained approved petitions for at least 10 "L" managers, executives or specialized knowledge professionals during the previous 12 months, have U.S. subsidiaries or affiliates with combined annual sales of at least 25 million dollars, or have a U.S. work force of at least 1,000 employees.

After approval of a blanket petition, you may file for individual employees to enter as an L-1A alien or L-1B specialized knowledge professional under the blanket petition. If the alien is outside the U.S., file Form I-129S. If the alien is already in the U.S., file the I-129 to request a change of status based on this blanket petition. The petition must be filed with:
- a copy of the approval notice for the blanket petition;
- a letter from the alien's foreign qualifying employer detailing his/her dates of employment, job duties, qualifications, and salary for the 3 previous years; and
- if the alien is a specialized knowledge professional, a copy of a U.S. degree, a foreign degree equivalent to a U.S. degree, or evidence establishing the combination of the beneficiary's education and experience is the equivalent of a U.S. degree.

O-1. An O-1 is an alien coming temporarily who has extraordinary ability in the sciences, education or business. A U.S. employer or foreign employer may file the petition. The petition must be filed with:
- a written consultation with a peer group in the alien's area of ability (see GENERAL EVIDENCE);
- a copy of any written contract between you and the alien or a summary of the terms of the oral agreement under which the alien will be employed.
- copies of evidence the services to be performed either:

- primarily involve a specific scientific or educational project, conference, convention, lecture, or exhibit sponsored by scientific or educational organizations or establishments, or
- consist of a specific business project that requires an extraordinary executive, manager, or highly technical person due to the complexity of the project;
- evidence the alien has received a major, internationally-recognized award, such as a Nobel Prize, or copies of evidence of at least three of the following:
  - receipt of nationally or internationally recognized prizes or awards for excellence in the field of endeavor,
  - membership in associations in the field which require outstanding achievements as judged by recognized international experts,
  - published material in professional or major trade publications or newspapers about the alien and his work in the field,
  - participation on a panel or individually as a judge of the work of others in the field or an allied field,
  - original scientific or scholarly research contributions of major significance in the field,
  - authorship of scholarly articles in the field in professional journals or other major media, or
  - evidence the alien commands a high salary or other high remuneration for services.

P-2. A P-2 is an alien coming temporarily to perform as an artist or entertainer, individually or as part of a group, under a reciprocal exchange program between an organization in the U.S. and an organization in another country. (See the separate instructions for accompanying personnel.) The petition must be filed by the sponsoring organization or employer in the U.S. It must be filed with:
- written consultation with an appropriate labor organization (see GENERAL EVIDENCE);

- a copy of the formal reciprocal exchange agreement between the U.S. organization(s) sponsoring the aliens, and the organization(s) in a foreign country which will receive the U.S. artist or entertainers;
- a statement from the sponsoring organization describing the reciprocal exchange, including the name of the receiving organization abroad, names and occupations of U.S. artists or entertainers being sent abroad, length of their stay, activities in which they will be engaged and the terms and conditions of their employment; and
- copies of evidence the aliens and the U.S. artists or entertainers are experienced artists with comparable skills and that the terms and conditions of employment are similar.

P-2 Accompanying Support Personnel. Accompanying support personnel are highly skilled aliens coming temporarily as an essential and integral part of the competition or performance of a P-2, or because they perform support services which cannot be readily performed by a U.S. worker and which are essential to the successful performance or services by the P-2. The aliens must each also have significant prior work experience with the P-2 alien. Write *P-2S* in the classification requested block on the petition. The petition must be filed in conjunction with the employment of a P-2 alien. The petition must be filed with:
- written consultation with a labor organization in the skill in which the alien will be involved (see GENERAL EVIDENCE);
- a statement describing the alien's prior and current essentiality, critical skills and experience with the P-2;
- statements or affidavits from persons with first hand knowledge that the alien has had substantial experience performing the critical skills and essential support services for the P-2, and
- a copy of any written contract between you and the alien or a summary of the terms of the oral agreement under which the alien will be employed.

Q. A Q is an alien coming temporarily to participate in an international cultural exchange program approved by the Attorney General for the sharing of the attitude, customs, history, heritage, philosophy, and/or traditions of the alien's country of nationality. The culture sharing must take place in a school, museum, business, or other establishment where the public is exposed to aspects of a foreign culture as part of a structured program. The work component of the program may not be independent of the cultural component, but must serve as the vehicle to achieve the objectives of the cultural component. A U.S. employer or foreign employer may file the petition; however, a foreign employer's petition must be signed by a U.S. citizen or permanent resident employed by the qualified employer on a permanent basis in an executive, managerial, or supervisory capacity for the prior year. File the petition with:

- evidence you:
  - maintain an established international cultural exchange program;
  - have designated a qualified employee to administer the program and serve as liaison with INS;
  - have been doing business in the U.S. for the past two years;
  - will offer the alien wages and working conditions comparable to those accorded local domestic workers similarly employed;
  - employ at least 5 full)time U.S. citizen or permanent resident workers
  - have the financial ability to remunerate the participant(s), as shown by your most recent annual report, business income tax return, or other form of certified accountant's report;
- catalogs, brochures or other types of material which illustrate that:
  - the cultural component is designed to give a overview of the attitude, customs, history, heritage, philosophy, tradition, and/or other cultural attributes of the participant's home country;
  - the employment or training takes place in a public setting where the sharing of the culture of their country of nationality can be achieved through direct interaction with the American public; and

- the American public will derive an obvious cultural benefit from the program.

However, if the proposed dates of employment are within 15 months of the approval of a prior "Q" petition filed by you for the same international cultural exchange program, and that earlier petition was filed with the above evidence of the program, you may submit a copy of the approval notice for that prior petition in lieu of the evidence about the program required above.

▶ **Petition only required for alien in the U.S. to change status or extend stay:** The following classifications do not require a petition for new employment if the alien is outside the U.S. The alien should instead contact a U.S. Consulate for information about a visa or admission. Use this form to petition for a change of status, concurrent employment, or an extension of stay.

A petition for change of status to one of the classifications described in this part must be filed with the initial evidence listed below and with the initial evidence required by the separate instructions for all petitions involving change of status. A petition for an extension of stay must be filed with the initial evidence listed below and with the initial evidence required by the separate instructions for all petitions for extension. However, a petition for an extension based on unchanged, previously approved employment need only be filed with the the initial evidence required by the separate extension of stay instructions.

E-1. An E-1 is a national of a country with which the U.S. has a treaty of friendship, commerce, and navigation who is coming to the U.S. to engage in substantial trade between the U.S. and the alien's country of nationality. Substantial trade means that your trading activities with the U.S. comprise more than 50% of your total volume of business transactions in the U.S. and that there is a continued course of international trade.

E-2. An E-2 is a national of a country with which the U.S. has a bilateral investment treaty or agreement, who is coming to the U.S. to direct and develop the operations of an enterprise in which he/she has invested or is in the process of investing substantially. A substantial investment is one in which personal funds or assets are put at risk in a real operating enterprise which generates services or goods. You must show that you are able to direct and develop the enterprise by having control over the business. You must also show that the investment is not your main source of income or that the proceeds from the investment are significantly greater than a subsistence income.

An **E-1** or **E-2** may also be an employee of a qualified treaty alien or treaty company. If so, the alien must be an executive or manager, an individual with specialized qualifications that are essential to the efficient operation of the employer's business enterprise, a highly trained technician, or start-up personnel (E-2 only).

E Petition requirements. A principal treaty trader or investor or the qualified employer may file the petition. It must be filed with copies of evidence of:
- ownership and nationality, including lists of investors with current status and nationality, stock certificates, certificates of ownership issued by the commercial section of a foreign embassy, and reports from a certified professional accountant (CPA);
- substantial trade if filing for an E-1, including copies of three or more of the following: bills of lading, customs receipts, letters of credit, insurance papers documenting commodities imported, purchase orders, carrier inventories, trade brochures, sales contracts.
- substantial investment if filing for an E-2, including copies of partnership agreements (with a statement on proportionate ownership), articles of incorporation, payments for the rental of business premises or office equipment, business licenses, stock certificates, office inventories (goods and equipment purchased for the business), insurance appraisals, advertising invoices, annual reports, net worth statements from certified professional accountants, business bank accounts containing funds for routine operations, funds held in escrow;

- if filing for an employee, evidence he/she is a manager or executive, or evidence of special knowledge, skills, training, or education, such as certificates, diplomas or transcripts, letters from employers describing job titles, duties, and the level of education and knowledge required, operators' manuals, and for non-executive/managerial employees, evidence that qualified U.S. workers are not available.

R-1. An R-1 is an alien who, for at least 2 years, has been a member of a religious denomination having a bona fide nonprofit, religious organization in the U.S., coming temporarily to work solely:
- as a minister of that denomination,
- in a professional capacity in a religious vocation or occupation for that organization, or
- in a religious vocation or occupation for the organization or its nonprofit affiliate.

The petition must be filed by a U.S. employer with:
- a letter from the authorizing official of the religious organization establishing that the proposed services and alien qualify above;
- a letter or letters from the authorizing officials of the religious denomination or organization attesting to the alien's membership in the religious denomination explaining, in detail, the person's religious work and all employment during the past 2 years and the proposed employment; and
- a copy of the tax-exempt certificate showing the religious organization, and any affiliate which will employ the person, is a bona fide nonprofit, religious organization in the U.S. and is exempt from taxation in accordance with section 501(c)(3) of the Internal Revenue Code of 1986;

TC. A TC is a Canadian citizen coming to the U.S. temporarily under the provisions of the United States-Canada Free-Trade Agreement. A U.S. employer or a foreign employer may file the petition. File the petition with:
- a letter stating the activity to be engaged in, the purpose of entry, the anticipated length of stay, and the arrangements for remuneration; and
- evidence the alien meets the educational and/or licensing requirements for the profession or occupation.

Change of status.

In addition to the initial evidence for the classification you are requesting, a petition requesting a change of status for an alien in the U.S. must be filed with a copy of the Form I-94, Nonimmigrant Arrival/Departure Record, of the employee(s). [Family members should use Form I-539 to apply for a change of status.] A nonimmigrant who must have a passport to be admitted must keep that passport valid during his/her entire stay. If a required passport is not valid, file a full explanation with your petition.

The following are **not eligible** to change status:
- an alien admitted under a visa waiver program;
- an alien in transit (C) or in transit without a visa (TWOV);
- a crewman (D);
- a fiance(e) or his/her dependent (K);
- a J-1 exchange visitor whose status was for the purpose of receiving graduate medical training;
- a J-1 exchange visitor subject to the foreign residence requirement who has not received a waiver of that requirement;
- an M-1 student to an H classification if training received as an M-1 helped him/her qualify for H classification.

Extension of stay.

A petition requesting an extension of stay for an employee in the U.S. must be filed with a copy of the Form I-94, Nonimmigrant Arrival/Departure Record, of the employee(s), and a letter from the petitioner explaining the reasons for the extension. [Family members should use Form I-539 to file for an extension of stay.] A nonimmigrant who must have a passport to be admitted must keep that passport valid during his/her entire stay. If a required passport is not valid, file a full explanation with your petition. Where there has been a change in the circumstances of employment, also submit the evidence required for a new petition.

Where there has been no change in the circumstances of employment, file your petition with the appropriate supplement and with your letter describing the continuing employment, and:

- if for H-1A status, submit a current copy of the Department of Labor's notice of acceptance of the petitioner's attestation.
- if for H-1B status, submit an approved labor condition application for the specialty occupation valid for the period of time requested.
- if for H-2B status, submit a labor certification valid for the dates of the extension.
- if for H-2A status, submit a labor certification valid for the dates of the extension unless it is based on a continuation of employment authorized by the approval of a previous petition filed with a certification and the extension will last no longer than the previously authorized employment and no longer than 2 weeks.

General Evidence.

Written consultation. Noted classifications require a written consultation with a recognized peer group, union, and/or management organization regarding the nature of the work to be done and the alien's qualifications before the petition may be approved. To obtain timely adjudication of a petition, you should obtain a written advisory opinion from an appropriate peer group, union, and/or management organization and submit it with the petition.

If you file a petition without the advisory opinion, it is advisable for you to send a copy of the petition and all supporting documents to the appropriate organization when you file the petition with INS, and indicate in the petition which organization you sent it to. Explain to the organization that they will be contacted by INS for an advisory opinion. If an accepted organization does not issue an advisory opinion within a given time period, a decision will be made based upon the evidence of record. If you do not know the name of an appropriate organization with which to consult, please indicate so on the petition. However, it will require a substantially longer period to process a petition filed without the actual advisory opinion.

Translations. Any foreign language document must be accompanied by a full English translation which the translator has certified as complete and correct, and by the translator's certification that he or she is competent to translate from the foreign language into English.

Copies. If these instructions state that a copy of a document may be filed with this petition, and you choose to send us the original, we may keep that original for our records.

H-1B and H-2B Notice.

The Immigration and Nationality Act makes a petitioner liable for the reasonable cost of return transportation for an H-1B or H-2B alien who is dismissed before the end of the authorized employment.

When To File.

File your petition as soon as possible, but no more than 4 months before the proposed employment will begin or the extension of stay is required. If you do not submit your petition at least 45 days before the employment will begin, petition processing, and subsequent visa issuance, may not be completed before the alien's services are required or previous employment authorization ends.

Where to File.

Mail this petition to the appropriate INS Service Center, except that:
- if the person is applying for admission as an L-1 under the U.S.-Canada Free Trade Agreement, the petition may be filed at the port of entry when the person applies for entry;
- if the services or training will be solely in Guam or the Virgin Islands, file the petition at the local INS office there.

In any other instance, mail this petition to the Service Center indicated below. If the services or training will be in more than one place, mail the petition to the Service Center with jurisdiction over the first work or training site. A blanket L petition should be mailed to the Service center with jurisdiction over the petitioner's location.

If the work or training will be in:
Alabama, Connecticut, Delaware, District of Columbia, Florida, Georgia, Maine, Maryland, Massachusetts, New Hampshire, New Jersey, New York, North Carolina, Pennsylvania, Puerto Rico, Rhode Island, South Carolina, Vermont, Virginia, or West Virginia; mail your petition to USINS, Eastern Service Center, 75 Lower Welden Street, St. Albans, VT 05479-0001.

If the work or training will be in:
Arizona, California, Hawaii, or Nevada; mail your petition to USINS, Western Service Center, P.O. Box 30040, Laguna Niguel, CA 92607-0040.

If the work or training will be elsewhere in the United States; mail your petition to USINS Northern Service Center, 100 Centennial Mall North, Room, B-26, Lincoln, NE 68508.

Fee.

The fee for this petition is a base fee of $70.00 + either:
- $10 per worker if you are requesting consulate or POE notification for visa issuance or admission [block (a) in Part 2, Question 4]; or
- $80 per worker if requesting a change of status [block (b) in Part 2, Question 4]; or
- $50 per worker if requesting an extension of stay [block (c) in Part 2, Question 4].

The fee must be submitted in the exact amount. It cannot be refunded. DO NOT MAIL CASH. All checks and money orders must be drawn on a bank or other institution located in the United States and must be payable in United States currency. The check or money order should be made payable to the Immigration and Naturalization Service, except that:
- If you live in Guam, and are filing this application in Guam, make your check or money order payable to the "Treasurer, Guam."
- If you live in the Virgin Islands, and are filing this application in the Virgin Islands, make your check or money order payable to the "Commissioner of Finance of the Virgin Islands."

Checks are accepted subject to collection. An uncollected check will render the application and any document issued invalid. A charge of $5.00 will be imposed if a check in payment of a fee is not honored by the bank on which it is drawn.

Processing Information.

Acceptance. Any petition that is not signed, or is not accompanied by the correct fee, will be rejected with a notice that the petition is deficient. You may correct the deficiency and resubmit the petition. A petition is not considered properly filed until accepted by the Service.

Initial processing. Once a petition has been accepted, it will be checked for completeness, including submission of the required initial evidence. If you do not completely fill out the form, or file if without required initial evidence, you will not establish a basis for eligibility, and we may deny your petition.

Requests for more information or interview. We may request more information or evidence, or we may request that you appear at an INS office for an interview. We may also request that you submit the originals of any copy. We will return these originals when they are no longer required.

Decision. The decision on a petition involves separate determinations of whether you have established that the alien is eligible for the requested classification based on the proposed employment, and whether he or she is eligible for any requested change of status or extension of stay. You will be notified of the decision in writing.

Penalties.

If you knowingly and willfully falsify or conceal a material fact or submit a false document with this request, we will deny the benefit you are filing for, and may deny any other immigration benefit. In addition, you will face severe penalties provided by law, and may be subject to criminal prosecution.

Privacy Act Notice.

We ask for the information on this form, and associated evidence, to determine if you have established eligibility for the immigration benefit you are filing for. Our legal right to ask for this information is in 8 USC 1154, 1184 and 1258. We may provide this information to other government agencies. Failure to provide this information, and any requested evidence, may delay a final decision or result in denial of your request.

Paperwork Reduction Act Notice.

We try to create forms and instructions that are accurate, can be easily understood, and which impose the least possible burden on you to provide us with information. Often this is difficult because some immigration laws are very complex. The estimated average time to complete and file this application is as follows: (1) 30 minutes to learn about the law and form; (2) 25 minutes to complete the form; and (3) 60 minutes to assemble and file the petition; for a total estimated average of 115 minutes per petition. If you have comments regarding the accuracy of this estimate, or suggestions for making this form simpler, you can write to both the Immigration and Naturalization Service, 425 I Street, N.W., Room 5304, Washington, D.C. 20536; and the Office of Management and Budget, Paperwork Reduction Project, OMB No. 1115-0168, Washington, D.C. 20503.

Purpose Of This Form.

This form is for an employer to petition for an alien to come to the U.S. temporarily to perform services or labor, or to receive training, as an H-1A, H-1B, H-2A, H-2B, H-3, L-1, O-1, P-2, or Q nonimmigrant worker.

This form is also for an employer to petition for an extension of stay or change of status for an alien as an E-1, E-2, R-1 or TC nonimmigrant. A petition is not required to apply for an E-1, E-2 or R-1 nonimmigrant visa or admission as a TC nonimmigrant. A petition is only required to apply for a change to such status or an extension of stay in such status.

This form consists of a basic petition, and different supplements that apply to each specific classification.

Who May File.

General. A U.S. employer may file to classify an alien in any nonimmigrant classification listed below. A foreign employer may file for certain classifications as indicated in the specific instructions.

Agents. A U.S. individual or company in business as an agent may file for types of workers who are traditionally self-employed or who traditionally use an agent to arrange short-term employment with numerous employers. A petition filed by an agent must include a complete itinerary of services or engagements, including dates, names and addresses of the actual employers, and the locations where the services will be performed. The agent must guarantee the wage offered and the other terms and conditions of employment by contract with the alien(s).

Including more than one alien in a petition. Aliens who will apply for their visas at the same consulate or, if they do not need visas, will enter at the same port of entry may be included in one petition filed by an employer or agent in the following classifications if the dates of employment are the same:
- H-1B if they are members of the same entertainment group or athletic team (accompanying aliens must be filed for on a separate petition);

- H-1B accompanying aliens if they will accompany the same H-1B or same H-1B group of artists, entertainers or athletes for the same period of time, in the same occupation, and in the same location(s);
- H2-A if they are included on the same labor certification and will perform the same duties;
- H-2B if they are included on the same labor certification and will perform the same duties;
- H-3 if they will receive the same training;
- P-2 if they are members of the same group (accompanying aliens must be filed for on a separate petition);
- P-2 accompanying aliens if they will accompany the same P-2 alien or group for the same period of time, in the same occupation, and in the same location(s);
- Q if they will be involved in the same international cultural exchange program.

Multiple locations. A petition for alien(s) to perform services or labor or receive training in more than one location must include an itinerary with the dates and locations where the services or training will take place.

Unnamed aliens. All aliens in a petition for an extension of stay or change of status must be named in the petition. All aliens included in any other petition must be named except:
- an H-2A petition for more than one worker may include unnamed aliens if they are unnamed on the labor certification;
- an H-2B petition for more than one worker may include unnamed aliens in emergent situations where you establish in the petition that you cannot yet provide names due to circumstances which you could not anticipate or control.

Where some or all of the aliens are not named, specify the total number of unnamed aliens and total number of aliens in the petition. Where the aliens must be named, petitions naming subsequent beneficiaries may be filed later with a copy of the same labor certification. Each petition must reference all previously filed petitions using that certification.

Appendix D
Form I-20 A-B

U.S. Department of Justice
Immigration and Naturalization Service
Please Read Instructions on Page 2

Certificate of Eligibility for Nonimmigrant (F-1) Student Status - For Academic and Language Students

OMB No. 1115-0051

Page 1

This page must be completed and signed in the U.S. by a designated school official.

1. Family Name (surname)

   First (given) name (do not enter middle name)

Country of birth	Date of birth (mo./day/year)

Country of citizenship	Admission number (Complete if known)

2. School (school district) name

   School official to be notified of student's arrival in U.S. (Name and Title)

   School address (include zip code)

   School code (including 3-digit suffix, if any) and approval date
   _____ 214F _____ approved on _____

For Immigration Official Use

Visa issuing post	Date Visa issued

Reinstated, extension granted to:

3. This certificate is issued to the student named above for:
   (Check and fill out as appropriate)
   a. ☐ Initial attendance at this school.
   b. ☐ Continued attendance at this school.
   c. ☐ School transfer.
      Transferred from _____
   d. ☐ Use by dependents for entering the United States.
   e. ☐ Other _____

4. Level of education the student is pursuing or will pursue in the United States:
   (check only one)
   a. ☐ Primary   e. ☐ Master's
   b. ☐ Secondary   f. ☐ Doctorate
   c. ☐ Associate   g. ☐ Language training
   d. ☐ Bachelor's   h. ☐ Other

5. The student named above has been accepted for a full course of study at
   this school, majoring in _____
   The student is expected to report to the school not later than (date)
   _____ and complete studies not later than (date) _____
   The normal length of study is _____

6. ☐ English proficiency is required:
   ☐ The student has the required English proficiency.
   ☐ The student is not yet proficient, English instructions will be given at
      the school.
   ☐ English proficiency is not required because _____

7. This school estimates the student's average costs for an academic term of
   _____ (up to 12) months to be:
   a. Tuition and fees $ _____
   b. Living expenses $ _____
   c. Expenses of dependents $ _____
   d. Other (specify): $ _____

   Total $ _____

8. This school has information showing the following as the student's means of
   support, estimated for an academic term of _____ months (Use the same
   number of months given in Item 7).
   a. Student's personal funds $ _____
   b. Funds from this school
      (specify type) $ _____
                                        _____
   c. Funds from another source
      (specify type and source) $ _____
                                        _____
   d. On-campus employment (if any) $ _____

   Total $ _____

9. Remarks: _____
   _____
   _____
   _____
   _____
   _____

10. **School Certification** I certify under penalty of perjury that all information provided above in items 1 through 8 was completed before I signed this form and is true and correct; I executed this form in the United States after review and evaluation in the United States by me or other officials of the school of the student's application, transcripts or other records of courses taken and proof of financial responsibility, which were received at the school prior to the execution of this form; the school has determined that the above named student's qualifications meet all standards for admission to the school; the student will be required to pursue a full course of study as defined by 8 CFR 214.2(f)(6); I am a designated official of the above named school and I am authorized to issue this form.

Signature of designated school official	Name of school official (print or type)	Title	Date issued	Place issued (city and state)

11. **Student Certification** I have read and agreed to comply with the terms and conditions of my admission and those of any extension of stay as specified on page 2. I certify that all information provided on this form refers specifically to me and is true and correct to the best of my knowledge. I certify that I seek to enter or remain in the United States temporarily, and solely for the purpose of pursuing a full course of study at the school named on Page 1 of this form. I also authorize the named school to release any information from my records which is needed by the INS pursuant to 8 CFR 214.3(g) to determine my nonimmigrant status.

Signature of student	Name of student	Date

Signature of parent or guardian if student is under 18	Name of parent/guardian (Print or type)	Address(city)	(State or province)	(Country)	(Date)

Form I-20 A-B/I-20ID (Rev 04-27-88)N

For official use only
Microfilm Index Number

I-20 SCHOOL

242

Authority for collecting the information on this and related student forms is contained in 8 U.S.C. 1101 and 1184. The information solicited will be used by the Department of State and the Immigration and Naturalization Service to determine eligibility for the benefits requested.

INSTRUCTIONS TO DESIGNATED SCHOOL OFFICIALS

1. **The law provides severe penalties for knowingly and willfully falsifying or concealing a material fact, or using any false document in the submission of this form.** Designated school officials should consult regulations pertaining to the issuance of Form I-20 A-B at 8 CFR 214.3 (K) before completing this form. Failure to comply with these regulations may result in the withdrawal of the school approval for attendance by foreign students by the Immigration and Naturalization Service (8 CFR 214.4).

2. **ISSUANCE OF FORM I-20 A-B.** Designated school officials may issue a Form I-20 A-B to a student who fits into one of the following categories, if the student has been accepted for full-time attendance at the institution: a) a prospective F-1 nonimmigrant student; b) an F-1 transfer student; c) an F-1 student advancing to a higher educational level at the same institution; d) an out of status student seeking reinstatement. The form may also be issued to the dependent spouse or child of an F-1 student for securing entry into the United States.

When issuing a Form I-20 A-B, designated school officials should complete the student's admission number whenever possible to ensure proper data entry and record keeping.

3. **ENDORSEMENT OF PAGE 4 FOR REENTRY.** Designated school officials may endorse page 4 of the Form I-20 A-B for reentry if the student and/or the F-2 dependents is to leave the United States temporarily. This should be done only when the information on the Form I-20 remains unchanged. If there have been substantial changes in item 4, 5, 7, or 8, a new Form I-20 A-B should be issued.

4. **REPORTING REQUIREMENT.** Designated school official should always forward the top page of the Form I-20 A-B to the INS data processing center at P.O. Box 140, London, Kentucky 40741 for data entry except when the form is issued to an F-1 student for initial entry or reentry into the United States, or for reinstatement to student status. (Requests for reinstatement should be sent to the Immigration and Naturalization Service district office having jurisdiction over the student's temporary residence in this country.)

The INS data processing center will return this top page to the issuing school for disposal after data entry and microfilming.

5. **CERTIFICATION.** Designated school officials should certify on the bottom part of page 1 of this form that the Form I-20 A-B is completed and issued in accordance with the pertinent regulations. The designated school official should remove the carbon sheet from the completed and signed Form I-20 A-B before forwarding it to the student.

6. **ADMISSION RECORDS.** Since the Immigration and Naturalization Service may request information concerning the student's immigration status for various reasons, designated school officials should retain all evidence which shows the scholastic ability and financial status on which admission was based, until the school has reported the student's termination of studies to the Immigration and Naturalization Service.

INSTRUCTIONS TO STUDENTS

1. **Student Certification.** You should read everything on this page carefully and be sure that you understand the terms and conditions concerning your admission and stay in the United States as a nonimmigrant student before you sign the student certification on the bottom part of page 1. **The law provides severe penalties for knowingly and willfully falsifying or concealing a material fact, or using any false document in the submission of this form.**

2. **ADMISSION.** A nonimmigrant student may be admitted for duration of status. This means that you are authorized to stay in the United States for the entire length of time during which you are enrolled as a full-time student in an educational program and any period of authorized practical training plus sixty days. While in the United States, you must maintain a valid foreign passport unless you are exempt from passport requirements.

You may continue from one educational level to another, such as progressing from high school to a bachelor's program or a bachelor's program to a master's program, etc., simply by invoking the procedures for school transfers

3. **SCHOOL.** For initial admission, you must attend the school specified on your visa. If you have a Form I-20 A-B from more than one school, it is important to have the name of the school you intend to attend specified on your visa by presenting a Form I-20 A-B from that school to the visa issuing consular officer. Failure to attend the specified school will result in the loss of your student status and subject you to deportation.

4. **REENTRY.** A nonimmigrant student may be readmitted after a temporary absence of five months or less from the United States, if the student is otherwise admissible. You may be readmitted by presenting a valid foreign passport, a valid visa, and either a new Form I-20 A-B or a page 4 of the Form I-20 A-B (the I-20 ID Copy) properly endorsed for reentry if the information on the I-20 form is current.

5. **TRANSFER.** A nonimmigrant student is permitted to transfer to a different school provided the transfer procedure is followed. To transfer school, you should first notify the school you are attending of the intent to transfer, then obtain a Form I-20 A-B from the school you intend to attend. Transfer will be effected only if you return the Form I-20 A-B to the designated school official within 15 days of beginning attendance at the new school. The designated school official will then report the transfer to the Immigration and Naturalization Service.

6. **EXTENSION OF STAY.** If you cannot complete the educational program after having been in student status for longer than the anticipated length of the program plus a grace period in a single educational level, or for more than eight consecutive years, you must apply for extension of stay. An application for extension of stay on a Form I-538 should be filed with the Immigration and Naturalization Service district office having jurisdiction over your school at least 15 days but no more than 60 days before the expiration of your authorized stay.

7. **EMPLOYMENT.** As an F-1 student, you are not permitted to work off-campus or to engage in business without specific employment authorization. After your first year in F-1 student status, you may apply for employment authorization on Form I-538 based on financial needs arising after receiving student status, or the need to obtain practical training.

8. **Notice of Address.** If you move, you must submit a notice within 10 days of the change of address to the Immigration and Naturalization Service. (Form AR-11 is available at any INS office.)

9. **Arrival/Departure.** When you leave the United States, you must surrender your Form I-94 Departure Record. Please see the back side of Form I-94 for detailed instructions. You do not have to turn in the I-94 if you are visiting Canada, Mexico, or adjacent islands other than Cuba for less than 30 days.

10. **Financial Support.** You must demonstrate that you are financially able to support yourself for the entire period of stay in the United States while pursuing a full course of study. You are required to attach documentary evidence of means of support.

11. **Authorization to Release Information by School.** To comply with requests from the United States Immigration & Naturalization Service for information concerning your immigration status, you are required to give authorization to the named school to release such information from your records. The school will provide the Service your name, country of birth, current address, and any other information on a regular basis or upon request.

12. **Penalty.** To maintain your nonimmigrant student status, you must be enrolled as a full-time student at the school you are authorized to attend. You may engage in employment only when you have received permission to work. Failure to comply with these regulations will result in the loss of your student status and subject you to deportation.

IF YOU NEED MORE INFORMATION CONCERNING YOUR F-1 NONIMMIGRANT STUDENT STATUS AND THE RELATING IMMIGRATION PROCEDURES, PLEASE CONTACT EITHER YOUR FOREIGN STUDENT ADVISOR ON CAMPUS OR A NEARBY IMMIGRATION AND NATURALIZATION SERVICE OFFICE.

THIS PAGE, WHEN PROPERLY ENDORSED, MAY BE USED FOR ENTRY OF THE SPOUSE AND CHILDREN OF AN F-1 STUDENT FOLLOWING TO JOIN THE STUDENT IN THE UNITED STATES OR FOR REENTRY OF THE STUDENT TO ATTEND THE SAME SCHOOL AFTER A TEMPORARY ABSENCE FROM THE UNITED STATES.

For reentry of the student and/or the F-2 dependents (EACH CERTIFICATION SIGNATURE IS VALID FOR ONLY ONE YEAR.)

Signature of Designated School Official	Name of School Official (print or type)	Title	Date
Signature of Designated School Official	Name of School Official (print or type)	Title	Date
Signature of Designated School Official	Name of School Official (print or type)	Title	Date
Signature of Designated School Official	Name of School Official (print or type)	Title	Date
Signature of Designated School Official	Name of School Official (print or type)	Title	Date
Signature of Designated School Official	Name of School Official (print or type)	Title	Date

Dependent spouse and children of the F-1 student who are seeking entry/reentry to the U.S.

Name family (caps) first	Date of birth	Country of birth	Relationship to the F-1 student

Student Employment Authorization and other Records

244

Appendix E
Form I-864

INSTRUCTIONS

Purpose of this Form
This form is required to show that an intending immigrant has adequate means of financial support and is not likely to become a public charge.

Sponsor's Obligation
The person completing this affidavit is the sponsor. A sponsor's obligation continues until the sponsored immigrant becomes a U.S. citizen, can be credited with 40 qualifying quarters of work, departs the United States permanently, or dies. Divorce does not terminate the obligation. By executing this form, you, the sponsor, agree to support the intending immigrant and any spouse and/or children immigrating with him or her and to reimburse any government agency or private entity that provides these sponsored immigrants with Federal, State, or local means-tested public benefits.

General Filing Instructions
Please answer all questions by typing or clearly printing in black ink only. Indicate that an item is not applicable with "N/A". If an answer is "none," please so state. If you need extra space to answer any item, attach a sheet of paper with your name and Social Security number, and indicate the number of the item to which the answer refers.

You must submit an affidavit of support for each applicant for immigrant status. You may submit photocopies of this affidavit and all supporting documentation for any spouse or children immigrating with an immigrant you are sponsoring, but the signature on each photocopied affidavit must be original. For purposes of this form, a spouse or child is immigrating with an immigrant you are sponsoring if he or she is: 1) listed in Part 3 of this affidavit of support; and 2) applies for an immigrant visa or adjustment of status within 6 months of the date this affidavit of support is originally completed and signed. The signature on the affidavit, including the signature on photocopies, must be notarized by a notary public or signed before an Immigration or a Consular Officer.

You should give the completed affidavit of support with all required documentation to the sponsored immigrant for submission to either a Consular Officer with Form OF-230, Application for Immigrant Visa and Alien Registration, or an Immigration Officer with Form I-485, Application to Register Permanent Residence or Adjust Status. You may enclose the affidavit of support and accompanying documents in a sealed envelope to be opened only by the designated Government official. The sponsored immigrant must submit the affidavit of support to the Government within 6 months of its signature.

Who Needs an Affidavit of Support under Section 213A?
This affidavit must be filed at the time an intending immigrant is applying for an immigrant visa or adjustment of status. It is required for:

- All immediate relatives, including orphans, and family-based immigrants. (Self-petitioning widow/ers and battered spouses and children are exempt from this requirement); and
- Employment-based immigrants where a relative filed the immigrant visa petition or has a significant ownership interest (5 percent or more) in the entity that filed the petition.

Who Completes an Affidavit of Support under Section 213A?
- For immediate relatives and family-based immigrants, the family member petitioning for the intending immigrant must be the sponsor.
- For employment-based immigrants, the petitioning relative or a relative with a significant ownership interest (5 percent or more) in the petitioning entity must be the sponsor. The term "relative," for these purposes, is defined as husband, wife, father, mother, child, adult son or daughter, brother, or sister.
- If the petitioner cannot meet the income requirements, a joint sponsor may submit an additional affidavit of support.

A sponsor, or joint sponsor, must also be:

- A citizen or national of the United States or an alien lawfully admitted to the United States for permanent residence;
- At least 18 years of age; and
- Domiciled in the United States or its territories and possessions.

Sponsor's Income Requirement
As a sponsor, your household income must equal or exceed 125 percent of the Federal poverty line for your household size. For the purpose of the affidavit of support, household size includes yourself, all persons related to you by birth, marriage, or adoption living in your residence, your dependents, any immigrants you have previously sponsored using INS Form I-864 if that obligation has not terminated, and the intending immigrant(s) in Part 3 of this affidavit of support. The poverty guidelines are calculated and published annually by the Department of Health and Human Services. Sponsors who are on active duty in the U.S. Armed Forces other than for training need only demonstrate income at 100 percent of the poverty line if they are submitting this affidavit for the purpose of sponsoring their spouse or child.

If you are currently employed and have an *individual* income which meets or exceeds 125 percent of the Federal poverty line or (100 percent, if applicable) for your household size, you do not need to list the income of any other person. When determining your income, you may include the income generated by individuals related to you by birth, marriage, or adoption who are living in your residence, if they have lived in your residence for the previous 6 months, or who are listed as dependents on your most recent Federal income tax return whether or not they live in your residence. For their income to be considered, these household members or dependents must be willing to make their income available for the support of the sponsored immigrant(s) if necessary, and to complete and sign Form I-864A, Contract Between Sponsor and Household Member. However, a household member who is the immigrant you are sponsoring only need complete Form I-864A if his or her income will be used to determine your ability to support a spouse and/or children immigrating with him or her.

If in any of the most recent 3 tax years, you and your spouse each reported income on a joint income tax return, but you want to use only your own income to qualify (and your spouse is not submitting a Form I-864A), you may provide a separate breakout of your individual income for these years. Your individual income will be based on the earnings from your W-2 forms, Wage and Tax Statement, submitted to IRS for any such years. If necessary to meet the income requirement, you may also submit evidence of other income listed on your tax returns which can be attributed to you. You must provide documentation of such reported income, including Forms 1099 sent by the payer, which show your name and Social Security number.

You must calculate your household size and total household income as indicated in Parts 4.C. and 4.D. of this form. You must compare your total household income with the minimum income requirement for your household size using the poverty guidelines. For the purposes of the affidavit of support, determination of your ability to meet the income requirements will be based on the most recent income-poverty guidelines published in the Federal Register at the time the Consular or Immigration Officer makes a decision on the intending immigrant's application for an immigrant visa or adjustment of status. Immigration and Consular Officers will begin to use updated poverty guidelines on the first day of the second month after the date the guidelines are published in the Federal Register.

If your total household income is equal to or higher than the minimum income requirement for your household size, you do not need to provide information on your assets, and you may *not* have a joint sponsor unless you are requested to do so by a Consular or Immigration Officer. If your total household income does not meet the minimum income requirement, the intending immigrant will be ineligible for an immigrant visa or adjustment of status, unless:

- You provide evidence of assets that meet the requirements outlined under "Evidence of Assets" below; and/or

- The immigrant you are sponsoring provides evidence of assets that meet the requirements under "Evidence of Assets" below; or

- A joint sponsor assumes the liability of the intending immigrant with you. A joint sponsor must execute a separate affidavit of support on behalf of the intending

immigrant and any accompanying family members. A joint sponsor must individually meet the minimum requirement of 125 percent of the poverty line based on his or her household size and income and/or assets, including any assets of the sponsored immigrant.

The Government may pursue verification of any information provided on or in support of this form, including employment, income, or assets with the employer, financial or other institutions, the Internal Revenue Service, or the Social Security Administration.

Evidence of Income

In order to complete this form you must submit the following evidence of income:

- A copy of your complete Federal income tax return, as filed with the Internal Revenue Service, for each of the most recent 3 tax years. If you were not required to file a tax return in any of the most recent 3 tax years, you must provide an explanation. If you filed a joint income tax return and are using only your own income to qualify, you must also submit copies of your W-2s for each of the most recent 3 tax years, and *if* necessary to meet the income requirement, evidence of other income reported on your tax returns, such as Forms 1099.

- If you rely on income of any members of your household or dependents in order to reach the minimum income requirement, copies of their Federal income tax returns for the most recent 3 tax years. These persons must each complete and sign a Form I-864A, Contract Between Sponsor and Household Member.

- Evidence of current employment or self-employment, such as a recent pay statement, *or* a statement from your employer on business stationery, showing beginning date of employment, type of work performed, and salary or wages paid. You must also provide evidence of current employment for any person whose income is used to qualify.

Evidence of Assets

If you want to use your assets, the assets of your household members or dependents, and/or the assets of the immigrant you are sponsoring to meet the minimum income requirement, you must provide evidence of assets with a cash value that equals at least five times the difference between your total household income and the minimum income requirement. For the assets of a household member, other than the immigrant(s) you are sponsoring, to be considered, the household member must complete and sign Form I-864A, Contract Between Sponsor and Household Member.

All assets must be supported with evidence to verify location, ownership, and value of each asset. Any liens and liabilities relating to the assets must be documented. List only assets that can be readily converted into cash within 1 year. Evidence of assets includes, but is not limited to the following:

- Bank statements covering the last 12 months, *or* a statement from an officer of the bank or other financial institution in which you have deposits, including deposit/withdrawal history for the last 12 months, and current balance;

- Evidence of ownership and value of stocks, bonds, and certificates of deposit, and date(s) acquired;

- Evidence of ownership and value of other personal property, and date(s) acquired; and

- Evidence of ownership and value of any real estate, and date(s) acquired.

Change of Sponsor's Address

You are required by 8 U.S.C. 1183a(d) and 8 CFR 213a.3 to report every change of address to the Immigration and Naturalization Service and the State(s) in which the sponsored immigrant(s) reside(s). You must report changes of address to INS on Form I-865, Sponsor's Notice of Change of Address, within 30 days of any change of address. You must also report any change in your address to the State(s) in which the sponsored immigrant(s) live.

Penalties

If you include in this affidavit of support any material information that you know to be false, you may be liable for criminal prosecution under the laws of the United States.

If you fail to give notice of your change of address, as required by 8 U.S.C. 1183a(d) and 8 CFR 213a.3, you may be liable for the civil penalty established by 8 U.S.C. 1183a(d)(2). The amount of the civil penalty will depend on whether you failed to give this notice because you were aware that the immigrant(s) you sponsored had received Federal, State, or local means-tested public benefits.

Privacy Act Notice

Authority for the collection of the information requested on this form is contained in 8 U.S.C. 1182(a)(4), 1183a, 1184(a), and 1258. The information will be used principally by the INS or by any Consular Officer to whom it is furnished, to support an alien's application for benefits under the Immigration and Nationality Act and specifically the assertion that he or she has adequate means of financial support and will not become a public charge. Submission of the information is voluntary. Failure to provide the information will result in denial of the application for an immigrant visa or adjustment of status.

The information may also, as a matter of routine use, be disclosed to other Federal, State, and local agencies or private entities providing means-tested public benefits for use in civil action against the sponsor for breach of contract. It may also be disclosed as a matter of routine use to other Federal, State, local, and foreign law enforcement and regulatory agencies to enable these entities to carry out their law enforcement responsibilites.

Reporting Burden

A person is not required to respond to a collection of information unless it displays a currently valid OMB control number. We try to create forms and instructions that are accurate, can be easily understood, and which impose the least possible burden on you to provide us with information. Often this is difficult because some immigration laws are very complex. The reporting burden for this collection of information on Form I-864 is computed as follows: 1) learning about the form, 17 minutes; 2) completing the form, 22 minutes; and 3) assembling and filing the form, 30 minutes, for an estimated average of 69 minutes per response. The reporting burden for collection of information on Form I-864A is computed as: 1) learning about the form, 5 minutes; 2) completing the form, 8 minutes; 3) assembling and filing the form, 2 minutes, for an estimated average of 15 minutes per response. If you have comments regarding the accuracy of this estimates, or suggestions for making this form simpler, you can write to the Immigration and Naturalization Service, 425 I Street, N.W., Room 5307, Washington, D.C. 20536. **DO NOT MAIL YOUR COMPLETED AFFIDAVIT OF SUPPORT TO THIS ADDRESS.**

CHECK LIST

The following items must be submitted with Form I-864, Affidavit of Support Under Section 213A:

For *ALL* sponsors:

This form, the **I-864, completed and signed** before a notary public or a Consular or Immigration Officer.

Proof of **current employment** or self employment.

Your individual Federal **income tax returns for the most recent 3 tax years,** or an explanation if fewer are submitted. Your **W-2s** for any of the most recent 3 tax years for which you filed a joint tax return but are using only your own income to qualify. Forms 1099 or evidence of other reported income *if* necessary to qualify.

For *SOME* sponsors:

If the immigrant you are sponsoring is bringing a spouse or children, **photocopies of the immigrant's affidavit of support and all supporting documentation with original notarized signatures** on each photocopy of the affidavit for each spouse and/or child immigrating with the immigrant you are sponsoring.

If you are on active duty in the Armed Forces and are sponsoring a spouse or child using the 100 percent of poverty level exception, **proof of your active military status.**

If you are using the income of persons in your household or dependents to qualify,

A separate **Form I-864A** for each person whose income you will use other than a sponsored immigrant/household member who is not immigrating with a spouse and/or child.

Proof of their **residency** and **relationship** to you if they are not listed as dependents on your income tax return for the most recent tax year.

Proof of their **current employment** or self-employment.

Copies of their individual Federal income tax returns for the 3 most recent tax years, or an explanation if fewer are submitted.

If you use your assets or the assets of the sponsored immigrant to qualify,

Documentation of assets establishing location, ownership, date of acquisition, and value. Evidence of any liens or liabilities against these assets.

A separate **Form I-864A** for each household member other than the sponsored immigrant/household member.

If you or a household member or dependent has used any type of means-tested public benefits in the last 3 years,

A list of the programs and dates.

If you are a joint sponsor or the relative of an employment-based immigrant requiring an affidavit of support, **proof of your citizenship status.**

For U.S. citizens or nationals, a copy of your birth certificate, passport, or certificate of naturalization or citizenship.

For lawful permanent residents, a copy of both sides of your I-551, Alien Registration Receipt Card.

U.S. Department of Justice
Immigration and Naturalization Service

OMB # 1115-0214

Affidavit of Support Under Section 213A of the Act

START HERE - Please Type or Print

Part 1. Information on Sponsor (You)

Last Name	First Name	Middle Name

Mailing Address *(Street Number and Name)*	Apt/ Suite Number

City	State or Province

Country	ZIP/ Postal Code	Telephone Number ( )

Place of Residence if different from above *(Street Number and Name)*	Apt/ Suite Number

FOR AGENCY USE ONLY

City	State or Province

This Affidavit | Receipt

[ ] Meets

Country	ZIP/Postal Code	Telephone Number ( )

[ ] Does not meet

Date of Birth *(Month, Day, Year)*	Place of Birth *(City, State, Country)*	Are you a U.S. Citizen? ☐ Yes ☐ No

Requirements of Section 213A

Social Security Number	A-Number *(If any)*

Part 2. Basis for Filing Affidavit of Support

I am filing this affidavit of support because *(check one)*:

a. ☐ I filed/am filing the alien relative petition.

b. ☐ I filed/am filing an alien worker petition on behalf of the intending immigrant, who is related to me as my _____.
(relationship)

c. ☐ I have ownership interest of at least 5% of _____.
(name of entity which filed visa petition)

which filed an alien worker petition on behalf of the intending immigrant, who is related to me as my _____.
(relationship)

d. ☐ I am a joint sponsor willing to accept the legal obligations with any other sponsor(s).

Officer's Signature

Location

Date

Part 3. Information on the Immigrant(s) You Are Sponsoring

Last Name	First Name	Middle Name

Date of Birth *(Month, Day, Year)*	Sex ☐ Male ☐ Female	Social Security Number *(If any)*

Country of Citizenship	A-Number *(If any)*

Current Address *(Street Number and Name)*	Apt/Suite Number	City

State/Province	Country	ZIP/Postal Code	Telephone Number ( )

List any spouse and/or children immigrating with the immigrant named above in this Part: *(Use additional sheet of paper if necessary.)*

Name	Relationship to Sponsored Immigrant			Date of Birth			A-Number *(If any)*	Social Security Number *(If any)*
	Spouse	Son	Daughter	Mo.	Day	Yr.		

250

Form I-864 (10/6/97)

Part 4.   Eligibility to Sponsor

To be a sponsor you must be a U.S. citizen or national or a lawful permanent resident. If you are not the petitioning relative, you must provide proof of status. To prove status, U.S. citizens or nationals must attach a copy of a document proving status, such as a U.S. passport, birth certificate, or certificate of naturalization, and lawful permanent residents must attach a copy of both sides of their Alien Registration Card (Form I-551).

The determination of your eligibility to sponsor an immigrant will be based on an evaluation of your demonstrated ability to maintain an annual income at or above 125 percent of the Federal poverty line (100 percent if you are a petitioner sponsoring your spouse or child and you are on active duty in the U.S. Armed Forces). The assessment of your ability to maintain an adequate income will include your current employment, household size, and household income as shown on the Federal income tax returns for the 3 most recent tax years. Assets that are readily converted to cash and that can be made available for the support of sponsored immigrants if necessary, including any such assets of the immigrant(s) you are sponsoring, may also be considered.

The greatest weight in determining eligibility will be placed on current employment and household income. If a petitioner is unable to demonstrate ability to meet the stated income and asset requirements, a joint sponsor who *can* meet the income and asset requirements is needed. Failure to provide adequate evidence of income and/ or assets or an affidavit of support completed by a joint sponsor will result in denial of the immigrant's application for an immigrant visa or adjustment to permanent resident status.

A. Sponsor's Employment

I am: 1.   ☐ Employed by _____ *(Provide evidence of employment)*
              Annual salary $_____ *or* hourly wage $ _____ *(for_____hours per week)*
       2.   ☐ Self employed _____ *(Name of business)*
              Nature of employment or business_____

       3.   ☐ Unemployed or retired since _____

B. Use of Benefits

Have you or anyone related to you by birth, marriage, or adoption living in your household or listed as a dependent on your most recent income tax return received any type of means-tested public benefit in the past 3 years?
   ☐ Yes   ☐ No *(If yes, provide details, including programs and dates, on a separate sheet of paper)*

C. Sponsor's Household Size   **Number**

1.   Number of persons (related to you by birth, marriage, or adoption) living in your residence, including yourself. *(Do NOT include persons being sponsored in this affidavit.)* _____
2.   Number of immigrants being sponsored in this affidavit *(Include all persons in Part 3.)* _____
3.   Number of immigrants **NOT** living in your household whom you are still obligated to support under a previously signed affidavit of support using Form I-864. _____
4.   Number of persons who are otherwise dependent on you, as claimed in your tax return for the most recent tax year. _____
5.   Total household size.   *(add lines 1 through 4.)*   **Total** _____

List persons below who are included in lines 1 or 3 for whom you previously have submitted INS Form I-864, *if your support obligation has not terminated.*
(If additional space is needed, use additional paper)

Name	A-Number	Date Affidavit of Support Signed	Relationship

D. Sponsor's Annual Household Income

Enter total unadjusted income from your Federal income tax return for the most recent tax year below.   If you last filed a joint income tax return but are using only your *own* income to qualify, list total earnings from your W-2 Forms, or, *if* necessary to reach the required income for your household size, include income from other sources listed on your tax return.   If your *individual* income does not meet the income requirement for your household size, you may also list total income for anyone related to you by birth, marriage, or adoption currently living with you in your residence if they   have lived in your residence for the previous 6 months, or any person shown as a dependent on your Federal income tax return for the most recent tax year, even if not living in the household.   For their income to be considered, household members   or dependents must be willing to make their income available for support of the sponsored immigrant(s) and to complete and sign Form I-864A, Contract Between Sponsor and Household Member.   A sponsored immigrant/household member only need   complete Form I-864A if his or her income will be used to determine your ability to support a spouse and/ or children immigrating with him or her.

You must attach evidence of current employment and copies of income tax returns as filed with the IRS for the most recent 3 tax years for yourself and all persons whose income is listed below.   See "Required Evidence" in Instructions. Income from all 3 years will be considered in determining your ability to support the immigrant(s) you are sponsoring.

- ☐ I filed a single/ separate tax return for the most recent tax year.
- ☐ I filed a joint return for the most recent tax year which includes only my own income.
- ☐ I filed a joint return for the most recent tax year which includes income for my spouse and myself.
    - ☐ I am submitting documentation of my individual income (Forms W-2 and 1099).
    - ☐ I am qualifying using my spouse's income; my spouse is submitting a Form I-864A.

Indicate most recent tax year   _____
                                                                        (tax year)

Sponsor's individual income $_____

or

Sponsor and spouse's combined income $_____
*(If joint tax return filed; spouse must submit
Form I-864A.)*

Income of other qualifying persons
*(List names; include spouse if applicable.
Each person must complete Form I-864A.)*

_____ $_____

_____ $_____

_____ $_____

Total Household Income $_____

Explain on separate sheet of paper if you or any of the above listed individuals are submitting Federal income tax returns for fewer than 3 years, or if other explanation of income, employment, or evidence is necessary.

E. Determination of Eligibility Based on Income

1.   ☐ I am subject to the 125 percent of poverty line requirement for sponsors.
     ☐ I am subject to the 100 percent of poverty line requirement for sponsors on active duty in the U.S. Armed Forces sponsoring their spouse or child.
2.   Sponsor's total household size, from Part 4.C., line 5 _____ .
3.   Minimum income requirement from the Poverty Guidelines chart for the year of _____ is $_____ for this household size.   *(year)*

If you are currently employed and your household income for your household size is equal to or greater than the applicable poverty line requirement (from line E.3.), you do not need to list assets (Parts   4.F. and 5) or have a joint sponsor (Part 6) unless you are requested to do so by a Consular or Immigration Officer.   You may skip to Part 7, Use of the Affidavit of Support to Overcome Public Charge Ground of Admissibility. **Otherwise, you should continue with Part 4.F.**

Part 4. Eligibility to Sponsor *(Continued)*

F. Sponsor's Assets and Liabilities

Your assets and those of your qualifying household members and dependents may be used to demonstrate ability to maintain an income at or above 125 percent (or 100 percent, if applicable) of the poverty line *if* they are available for the support of the sponsored immigrant(s) and can readily be converted into cash within 1 year. The household member, other than the immigrant(s) you are sponsoring, must complete and sign Form I-864A, Contract Between Sponsor and Household Member. List the cash value of each asset *after* any debts or liens are subtracted. Supporting evidence must be attached to establish location, ownership, date of acquisition, and value of each asset listed, including any liens and liabilities related to each asset listed. See "Evidence of Assets" in Instructions.

Type of Asset	Cash Value of Assets *(Subtract any debts)*
Savings deposits	$
Stocks, bonds, certificates of deposit	$
Life insurance cash value	$
Real estate	$
Other *(specify)*	$
Total Cash Value of Assets	$_____

Part 5. Immigrant's Assets and Offsetting Liabilities

The sponsored immigrant's assets may also be used in support of your ability to maintain income at or above 125 percent of the poverty line *if* the assets are or will be available in the United States for the support of the sponsored immigrant(s) and can readily be converted into cash within 1 year.

The sponsored immigrant should provide information on his or her assets in a format similar to part 4.F. above. Supporting evidence must be attached to establish location, ownership, and value of each asset listed, including any liens and liabilities for each asset listed. See "Evidence of Assets" in Instructions.

Part 6. Joint Sponsors

If household income and assets do not meet the appropriate poverty line for your household size, a joint sponsor is required. There may be more than one joint sponsor, but each joint sponsor must individually meet the 125 percent of poverty line requirement based on his or her household income and.or assets, including any assets of the sponsored immigrant. By submitting a separate Affidavit of Support under Section 213A of the Act (Form I-864), a joint sponsor accepts joint responsibility with the petitioner for the sponsored immigrant(s) until they become U.S. citizens, can be credited with 40 quarters of work, leave the United States permanently, or die.

Part 7. Use of the Affidavit of Support to Overcome Public Charge Ground of Inadmissibility

Section 212(a)(4)(C) of the Immigration and Nationality Act provides that an alien seeking permanent residence as an immediate relative (including an orphan), as a family-sponsored immigrant, or as an alien who will accompany or follow to join another alien is considered to be likely to become a public charge and is inadmissible to the United States unless a sponsor submits a legally enforceable affidavit of support on behalf of the alien. Section 212(a)(4)(D) imposes the same requirement on an employment-based immigrant, and those aliens who accompany or follow to join the employment-based immigrant, if the employment-based immigrant will be employed by a relative, or by a firm in which a relative owns a significant interest. Separate affidavits of support are required for family members at the time they immigrate if they are not included on this affidavit of support or do not apply for an immigrant visa or adjustment of status within 6 months of the date this affidavit of support is originally signed. The sponsor must provide the sponsored immigrant(s) whatever support is necessary to maintain them at an income that is at least 125 percent of the Federal poverty guidelines.

I submit this affidavit of support in consideration of the sponsored immigrant(s) not being found inadmissible to the United States under section 212(a)(4)(C) (or 212(a)(4)(D) for an employment-based immigrant) and to enable the sponsored immigrant(s) to overcome this ground of inadmissibility. I agree to provide the sponsored immigrant(s) whatever support is necessary to maintain the sponsored immigrant(s) at an income that is at least 125 percent of the Federal poverty guidelines. I understand that my obligation will continue until my death or the sponsored immigrant(s) have become U.S. citizens, can be credited with 40 quarters of work, depart the United States permanently, or die.

Notice of Change of Address.

Sponsors are required to provide written notice of any change of address within 30 days of the change in address until the sponsored immigrant(s) have become U.S. citizens, can be credited with 40 quarters of work, depart the United States permanently, or die. To comply with this requirement, the sponsor must complete INS Form I-865. Failure to give this notice may subject the sponsor to the civil penalty established under section 213A(d)(2) which ranges from $250 to $2,000, unless the failure to report occurred with the knowledge that the sponsored immigrant(s) had received means-tested public benefits, in which case the penalty ranges from $2,000 to $5,000.

> *If my address changes for any reason before my obligations under this affidavit of support terminate, I will complete and file INS Form I-865, Sponsor's Notice of Change of Address, within 30 days of the change of address. I understand that failure to give this notice may subject me to civil penalties.*

Means-tested Public Benefit Prohibitions and Exceptions.

Under section 403(a) of Public Law 104-193 (Welfare Reform Act), aliens lawfully admitted for permanent residence in the United States, with certain exceptions, are ineligible for most Federally-funded means-tested public benefits during their first 5 years in the United States. This provision does not apply to public benefits specified in section 403(c) of the Welfare Reform Act or to State public benefits, including emergency Medicaid; short-term, non-cash emergency relief; services provided under the National School Lunch and Child Nutrition Acts; immunizations and testing and treatment for communicable diseases; student assistance under the Higher Education Act and the Public Health Service Act; certain forms of foster-care or adoption assistance under the Social Security Act; Head Start programs; means-tested programs under the Elementary and Secondary Education Act; and Job Training Partnership Act programs.

Consideration of Sponsor's Income in Determining Eligibility for Benefits.

If a permanent resident alien is no longer statutorily barred from a Federally-funded means-tested public benefit program and applies for such a benefit, the income and resources of the sponsor and the sponsor's spouse will be considered (or deemed) to be the income and resources of the sponsored immigrant in determining the immigrant's eligibility for Federal means-tested public benefits. Any State or local government may also choose to consider (or deem) the income and resources of the sponsor and the sponsor's spouse to be the income and resources of the immigrant for the purposes of determining eligibility for their means-tested public benefits. The attribution of the income and resources of the sponsor and the sponsor's spouse to the immigrant will continue until the immigrant becomes a U.S. citizen or has worked or can be credited with 40 qualifying quarters of work, provided that the immigrant or the worker crediting the quarters to the immigrant has not received any Federal means-tested public benefit during any creditable quarter for any period after December 31, 1996.

> *I understand that, under section 213A of the Immigration and Nationality Act (the Act), as amended, this affidavit of support constitutes a contract between me and the U.S. Government. This contract is designed to protect the United States Government, and State and local government agencies or private entities that provide means-tested public benefits, from having to pay benefits to or on behalf of the sponsored immigrant(s), for as long as I am obligated to support them under this affidavit of support. I understand that the sponsored immigrants, or any Federal, State, local, or private entity that pays any means-tested benefit to or on behalf of the sponsored immigrant(s), are entitled to sue me if I fail to meet my obligations under this affidavit of support, as defined by section 213A and INS regulations.*

Civil Action to Enforce.

If the immigrant on whose behalf this affidavit of support is executed receives any Federal, State, or local means-tested public benefit before this obligation terminates, the Federal, State, or local agency or private entity may request reimbursement from the sponsor who signed this affidavit. If the sponsor fails to honor the request for reimbursement, the agency may sue the sponsor in any U.S. District Court or any State court with jurisdiction of civil actions for breach of contract. INS will provide names, addresses, and Social Security account numbers of sponsors to benefit-providing agencies for this purpose. Sponsors may also be liable for paying the costs of collection, including legal fees.

Part 7. Use of the Affidavit of Support to Overcome Public Charge Grounds *(Continued)*

I acknowledge that section 213A(a)(1)(B) of the Act grants the sponsored immigrant(s) and any Federal, State, local, or private agency that pays any means-tested public benefit to or on behalf of the sponsored immigrant(s) standing to sue me for failing to meet my obligations under this affidavit of support. I agree to submit to the personal jurisdiction of any court of the United States or of any State, territory, or possession of the United States if the court has subject matter jurisdiction of a civil lawsuit to enforce this affidavit of support. I agree that no lawsuit to enforce this affidavit of support shall be barred by any statute of limitations that might otherwise apply, so long as the plaintiff initiates the civil lawsuit no later than ten (10) years after the date on which a sponsored immigrant last received any means-tested public benefits.

Collection of Judgment.

I acknowledge that a plaintiff may seek specific performance of my support obligation. Furthermore, any money judgment against me based on this affidavit of support may be collected through the use of a judgment lien under 28 U.S.C. 3201, a writ of execution under 28 U.S.C. 3203, a judicial installment payment order under 28 U.S.C. 3204, garnishment under 28 U.S.C. 3205, or through the use of any corresponding remedy under State law. I may also be held liable for costs of collection, including attorney fees.

Concluding Provisions.

I, _____, certify under penalty of perjury under the laws of the United States that:

    (a) *I know the contents of this affidavit of support signed by me;*
    (b) *All the statements in this affidavit of support are true and correct;*
    (c) *I make this affidavit of support for the consideration stated in Part 7, freely, and without any mental reservation or purpose of evasion;*
    (d) *Income tax returns submitted in support of this affidavit are true copies of the returns filed with the Internal Revenue Service; and*
    (e) *Any other evidence submitted is true and correct.*

_____   _____
(Sponsor's Signature)   *(Date)*

Subscribed and sworn to *(affirmed)* before me this

_____ day of _____, _____
               (Month)   *(Year)*

at _____.

My commission expires on _____.

_____
(Signature of Notary Public or Officer Administering Oath)

_____
(Title)

Part 8. If someone other than the sponsor prepared this affidavit of support, that person must complete the following:

I certify under penalty of perjury under the laws of the United States that I prepared this affidavit of support at the sponsor's request, and that this affidavit of support is based on all information of which I have knowledge.

Signature	Print Your Name	Date	Daytime Telephone Number ( )

Firm Name and Address

Appendix F
Form OF-156

PLEASE TYPE OR PRINT YOUR ANSWERS IN THE SPACE PROVIDED BELOW EACH ITEM.

1. SURNAMES OR FAMILY NAMES (Exactly as in Passport)

2. FIRST NAME AND MIDDLE NAME (Exactly as in Passport)

3. OTHER NAMES (Maiden, Religious, Professional, Aliases)

4. DATE OF BIRTH (Day, Month, Year)

8. PASSPORT NUMBER

5. PLACE OF BIRTH
City, Province | Country

DATE PASSPORT ISSUED
(Day, Month, Year)

6. NATIONALITY

7. SEX
☐ MALE
☐ FEMALE

DATE PASSPORT EXPIRES
(Day, Month, Year)

9. HOME ADDRESS (Include apartment no., street, city, province, and postal zone)

10. NAME AND STREET ADDRESS OF PRESENT EMPLOYER OR SCHOOL (Postal box number unacceptable)

11. HOME TELEPHONE NO.

12. BUSINESS TELEPHONE NO.

13. COLOR OF HAIR

14. COLOR OF EYES

15. COMPLEXION

16. HEIGHT

17. MARKS OF IDENTIFICATION

18. MARITAL STATUS
☐ Married ☐ Single ☐ Widowed ☐ Divorced ☐ Separated
If married, give name and nationality of spouse.

19. NAMES AND RELATIONSHIPS OF PERSONS TRAVELING WITH YOU (NOTE: A separate application must be made for a visa for each traveler, regardless of age.)

20. HAVE YOU EVER APPLIED FOR A U.S. VISA BEFORE, WHETHER IMMIGRANT OR NONIMMIGRANT?
☐ No
☐ Yes   Where? _____
When? _____ Type of visa? _____
☐ Visa was issued   ☐ Visa was refused

21. HAS YOUR U.S. VISA EVER BEEN CANCELED?
☐ No
☐ Yes   Where? _____
When? _____ By whom? _____

22. Bearers of visitors visas may generally not work or study in the U.S.
DO YOU INTEND TO WORK IN THE U.S.?   ☐ No ☐ Yes
If YES, explain.

23. DO YOU INTEND TO STUDY IN THE U.S.?   ☐ No ☐ Yes
If YES, write name and address of school as it appears on form I-20.

DO NOT WRITE IN THIS SPACE

B-1/B-2 MAX   B-1 MAX   B-2 MAX

OTHER_____MAX
Visa Classification

MULT OR _____
Number Applications

MONTHS_____
Validity

L.O. CHECKED_____

ISSUED/REFUSED

ON _____ BY _____

UNDER SEC. _____ INA

REFUSAL REVIEWED BY _____

24. PRESENT OCCUPATION (If retired, state past occupation)

25. WHO WILL FURNISH FINANCIAL SUPPORT, INCLUDING TICKETS?

26. AT WHAT ADDRESS WILL YOU STAY IN THE U.S.A.? (City and State)

27. WHAT IS THE PURPOSE OF YOUR TRIP?

28. WHEN DO YOU INTEND TO ARRIVE IN THE U.S.A.?

29. HOW LONG DO YOU PLAN TO STAY IN THE U.S.A.?

30. HAVE YOU EVER BEEN IN THE U.S.A.?
☐ No
☐ Yes   When? _____
For how long? _____

NONIMMIGRANT VISA APPLICATION

COMPLETE ALL QUESTIONS ON REVERSE OF FORM

OPTIONAL FORM 156 (Rev. 7/94) PAGE 1   50156-106
Department of State

31. (a) HAVE YOU OR ANYONE ACTING FOR YOU EVER INDICATED TO A U.S. CONSULAR OR IMMIGRATION EMPLOYEE A DESIRE TO IMMIGRATE TO THE U.S.? (b) HAS ANYONE EVER FILED AN IMMIGRANT VISA PETITION ON YOUR BEHALF? (c) HAS LABOR CERTIFICATION FOR EMPLOYMENT IN THE U.S. EVER BEEN REQUESTED BY YOU OR ON YOUR BEHALF?

(a) ☐ No ☐ Yes   (b) ☐ No ☐ Yes   (c) ☐ No ☐ Yes

32. ARE ANY OF THE FOLLOWING IN THE U.S.? (If YES, circle appropriate relationship and indicate that person's status in the U.S., i.e. studying, working, U.S. permanent resident, U.S. citizen, etc.)

HUSBAND/WIFE _____ FIANCE/FIANCEE _____ BROTHER/SISTER _____

FATHER/MOTHER _____ SON/DAUGHTER _____

33. PLEASE LIST THE COUNTRIES WHERE YOU HAVE LIVED FOR MORE THAN 6 MONTHS DURING THE PAST 5 YEARS. BEGIN WITH YOUR PRESENT RESIDENCE.

Countries   Cities   Approximate Dates

34. IMPORTANT: ALL APPLICANTS MUST READ AND CHECK THE APPROPRIATE BOX FOR EACH ITEM:

A visa may not be issued to persons who are within specific categories defined by law as inadmissible to the United States (except when a waiver is obtained in advance). Are any of the following applicable to you?

- Have you ever been afflicted with a communicable disease of public health significance, a dangerous physical or mental disorder, or been a drug abuser or addict? . . . . ☐ Yes ☐ No

- Have you ever been arrested or convicted for any offense or crime, even though subject of a pardon, amnesty, or other such legal action? . . . . ☐ Yes ☐ No

- Have you ever been a controlled substance (drug) trafficker, or a prostitute or procurer? . . . . . ☐ Yes ☐ No

- Have you ever sought to obtain or assist others to obtain a visa, entry into the U.S., or any U.S. Immigration benefit by fraud or willful misrepresentation? . . . . ☐ Yes ☐ No

- Were you deported from the U.S.A. within the last 5 years? . . . . ☐ Yes ☐ No

- Do you seek to enter the United States to engage in export control violations, subversive or terrorist activities, or any unlawful purpose? . . . . ☐ Yes ☐ No

- Have you ever ordered, incited, assisted, or otherwise participated in the persecution of any person because of race, religion, national origin, or political opinion under the control, direct or indirect of the Nazi Government of Germany, or of the government of any area occupied by, or allied with, the Nazi Government of Germany; or have you ever participated in genocide? . . . . ☐ Yes ☐ No

A YES answer does not automatically signify ineligibility for a visa, but if you answered YES to any of the above, or if you have any question in this regard, personal appearance at this office is recommended. If appearance is not possible at this time, attach a statement of facts in your case to this application.

35. I certify that I have read and understood all the questions set forth in this application and the answers I have furnished on this form are true and correct to the best of my knowledge and belief. I understand that any false or misleading statement may result in the permanent refusal of a visa or denial of entry into the United States. I understand that possession of a visa does not entitle the bearer to enter the United States of America upon arrival at port of entry if he or she is found inadmissible.

DATE OF APPLICATION _____

APPLICANT'S SIGNATURE _____

If this application has been prepared by a travel agency or another person on your behalf, the agent should indicate name and address of agency or person with appropriate signature of individual preparing form.

SIGNATURE OF PERSON PREPARING FORM _____
(If other than applicant)

DO NOT WRITE IN THIS SPACE

37 mm x 37 mm

PHOTO

Glue or staple
photo here

CUT ALONG DOTTED LINE

260

INDEX

Your #1 Source for Real World Legal Information...

Sphinx® Publishing
A Division of Sourcebooks, Inc.

- Written by lawyers
- Simple English explanation of the law
- Forms and instructions included

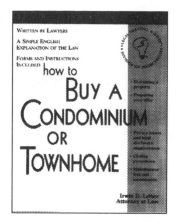

HOW TO BUY A CONDOMINIUM OR TOWNHOME

Provides information on forms of ownership, rights and duties of owners, associations, sample forms and state-by-state listing of statutes.

176 pages; $16.95;
ISBN 1-57071-164-X

HOW TO MAKE YOUR OWN WILL

Valid in 50 states, this book contains 14 different legal forms that will help you put your financial affairs in order. Also discusses inheritance laws.

144 pages; $12.95;
ISBN 1-57071-228-X

HOW TO WRITE YOUR OWN LIVING WILL

Step-by-step guide to writing living wills in all 50 states and the District of Columbia, complete with necessary forms.

160 pages; $9.95;
ISBN 1-57071-167-4

See the following order form for books written specifically for California, Florida, Georgia, Illinois, Massachusetts, Michigan, Minnesota, New York, North Carolina, Pennsylvania, and Texas! *Coming in 1999: Ohio!*

What our customers say about our books:

"It couldn't be more clear for the lay person." —R.D.

"I want you to know I really appreciate your book. It has saved me a lot of time and money." —L.T.

"Your real estate contracts book has saved me nearly $12,000.00 in closing costs over the past year." —A.B.

"...many of the legal questions that I have had over the years were answered clearly and concisely through your plain English interpretation of the law." —C.E.H.

"If there weren't people out there like you I'd be lost. You have the best books of this type out there." —S.B.

"...your forms and directions are easy to follow." —C.V.M.

Sphinx Publishing's Legal Survival Guides
are directly available from the Sourcebooks, Inc., or from your local bookstores.
For credit card orders call 1–800–43–BRIGHT, write P.O. Box 372, Naperville, IL 60566,
or fax 630-961-2168

SPHINX® PUBLISHING NATIONAL TITLES

Valid in All 50 States

LEGAL SURVIVAL IN BUSINESS

How to Form Your Own Corporation (2E)	$19.95
How to Form Your Own Partnership	$19.95
How to Register Your Own Copyright (2E)	$19.95
How to Register Your Own Trademark (2E)	$19.95
Most Valuable Business Legal Forms You'll Ever Need (2E)	$19.95
Most Valuable Corporate Forms You'll Ever Need (2E)	$24.95
Software Law (with diskette)	$29.95

LEGAL SURVIVAL IN COURT

Crime Victim's Guide to Justice	$19.95
Debtors' Rights (3E)	$12.95
Defend Yourself Against Criminal Charges	$19.95
Grandparents' Rights	$19.95
Help Your Lawyer Win Your Case	$12.95
Jurors' Rights (2E)	$9.95
Legal Malpractice and Other Claims Against Your Lawyer	$18.95
Legal Research Made Easy (2E)	$14.95
Simple Ways to Protect Yourself From Lawsuits	$24.95
Victims' Rights	$12.95
Winning Your Personal Injury Claim	$19.95

LEGAL SURVIVAL IN REAL ESTATE

How to Buy a Condominium or Townhome	$16.95
How to Negotiate Real Estate Contracts (3E)	$16.95
How to Negotiate Real Estate Leases (3E)	$16.95
Successful Real Estate Brokerage Management	$19.95

LEGAL SURVIVAL IN PERSONAL AFFAIRS

How to File Your Own Bankruptcy (4E)	$19.95
How to File Your Own Divorce (3E)	$19.95
How to Make Your Own Will	$12.95
How to Write Your Own Living Will	$9.95
How to Write Your Own Premarital Agreement (2E)	$19.95
How to Win Your Unemployment Compensation Claim	$19.95
Living Trusts and Simple Ways to Avoid Probate (2E)	$19.95
Most Valuable Personal Legal Forms You'll Ever Need	$14.95
Neighbor vs. Neighbor	$12.95
The Power of Attorney Handbook (3E)	$19.95
Simple Ways to Protect Yourself from Lawsuits	$24.95
Social Security Benefits Handbook (2E)	$14.95
Unmarried Parents' Rights	$19.95
U.S.A. Immigration Guide (3E)	$19.95
Guia de Inmigracion a Estados Unidos	$19.95

Sphinx Publishing's Legal Survival Guides
are directly available from Sourcebooks, Inc., or from your local bookstores.
For credit card orders call 1–800–43–BRIGHT, write P.O. Box 372, Naperville, IL 60566,
or fax 630-961-2168

SPHINX® PUBLISHING ORDER FORM

BILL TO:		SHIP TO:		
Phone #	Terms	F.O.B. Chicago, IL		Ship Date

Charge my: ☐ VISA   ☐ MasterCard   ☐ American Express

☐ **Money Order or Personal Check**

Credit Card Number

Expiration Date

Qty	ISBN	Title	Retail	Ext.
		SPHINX® PUBLISHING NATIONAL TITLES		
____	1-57071-166-6	Crime Victim's Guide to Justice	$19.95	____
____	1-57071-342-1	Debtors' Rights (3E)	$12.95	____
____	1-57071-162-3	Defend Yourself Against Criminal Charges	$19.95	____
____	1-57248-001-7	Grandparents' Rights	$19.95	____
____	0-913825-99-9	Guia de Inmigracion a Estados Unidos	$19.95	____
____	1-57248-021-1	Help Your Lawyer Win Your Case	$12.95	____
____	1-57071-164-X	How to Buy a Condominium or Townhome	$16.95	____
____	1-57071-223-9	How to File Your Own Bankruptcy (4E)	$19.95	____
____	1-57071-224-7	How to File Your Own Divorce (3E)	$19.95	____
____	1-57071-227-1	How to Form Your Own Corporation (2E)	$19.95	____
____	1-57071-343-X	How to Form Your Own Partnership	$19.95	____
____	1-57071-228-X	How to Make Your Own Will	$12.95	____
____	1-57071-331-6	How to Negotiate Real Estate Contracts (3E)	$16.95	____
____	1-57071-332-4	How to Negotiate Real Estate Leases (3E)	$16.95	____
____	1-57071-225-5	How to Register Your Own Copyright (2E)	$19.95	____
____	1-57071-226-3	How to Register Your Own Trademark (2E)	$19.95	____
____	1-57071-349-9	How to Win Your Unemployment Compensation Claim	$19.95	____
____	1-57071-167-4	How to Write Your Own Living Will	$9.95	____
____	1-57071-344-8	How to Write Your Own Premarital Agreement (2E)	$19.95	____
____	1-57071-333-2	Jurors' Rights (2E)	$9.95	____
____	1-57248-032-7	Legal Malpractice and Other Claims Against...	$18.95	____
____	1-57071-400-2	Legal Research Made Easy (2E)	$14.95	____
____	1-57071-336-7	Living Trusts and Simple Ways to Avoid Probate (2E)	$19.95	____
____	1-57071-345-6	Most Valuable Bus. Legal Forms You'll Ever Need (2E)	$19.95	____
____	1-57071-346-4	Most Valuable Corporate Forms You'll Ever Need (2E)	$24.95	____
____	1-57071-347-2	Most Valuable Personal Legal Forms You'll Ever Need	$14.95	____

Qty	ISBN	Title	Retail	Ext.
____	0-913825-41-7	Neighbor vs. Neighbor	$12.95	____
____	1-57071-348-0	The Power of Attorney Handbook (3E)	$19.95	____
____	1-57248-020-3	Simple Ways to Protect Yourself from Lawsuits	$24.95	____
____	1-57071-337-5	Social Security Benefits Handbook (2E)	$14.95	____
____	1-57071-163-1	Software Law (w/diskette)	$29.95	____
____	0-913825-86-7	Successful Real Estate Brokerage Mgmt.	$19.95	____
____	1-57071-399-5	Unmarried Parents' Rights	$19.95	____
____	1-57071-354-5	U.S.A. Immigration Guide (3E)	$19.95	____
____	0-913825-82-4	Victims' Rights	$12.95	____
____	1-57071-165-8	Winning Your Personal Injury Claim	$19.95	____
		CALIFORNIA TITLES		
____	1-57071-360-X	CA Power of Attorney Handbook	$12.95	____
____	1-57071-355-3	How to File for Divorce in CA	$19.95	____
____	1-57071-356-1	How to Make a CA Will	$12.95	____
____	1-57071-408-8	How to Probate an Estate in CA	$19.95	____
____	1-57071-357-X	How to Start a Business in CA	$16.95	____
____	1-57071-358-8	How to Win in Small Claims Court in CA	$14.95	____
____	1-57071-359-6	Landlords' Rights and Duties in CA	$19.95	____
		FLORIDA TITLES		
____	1-57071-363-4	Florida Power of Attorney Handbook (2E)	$9.95	____
____	1-57071-403-7	How to File for Divorce in FL (5E)	$21.95	____
____	1-57071-401-0	How to Form a Partnership in FL	$19.95	____
____	1-57248-004-1	How to Form a Nonprofit Corp. in FL (3E)	$19.95	____
____	1-57071-380-4	How to Form a Corporation in FL (4E)	$19.95	____
____	1-57071-361-8	How to Make a FL Will (5E)	$12.95	____

____ *Form Continued on Following Page*   **SUBTOTAL** ____

To order, call Sourcebooks at 1-800-43-BRIGHT or FAX (630)961-2168 (Bookstores, libraries, wholesalers—please call for discount)

SPHINX® PUBLISHING ORDER FORM

Qty	ISBN	Title	Retail	Ext.
		FLORIDA TITLES (CONT'D)		
____	1-57248-056-4	How to Modify Your FL Divorce Judgement (3E)	$22.95	____
____	1-57071-364-2	How to Probate an Estate in FL (3E)	$24.95	____
____	1-57248-005-X	How to Start a Business in FL (4E)	$16.95	____
____	1-57071-362-6	How to Win in Small Claims Court in FL (6E)	$14.95	____
____	1-57071-335-9	Landlords' Rights and Duties in FL (7E)	$19.95	____
____	1-57071-334-0	Land Trusts in FL (5E)	$24.95	____
____	0-913825-73-5	Women's Legal Rights in FL	$19.95	____
		GEORGIA TITLES		
____	1-57071-387-1	How to File for Divorce in GA (3E)	$19.95	____
____	1-57248-047-5	How to Make a GA Will (2E)	$9.95	____
____	1-57248-026-2	How to Start and Run a GA Business (2E)	$18.95	____
		ILLINOIS TITLES		
____	1-57071-405-3	How to File for Divorce in IL (2E)	$19.95	____
____	1-57071-415-0	How to Make an IL Will (2E)	$12.95	____
____	1-57071-416-9	How to Start a Business in IL (2E)	$16.95	____
		MASSACHUSETTS TITLES		
____	1-57071-329-4	How to File for Divorce in MA (2E)	$19.95	____
____	1-57248-050-5	How to Make a MA Will	$9.95	____
____	1-57248-053-X	How to Probate an Estate in MA	$19.95	____
____	1-57248-054-8	How to Start a Business in MA	$16.95	____
____	1-57248-055-6	Landlords' Rights and Duties in MA	$19.95	____
		MICHIGAN TITLES		
____	1-57071-409-6	How to File for Divorce in MI (2E)	$19.95	____
____	1-57248-015-7	How to Make a MI Will	$9.95	____
____	1-57071-407-X	How to Start a Business in MI (2E)	$16.95	____
		MINNESOTA TITLES		
____	1-57248-039-4	How to File for Divorce in MN	$19.95	____
____	1-57248-040-8	How to Form a Simple Corporation in MN	$19.95	____
____	1-57248-037-8	How to Make a MN Will	$9.95	____
____	1-57248-038-6	How to Start a Business in MN	$16.95	____
		NEW YORK TITLES		
____	1-57071-184-4	How to File for Divorce in NY	$19.95	____
____	1-57071-183-6	How to Make a NY Will	$12.95	____
____	1-57071-185-2	How to Start a Business in NY	$16.95	____
____	1-57071-187-9	How to Win in Small Claims Court in NY	$14.95	____
____	1-57071-186-0	Landlords' Rights and Duties in NY	$19.95	____
____	1-57071-188-7	New York Power of Attorney Handbook	$19.95	____
		NORTH CAROLINA TITLES		
____	1-57071-326-X	How to File for Divorce in NC (2E)	$19.95	____
____	1-57071-327-8	How to Make a NC Will (2E)	$12.95	____
____	0-913825-93-X	How to Start a Business in NC	$16.95	____
		PENNSYLVANIA TITLES		
____	1-57071-177-1	How to File for Divorce in PA	$19.95	____
____	1-57071-176-3	How to Make a PA Will	$12.95	____
____	1-57071-178-X	How to Start a Business in PA	$16.95	____
____	1-57071-179-8	Landlords' Rights and Duties in PA	$19.95	____
		TEXAS TITLES		
____	1-57071-330-8	How to File for Divorce in TX (2E)	$19.95	____
____	1-57248-009-2	How to Form a Simple Corporation in TX	$19.95	____
____	1-57071-417-7	How to Make a TX Will (2E)	$12.95	____
____	1-57071-418-5	How to Probate an Estate in TX (2E)	$19.95	____
____	1-57071-365-0	How to Start a Business in TX (2E)	$16.95	____
____	1-57248-012-2	How to Win in Small Claims Court in TX	$14.95	____
____	1-57248-011-4	Landlords' Rights and Duties in TX	$19.95	____

SUBTOTAL THIS PAGE ____

SUBTOTAL PREVIOUS PAGE ____

Illinois residents add 6.75% sales tax

Florida residents add 6% state sales tax plus applicable discretionary surtax

Shipping— $4.00 for 1st book, $1.00 each additional ____

TOTAL ____